D0369502

COURAGEOUS RESISTANCE

COURAGEOUS RESISTANCE

THE POWER OF ORDINARY PEOPLE

Kristina E. Thalhammer,
St. Olaf College

Paula L. O'Loughlin,
University of Minnesota, Morris

Sam McFarland,
Western Kentucky University

Myron Peretz Glazer,
Smith College

Penina Migdal Glazer,
Hampshire College

Sharon Toffey Shepela,
University of Hartford

Nathan Stoltzfus,
Florida State University

palgrave
macmillan

COURAGEOUS RESISTANCE: THE POWER OF ORDINARY PEOPLE
Copyright © Kristina E. Thalhammer et al., 2007.
All rights reserved. No part of this book may be used or reproduced in any
manner whatsoever without written permission except in the case of brief quotations embodied in critical articles or reviews.

First published in 2007 by
PALGRAVE MACMILLAN™
175 Fifth Avenue, New York, N.Y. 10010 and
Houndmills, Basingstoke, Hampshire, England RG21 6XS.
Companies and representatives throughout the world.

PALGRAVE MACMILLAN is the global academic imprint of the Palgrave
Macmillan division of St. Martin's Press, LLC and of Palgrave Macmillan Ltd.
Macmillan® is a registered trademark in the United States, United Kingdom and
other countries. Palgrave is a registered trademark in the European Union and
other countries.

ISBN-13: 978-1-4039-8498-2
ISBN-10: 1-4039-8498-0

Library of Congress Cataloging-in-Publication Data

A catalogue record of the book is available from the British Library.

Design by Scribe Inc.

First edition: August 2007

10 9 8 7 6 5 4 3 2 1

Printed in the United States of America.

Transferred to digital printing in 2007.

To those who struggle for justice against all odds

CONTENTS

List of Tables and Figures

ACKNOWLEDGMENTS

We thank all those who were interviewed for this book.

SPECIAL thanks for assistance in research and editing to: Shawn Paulson, Gloria MacWilliams-Brooks, Meghan Swanson, Isaac Linehan-Clodfelter, John Hansen, Argie Manolis, Rachel Bjorhus, Melanie Meinzer, Tony Olson, Jennifer Archbold, Elida Araujo and Alicia Astromujoff.

Thanks for the love, support and sacrifice of family and friends, especially David Anderson, Daniel and Anna Anderson-Thalhammer, Maria Foscarinis, Jessica, Joshua, Tamar, Einav and Natan Glazer, Cheryl McFarland, Francesca and Kevin O'Loughlin-Villa, Tara Tieso and Adam Shepela.

This project could never have come together without generous support from all of our institutions. We would like to acknowledge support for this project from St. Olaf College, especially the Dean of the Faculty, Dean of the Social Sciences, Globalization Conference Committee, the Kloeck-Jenson Endowment for Peace and Justice, and the Department of Political Science. We thank Smith College and especially the Project on Women and Social Change for their generous support of this project. We deeply appreciate the opportunity they gave us to come together as part of their 14th Annual Kathleen Ridder Conference, "Ordinary People: Extraordinary Courage and Hope." We are indebted to Christine Shelton and Kathleen Gauger for the organization of this conference. We thank Western Kentucky University's Honors Program and the Psychology Department at Western Kentucky for their support. We thank Dean David Goldenberg of Hillyer College and the University of Hartford for his support and encouragement. Thanks also to the University of Minnesota, Morris, Hampshire College and Florida State University. We are indebted to University of Minnesota Professors John Sullivan and Kathryn Sikkink, whose teaching and interest in political psychology and human rights unknowingly planted the seeds for this book within two of its authors many years ago. Finally, we thank the Honors students in Resisting Evil at Hartford College for Women who helped clarify how the Latane and Darley model can describe the path to courageous resistance.

CHAPTER 1

PATHWAYS TO COURAGEOUS RESISTANCE: ORDINARY PEOPLE, GROUPS, AND INSTITUTIONS CONFRONT INJUSTICE

> How wonderful it is that nobody need wait a single moment before
> starting to improve the world.
>
> —Anne Frank, *Diary of a Young Girl*

INTRODUCTION

RWANDAN GENOCIDE AND A HOTEL MANAGER'S SANCTUARY

In April 1994, the east African country of Rwanda exploded into a nightmare of mass killing. Following the lead of the Presidential Guard and military, the fiercely ethnocentric Hutu Interahamwe militia, purporting to be saving the country from disloyal Tutsi and Hutu moderates, urged the Hutu majority to purge the country of the "cockroach" Tutsi minority. Many Hutu civilians began killing their countrymen encouraged by incendiary rhetoric on the radio. Hundreds of thousands of unarmed men, women and children were slaughtered over a 100 day period, "Neighbors hacked neighbors to death in their homes, and colleagues hacked colleagues to death in their workplaces. Doctors killed their patients and schoolteachers killed their pupils. Within days, the Tutsi populations of many villages were all but eliminated"(Gourevitch 1998, 115).

As the mass killings spread throughout Rwanda, they became more organized and coldly efficient. Members of the Tutsi minority were encouraged to gather together in central locations like churches and hospitals for ostensible protection. Rather than providing safety and sanctuary for the Tutsi, however, these sites became venues for more efficient slaughter, as Hutus were able to kill large numbers of Tutsi at one time. Rwandans would note in later interviews, "It was like sweeping dry banana leaves into a pile to burn them more easily" (Human Rights Watch 1999).

By the middle of the summer, grim evidence of the mass killings and other atrocities littered the country:

> The sweetly sickening odor of decomposing bodies hung over many parts of Rwanda in July 1994: on the Nyanza ridge, overlooking the capital, Kigali, where skulls and bones, torn clothing, and scraps of paper were scattered among the bushes; at Nyamata where bodies lay twisted and heaped on benches and the floor of a church; at Nyarbuye in eastern Rwanda, where the cadaver of a little girl, otherwise intact, had been flattened by passing vehicles to the thinness of cardboard in front on the church steps. (Human Rights Watch 1999)

Yet the United Nations peacekeeping forces stationed in Rwanda were ordered not to intervene in any way, other than to help foreign nationals leave Rwanda. By the time the rebel military finally defeated the military junta in July 1994, more than eight hundred thousand Rwandans—one tenth of the entire country's population and half the Tutsis in Rwanda—were dead (Gourevitch 1998).

In the midst of this terror, Paul Rusesabagina, a Rwandan Hutu married to a Tutsi, used his wits and courage to keep 1,268 Tutsis and moderate Hutus alive, sheltering them at the *Hotel des Mille Collines*, Kigali's premier international hotel, where Rusesabagina worked as interim general manager. Author Philip Gourevitch describes Rusesabagina as "armed with nothing but a liquor cabinet, a phone line, an internationally famous address and his spirit of resistance" (Gourevitch 1998, 142). With the alcohol, he bribed and softened up members of the militia and high-ranking military officers. Rusesabagina, whose story is told in the film *Hotel Rwanda*, also drew on his connections and the cash in the hotel safe to buy sweet potatoes to feed the hundreds of people who had moved onto the hotel's grounds. He used the hotel's phone and fax machine, the impressive international connections of Sabena, his Belgian-based corporate employer, and his guests to send out information around the world and around the clock, trying to inspire sufficient pressure to end the killings.

For weeks, Rusesabagina faced this pressure-filled nightmare, trying to protect the hundreds within the hotel from the fate that befell others outside the hotel's walls. Marauding militia and others repeatedly tried to take the refugees away, but each time Rusesabagina managed to stop them by using bribes, free drinks, bad directions, and other tactics. The stress and danger were always present. As Rusesabagina struggled to feed and shelter the refugees, he and the others could hear the screams of the dying and the hacking of people to death on the other side of the hotel walls.

Rusesabagina also recognized that the sanctuary of the hotel could not last forever. Knowing that his guests' long-term safety depended on evacuation from Rwanda, Rusesabagina tried to move them using truck convoys protected by UN forces. These initial evacuation efforts failed as the refugees were attacked and the UN troops were prevented from interfering (Gourevitch 1998, 142). Eventually, Rusesabagina safely evacuated all his guests, but only after a change in the political context occurred. Threatened by the advance of the rebel military opposed to the genocide, Hutu forces in Kigali slowly began to allow the refugees to leave the hotel.

Even as the evacuation began, the danger remained for Rusesabagina and the people still inside the hotel. Rusesabagina steadfastly continued to use all his resources and connections to protect the last remaining hotel residents:

> On June 17, when only a handful of refugees remained at the Mille Collines, Paul went to the Hotel des Diplomates . . . in search of liquor for General Bizimungu. When he returned to the Mille Collines, he found that a mob of *Interahamwe* had broken into the suite where he was staying with his family. His wife and children hid in the bathroom, while the militia tore up the living room. Paul ran into some of the invaders in the corridor . . . he sent them off in the other direction. Then he went looking for General Bizimungu, who was waiting for his liquor handout. The general instructed one of his sergeants to chase the militia out. (Gourevitch 1998, 144)

In the end, due to Rusesabagina's efforts, none of the people who took shelter at the hotel were killed. Notably, his hotel was the only one of the small number of sanctuaries operating without foreign protection that was able to protect all who sought refuge there during the Rwandan genocide (Human Rights Watch 1999).

EXPLAINING COURAGEOUS RESISTANCE

Why do Paul Rusesabegina and others like him choose to put their own lives at risk to help others? This book attempts to answer this question by focusing on the decisions of people who live during times of grave injustice. The choices ordinary people make in these threatening periods—including extreme circumstances such as those involving torture, mass murder, and genocide—can transform the decision maker, but can also alter the fate of potential victims, influence the behaviors of perpetrators, and modify the context in ways that make future abuses more or less likely to occur. The individuals who choose to courageously resist the powerful forces that threaten to harm others despite high risks are the focus of this book. Perpetrators have the power to destroy lives and communities, but the effects of their deeds may be mitigated by courageous resisters who act against injustice. People who act in these dangerous situations to protect others can sometimes halt seemingly unstoppable abuses of power or save some lives otherwise destined for destruction. In contrast, the destruction unleashed by perpetrators becomes even more potent with the support or quiescence of bystanders, who may recognize what is happening but fail to challenge destructive policies and actions.

People who live during such periods of injustice encounter a series of decisive crossroads, points where they must choose whether to actively side with victims, to remain mute, or perhaps to even join perpetrators of harm. Facing these crossroads, people become bystanders, perpetrators, or courageous resisters. Their choices depend on who they, as individuals, are, who they know, and the nature of the environment. Bystanders, perpetrators, and courageous resisters can be individuals, collectives, or institutions.[1]

We define bystanders as those who are neither the direct perpetrators of unjust acts nor the victims and who also do not engage in active resistance to such actions. They may be passive supporters of the perpetrators' actions, they may disapprove of the actions, or they may hold no particular judgment about them. Others may know what harm is being done, and object to it, but interpret the situation as so overwhelming or risky that they dare not resist it. People also might not respond because they are totally unaware that victims are being targeted for maltreatment. Such "unaware" persons are bystanders if their ignorance is the result of a choice they have made to be unaware—they do not want to know, and they avoid the information. While bystanders may see their silence in the face of violence as having a morally neutral effect, they often actually contribute to the power of the perpetrators. Perpetrators and their peers often interpret bystanders' inaction as tacit support for their malevolent actions.

Perpetrators are individuals, collectives, or institutions whose actions and policies result in the serious mistreatment of a subgroup, often escalating attacks possibly until the group itself is destroyed. The key characteristics of perpetrators are the potentially coordinated nature of their destructive acts and the effects of their actions on societal subgroups. This book focuses on destructive acts that target members of subgroups of society (momentarily created or historically established), where such targeting lends itself to the potential for a greater number of victims. While every individual's suffering is a tragedy, a greater number of victims compounds catastrophe. Individual episodes of criminal behavior— bullying, robbery, sexual or domestic assault, and even murder—are not the focus of our analysis unless they form part of a larger pattern of socially or state condoned injustice. Perpetrators' levels of organization, access to resources, and international contexts may vary significantly. The Interahamwe militias of Rwanda and the German Nazis who carried out the Final Solution are both prime examples of perpetrators.

We define *courageous resisters* along three dimensions: First, they are those who voluntarily engage in other-oriented, largely selfless behavior with a significantly high risk or cost to themselves or their associates. Second, their actions are the result of a conscious decision. Third, their efforts are sustained over time. The latter two dimensions distinguish courageous resistance as a more sustained and deliberative series of actions, in contrast to risky interventions by heroes which might be relatively spontaneous and brief.[2] Courageous resisters begin as people who could choose to minimize their own risks by blending into the ranks of bystanders. Instead, they decide to act against injustice and on behalf of others, despite likely risks (Shepela et al. 1999, 787). While the choice to act using nonviolent tactics is not required for courageous resistance, the kind of courageous resistance we examine here is that of actors who show a strong preference for nonviolent strategies.

We recognize that there are instances where nonviolent courageous resistance may not be possible. For example, Jewish resistance in the ghettos and concentration camps necessitated secretly securing guns and explosives to counter the Nazis' mass murders. At other times, nonviolent methods may simply be insufficient. While Paul Rusesabagina provided refuge, without using violence, at the Hotel des Mille Collines for approximately 1,200 people fleeing the Hutu massacre, he was unable to help more people. General Dallaire, the head of the UN forces in Rwanda during the genocide, concluded that the UN mandate that prohibited its troops from using force, except in self-defense, cost hundreds of thousands of innocent Rwandan lives (Dallaire 2003). Nevertheless, nonviolent courageous resistance is the primary focus here for several reasons. Potentially, anyone can be a nonviolent courageous resister. Nonviolent courageous resistance does not require access to specialized resources such as weaponry. Courageous resisters who choose nonviolent tactics also do not legitimate perpetrators' use of force as necessary. As such, the choice of nonviolent resistance accentuates the differences between perpetrators' and resisters' actions for the rest of their society. Nonviolent courageous resistance is also fundamentally different in the kinds of preconditions that are likely to encourage it, in the impact it has on the resister and on others, and on the likelihood that such actions will be successful in addressing the injustice. We also believe that nonviolent courageous resisters offer the fullest expression of pro-social behavior possible. For example, despite the heinous actions of perpetrators, nonviolent courageous resisters may see perpetrators as still deserving of basic human dignity and the protection of life.[3]

Paul Rusesabagina offers an excellent example of what we term courageous resistance. Rusesabagina's actions—and those of other courageous resisters—can be best understood by considering the interaction of three factors: *preconditions,* Rusesabagina's own previous attitudes, experiences, and internal resources; his *networks,* his ongoing relationships with people and organizations that offered information, resources, and assistance; and the *context* itself, the institutions, political climate, and other factors that made certain paths of response more feasible even as others became less available. In other words, it was the combination of who he was, who he knew, and the nature of the environment that made it possible for Rusesabagina to shelter more than a thousand people until others could liberate his country from genocide.

Rusesabagina's courage and attention to the needs of others were reflections of the preconditions he brought to the situation—who he was and is as a person. Paul's parents had sheltered refugees from a massacre when he was a small boy (Rusesabagina 2006). In his autobiography, he asserts that he never believed in the validity of identifying Rwandans as Tutsi or Hutu, recognizing even as a child that his own lineage was mixed (20).

In 1994 Paul Rusesabagina became aware of the massacre early on as his Tutsi wife, his children, and many Tutsi and moderate Hutu neighbors sought out his leadership and help. In an interview nearly a decade later, Rusesabagina tried to explain his actions: "I really don't know. I felt I was responsible [for their well-being]" (Meyer 2005). While Rusesabagina's actions stand as a remarkable exception to the widespread barbarity of those one hundred days, he did not see himself as unusual:

I am nothing more or less than a hotel manager trained to negotiate contracts and charged to give shelter to those who need it. My job did not change in the genocide, even though I was thrust into a sea of fire. I only spoke the words that seemed normal and sane to me. I did what I believed to be the ordinary things that an ordinary man would do. I said no to outrageous actions the way I thought that anybody would, and it still mystifies me that so many others could say yes. (Rusesabagina 2006, xvi)

Rusesabagina's networks facilitated his courageous resistance. For example, his phone conversation with the key officers of the Sabena hotel chain headquarters in Belgium apparently inspired an urgent phone call to government ministers in the French cabinet. Because the French government was the key supplier of arms to the Rwandan military, a message from one of the ministers to the Rwandan government, expressing concern about an impending attack at the hotel, stopped—at least temporarily—a planned raid on the Mille Collines:

[O]n May 13, a captain came to the hotel in the morning to warn that there would be an attack at 4 in the afternoon. On that day, the French Foreign Ministry "received a fax from the hotel saying that Rwandan government forces plan to massacre all the occupants of the hotel in the next few hours." It directed its representative at the U.N. to inform the secretariat of the threat and presumably also brought pressure to bear directly on authorities in Kigali, as others may have done also. The attack never took place. (Human Rights Watch 1999)

Similarly, Rusesabagina's prior connections to important Rwandans (from food suppliers to high-ranking members of the Rwandan army) provided resources, information, and access to influential people.

Rusesabagina's actions were also influenced by the genocide's context. As noted above, France's close relations with the Rwandan military offered an opening for French influence. The UN's unwillingness to step in and stop the slaughter also shaped Rusesabagina's actions. The UN troops' orders to not intervene except in self-defense meant sanctuaries such as the Hotel des Mille Collines offered the only safety for many. Similarly, Rusesabagina's efforts to evacuate his guests were not successful until the Kigali political environment changed.

Although Paul Rusesabagina is a single individual, collectives and institutions can also engage in courageous resistance to injustice. Consider another case that emerged during the Nazi Holocaust, which is the most well-researched and well-documented case of genocide in world history. While millions were killed, residents of a remote plateau in occupied

France during World War II, despite great risk and deprivation, sheltered several thousand people targeted by the Nazis. These efforts, documented in the award-winning film, *Weapons of the Spirit*, illustrate the impact that collective courageous resistance, challenging horrific policies and saving lives, can have. The choices of the farmers and villagers in the mountain region of Vivarais-Lignon highlight not only how preconditions, networks, and context can combine to make possible sustained collective courageous resistance, but also how such actions can have some influence on the behavior of would-be perpetrators.

LE CHAMBON: A COMMUNITY THAT DEFIED HITLER

When Adolf Hitler rose to power in Germany in 1933, Nazi policy began to threaten the lives of millions in Europe.[4] While many ordinary people in Germany and occupied Europe complied with the Nazi authorities, there were thousands of people who risked their own safety to rescue those threatened by the Nazi policies. In occupied France, residents of the village of Le Chambon and twelve other predominantly Protestant farming communities on the Vivarais-Lignon plateau saved the lives of five thousand refugees in total, including as many as thirty-five hundred Jews, many of them children (Henry 2002).

The residents of the Vivarais-Lignon plateau were in some ways uniquely ready to shelter Jewish refugees from the Nazis. Located in a remote mountain region, people in the area were used to thinking and acting independently, had little connection with the state, and had a deep-rooted suspicion of government authorities even before the Nazi conquest. They were used to making do with little, as farming was the primary livelihood in their tough climate. The local populace had remained relatively stable for nearly five hundred years but also had a tradition of opening their community to strangers. The people living on the plateau relied on tourism as a source of secondary income. Many households had a fairly long history of renting out extra rooms in the summer and opening their houses to those trying to escape France's polluted industrial and urban sectors. The history of the region also made the plateau's residents identify with victims of persecution and inclined to resist oppression. Most of the year-round residents of the plateau were Protestants in a largely Catholic country. These residents were descendants of persecuted Huguenots, who had centuries before sought refuge in this remote area and whose struggles, resistance, and punishments were recalled regularly in hymns and sermons in the local Protestant churches. In the 1930s, the regional climate of support for resistance to oppression and openness to strangers grew even stronger as the villagers of Le Chambon, led by Pastor Andre Trocme and Assistant Pastor Edouard Theis, developed the Cevenol school, which featured an education curriculum focused on non-violence and internationalism. The school's distinctive curriculum attracted new well-educated immigrants with worldviews complementary to those of the area residents.

When Nazi Germany defeated France in 1940, the plateau's long-standing independently-minded culture was stronger than ever. The Vivarais-Lignon plateau was already hosting some particularly creative and articulate individuals who became models of resistance to state authority, especially the two Protestant ministers devoted to nonviolence, Trocme and Theis. Philip Hallie, author of the best known work on this case, *Lest Innocent Blood Be Shed*, notes that Trocme and Theis' emphasis on resisting Nazism went beyond individual behavior and called on nations and groups to act against evil:

> Theis and Trocme preached resistance against the hatred, betrayal, and naked destruction that Nazi Germany stood for. They insisted, in those times when some nations were trying to appease Hitler, that a nation, like an individual, must do all it can to resist *le mal* (grievous harm) because when such evil was being loosened upon the world, those who were neutral were complicit (Hallie 1979, 85).

Pastor Trocme preached that the collaborationist Vichy government, headed by Marshal Pétain, and the anti-Semitic laws promulgated to appease German occupiers must not be obeyed; the reality of round-ups and deportation must not be ignored.

The result of combining such messages from community leaders with the villagers' previous experiences and cultural traditions was that the people of Le Chambon were engaged in various forms of resistance to the Vichy regime almost from the beginning of the occupation. Many of the villagers refused to perform the ritualized daily straight-armed salute to the French flag mandated by the state and rejected state orders to ring church bells in tribute to Pétain's government. Although not a member of Trocme's church herself, church custodian Amelie defied outsiders' pressure to ring the bells: "I told them that the bell does not belong to the marshal, but to God. It is rung for God—otherwise it is not rung. Otherwise—no!" (96). When a French official and German prefect visited the village to recruit youthful support for the Nazi cause in 1942, they were ignored by many and challenged by others. The older students of the Cevinol school handed them a letter stating, "We make no distinction between Jews and non-Jews. It is contrary to the Gospel teaching. If our comrades, whose only fault is to be born in another religion, received the order to let themselves be deported, or even examined, they would disobey the orders received and we would try to hide them as best we could" (102).

According to Hallie, the plateau's rescue efforts began on a snowy night in 1940 when a lone Jewish woman came to the home of Le Chambon's Protestant pastor seeking shelter from the storm and from arrest. Magda Trocme, the Italian-born wife of the pastor and herself a major rescuer, immediately welcomed the stranger in (120). Another villager who sheltered Jews said, "Look, look. Who else would have taken care of them (the Jews) if we didn't? They needed our help and they needed it *then.*" (127). Refugees began as a trickle and later flooded the area. Rescuers not only housed and hid refugees when necessary, but also educated them as well. Some Jews took up residence in existing pensions, farmhouses, and the buildings of the Cevenol School.

Although the elders of Trocme's parish made a collective decision to create a place of refuge for persecuted Jews, many of the farm families and villagers who participated in rescuing behaviors did so in relative isolation. For reasons of safety, most rescuers did not know which other families had a Jewish child or family living with them, though they were likely all aware that there were many refugee children living in the dormitories and pensions of Le Chambon, as well as in isolated farmhouses in the wooded countryside. People of the area were enormously resourceful, managing to feed the many nonpaying guests for months and even years, despite their own close-to-the-bone existences. Some even managed to help Orthodox Jews remain kosher while their families merged (Sauvage 1989). A women's group, *Le Cimade*, eventually led many of the refugees across the border to neutral Switzerland.

The villagers' motivations for resistance varied. Deep religious commitments were central to the actions of some such as Pastor Trocme. Such people maintained that the highest authority was neither found in the Vichy government nor in Berlin, but in Jesus and the commandment to love your neighbor as yourself, particularly the neighbor in imminent danger. Others were motivated by humanitarian beliefs or their own principles. A villager who provided refuge for the Jews explained why she participated: "Oh, well it was a matter of conscience. Whatever they asked for was just what my conscience would want. Why—I just could not have done anything else but help them and the refugees." (180)

Villagers gradually learned to handle their fears and challenges to their actions as the context changed. When the rescue efforts began, Pastor Trocme was ordered by his superior in the Reformed Protestant Church to discontinue these activities lest they lead to problems between the French Protestant Church and the government. He refused to stop (143–44). The risks of being discovered and punished intensified as other villages in France were burned to the ground by the Germans in retribution for their resistance. German soldiers were sent from the front to recuperate and relax in the plateau. Direct German occupation replaced the Vichy France puppet government of Marshall Pétain. Pastors Trocme, Theis, and another leader of the community were arrested and sent to an internment camp for several months before they were released. Official raids attempted to round up Jews in Le Chambon in 1942 but found no one. But in a raid during the summer of 1943, Daniel Trocme, the Trocmes's nephew and a teacher at the Cevinol school, and a houseful of his Jewish students were arrested by the Gestapo and deported to the concentration camps, where they were killed. Some refugees and their guides were captured or killed on their way to the border. Hallie later reported that evidence of the growing risks actually reaffirmed to rescuers the depth of the dangers the refugees faced were they to be discovered. This awareness further deepened the locals' commitment to help them (205).

Just as the plateau's history and the values of the individual villager enhanced the likelihood of resistance, external factors also helped facilitate the actions of the people of the plateau. Before Nazi raids to round up Jews in the area, villagers received anonymous warnings, which gave them time to find more secure places for the refugees to hide. It also appears that in official reports and correspondence, some French officials deliberately downplayed the numbers of Jews they knew to be in the area. This tacit and anonymous assistance by a few who might just as easily have helped to destroy the village was crucial in enabling the rescue efforts to succeed.

The Trocmes' and Theis' international connections, especially to such organizations as the Quakers, American Congregationalists, the Swiss Red Cross, and the Swedish government, provided crucial support for the rescuers' efforts as well. On the most basic level, this international network's backing affirmed the legitimacy of the rescuers' actions. Equally important, members of this network supplied resources to build and fund dormitories, which rapidly filled with refugee children. These connections also helped with information and international contacts to help get some of the refugees out of France.

Even with this assistance, resources were always strained with hundreds of refugees arriving daily. Nonetheless, Hallie reports, "[N]o Chambonnais ever turned away a refugee, and no Chambonnais ever denounced or betrayed a refugee. . . . In the end, each private home, each pension, even each funded house simply coped on its own. . . . They (rescue activities) were *discrete* in the sense of being separate from each other, distinct, and they were *discreet* in the sense that they were silent, even cautious with each other" (196–97). The Trocmes and the people of Le Chambon took great risks to show compassion for those in danger. Hundreds, then several thousand refugees came, and all were sheltered, welcomed, hidden, and educated by the residents of the Vivarais-Lignon plateau.

The story of Le Chambon is inspiring and illustrates the interconnection of preconditions, networks, and context in propelling collective courageous resistance. The villagers' previous experiences and cultural traditions, coupled with the messages of community leaders such as Theis and the Trocmes, likely made the villagers exceptionally open to courageous resistance. These preconditions on their own, however, do not explain what made the Chambonnais rescue Jews. The villagers' local networks and links to international organizations were also important in making their courageous resistance possible. Certain aspects of the villagers' environment also seem to have made their courageous resistance more likely. Individuals within some of the key institutions of the Occupation (e.g., Major Schmähling, who is discussed in Chapter 4) gave the villagers warning when raids were going to happen and intentionally misdirected Nazi efforts by downplaying the number of Jews in the area.

Courageous resistance does not always require such dramatic efforts. One less dramatic, but equally powerful way people could act against injustice is by creating institutions. By building institutions that challenge injustice, people transform the context and enhance prospects for courageous resistance. These institutions then provide an additional set of resources or tools for their creators and other courageous resisters in the future. Institutions have been particularly important forces in the struggle against abuses of human rights, "literally the rights that one has simply because one is a human being" (Donnelly 2003, 10). Consider how the founding of Human Rights Watch changed the international environment regarding human rights abuses.

HUMAN RIGHTS WATCH: INSTITUTIONS KEEPING AN EYE ON HUMAN RIGHTS ABUSES

In 1975, Canada, the United States, and thirty-three European nations, including the USSR and other Eastern bloc countries signed the *Helsinki Final Act*. The signatory nations agreed to "respect human rights and fundamental freedoms, including the freedom of thought, conscience, religion or belief, for all without distinction as to race, sex, language or religion" and to "promote and encourage the effective exercise of civil, political, economic, social, cultural and other rights and freedoms" (*Helsinki Final Act*). The effects of the *Helsinki Final Act's* human rights provisions were profound. In the Soviet Union and Eastern Europe, activists began publicizing and protesting their governments' human rights abuses. Using the Helsinki Accords as their justification, groups such as the Moscow Helsinki Group in the Soviet Union and Charter 77 in Czechoslovakia formed and called for broad human rights in their own societies. The efforts of these dissidents profoundly affected Robert Bernstein, head of Random House publishing company, when he visited the Soviet Union in 1976. In 1978, with the assistance of the Ford Foundation, he founded Helsinki Watch. Helsinki Watch's mission was to document and publicize human rights abuses in the Soviet Union and Eastern Europe and to pressure countries to fulfill the human rights protections in the Helsinki Accords. Bernstein had some previous experience in creating organizations against injustice. In 1976 he had started the Fund for Free Expression to work with Soviet writers whose works were banned (Montgomery 2002).

The creation of Helsinki Watch fundamentally altered the international environment regarding human rights. Helsinki Watch soon inspired the creation of similar organizations, such as Americas Watch and Asia Watch, to report and publicize human rights abuses in other regions of the world. In 1988, all of the Watch groups came together to form the umbrella organization Human Rights Watch (HRW).[5]

The actions of Human Rights Watch advanced the protection of human rights throughout the world. By helping build other human rights institutions, HRW created a more favorable environment for others working to stop human rights abuses. For example, HRW was a principal advocate for a permanent International Criminal Court, which was established in 2002.[6] The United Nations 1997 Mine Ban Treaty resulted from the efforts of HRW's Arms Project, as well as others. HRW led the lobbying for the UN to adopt an optional Protocol to the Convention on the Rights of the Child in 2002, which prohibits drafting children into armed forces. Domestic human rights activists in a wide range of countries have also found HRW to be a valuable resource. For instance, HRW helped to document and publicize the atrocities in Rwanda, which were discussed earlier in this chapter, and the organization was among the first to call for international war crimes tribunals following the wars and atrocities in the former Yugoslavia and Rwanda. It also documented Saddam Hussein's genocide against the Kurds in the late 1980s.

The story of HRW shows how courageous resistance to injustice can occur through the seemingly mundane creation of institutions. Since its founding, HRW has been a major force against human rights abuses throughout the world. Others who fight against human rights abuses benefit from the more supportive environment that HRW's presence has created. HRW also illustrates how the institutions that fight injustice develop out of the same kinds of dynamic interactions that lead to courageous resistance on the part of individuals and groups. Helsinki Watch was not Bernstein's first effort against oppression; he had a longstanding interest in issues of injustice. Dissident networks in the Soviet Union and Czechoslovakia also contributed to the creation of Helsinki Watch. In turn, Helsinki Watch, as part of the transnational human rights network, shaped an international environment conducive to the creation of HRW.

Even if people have preconditions supportive of courageous resistance, there is no guarantee that they will become courageous resisters. Just as a potential actor's networks and environment can strengthen his likelihood of standing against injustices, so too can they contribute to him making different choices at crossroads and not intervening when injustice occurs. A return to the case of Rwanda and the very different story of General Roméo Dallaire that follows illustrate how elements of the context—in this case, the stance of international institutions—may lead people otherwise inclined toward courageous resistance to become bystanders.

GENERAL DALLAIRE AND THE RWANDAN GENOCIDE: THE CREATION OF A BYSTANDER

Canadian General Roméo Dallaire headed the UN peacekeeping troops in Rwanda in April 1994. When the Rwandan president's plane was shot down on April 6, 1994, Dallaire immediately recognized the likely potential for unrest and tried to stabilize the situation. Dallaire sent Belgian UN troops to protect the Rwandan prime minister and preserve the continuity of government, but his efforts were to no avail. Both the Rwandan prime minister and the troops sent to rescue her were tortured and killed within a day. In response, the Belgian government ordered its remaining contingent of UN forces to withdraw from Rwanda. Dallaire quickly asked the UN for more troops and for permission to launch a preemptive strike against those organizing the ethnic cleansing campaign, but his requests were denied. As the mass killings intensified, General Dallaire repeatedly appealed to the United Nations for more troops, supplies, and authorization to intervene aggressively in order to halt the violence. UN officials responded that he should take no action; his troops could only respond if attacked.

Frustrated, Dallaire found himself in an untenable position. Recalling the days immediately before and after the genocide began, Dallaire later said, "[T]here were five hundred French para-commandos working out of the airport, and a thousand Belgian paras in Nairobi. To that I could add the 250 U.S. Marines in Bujumbara. A force of that size could possibly bring an end to the killings. But such an option wasn't even being discussed" (Dallaire 2003, 284). As the violence grew, Dallaire's superior officers at the UN ordered him and his troops to leave Rwanda as well. Dallaire refused. He and some of his men remained throughout the slaughter, offering whatever assistance they could but unable to use their weapons except in self-defense. After the militia's defeat and the end to the killings, Dallaire remained distraught about the killings. He stayed in Rwanda, trying to provide assistance to the genocide's victims. However, the activities provided Dallaire little consolation. He had been forced to stand by while the Rwandan genocide had occurred, causing him to suffer emotionally and physically from the experience of being a bystander to the mass slaughter: "After Rwanda, Dallaire blamed himself for everything. He sank deep into despair. He attempted suicide. Three years ago he sat on a park bench in Ottawa and drank from a bottle of alcohol. He's forbidden to drink because of the drugs he takes for depression. The mixture almost put him into a coma. Police had to take him to hospital" ("Indepth: Roméo Dallaire," *CBS News* 2003).

Dallaire recovered, but the Rwandan genocide continues to haunt him to this day. He remains frustrated and feels guilty that he could not do more. He recently published his memoirs of the genocide in an attempt to hold accountable international leaders and to inspire the international community to respond more effectively in future emergencies. He also has been helping in the UN-sponsored trials of the genocide's key leaders in Arusha. Testifying for this tribunal, Dallaire noted how institutions of a stronger international community, united and more resolute around the protection of human rights, could have stopped the genocide:

> To properly mourn the dead and respect the potential of the living, we need accountability, not blame. We need to eliminate from this earth the impunity with which the genocidaires were able to act, and re-emphasize the principle of justice for all, so that no one for even a moment will make the ethical and moral mistake of ranking some humans as more human than others, a mistake that the international community endorsed by its indifference in 1994" (Dallaire 2003, 513).

Dallaire's story highlights the dynamic and unpredictable ways that external forces interact with peoples' individual preconditions during times of injustice to shape whether they become courageous resisters, bystanders, or perpetrators. Dallaire and Rusesabagina lived through the same nightmare of mass killing that was Rwanda in the spring and summer of 1994. Dallaire wanted to resist and protect Rwandans from the slaughter just as Rusesabagina did; however, in contrast to Rusesabagina, Dallaire never took action. Despite his desire to stop the ongoing injustices, the UN would not allow him to intervene.

The stories presented above show that courageous resistance has happened at many times in varied places and multiple forms. As inspiring as these stories are, however, they leave crucial questions unresolved. Why do some people look out for others' welfare in the most high-cost settings? What individual preconditions make people more likely to take such actions against injustice? How do external forces beyond the potential actors' preconditions, such as their networks and their context, affect how they respond to injustice? What kinds of networks and contextual circumstances make courageous resistance most likely to occur? How do efforts for justice at the individual, collective, and institutional levels influence each other? How and why are individuals, groups, and institutions able to combat human rights abuses at some points and not at others? If we can address these issues, we can better understand how people become courageous resisters and ideally achieve more success in creating a world in which grave injustices are less likely to occur.

OUR FRAMEWORK

We contend that certain preconditions and external factors heighten the likelihood of people becoming courageous resisters rather than perpetrators or bystanders. Preconditions at the individual level and external factors interact in a variety of ways as people interpret events and determine the degree to which they are individually responsible and need to take action (see Figure 1.1). Our predispositions help shape our knowledge and our perspective on the world as well as our relationships to others. For example, one important predisposition many courageous resisters have is an *extensive worldview*. They see large sectors of the population as part of their in-group (that is, "people like me") and therefore entitled to equal treatment. Illustrative of this is Paul Rusesabagina's refusal to discriminate against those labeled as Tutsis when they needed protection in the Rwandan genocide. When injustice occurs, such factors influence how potential actors interpret available information and how they act in response.

Specific external factors can also influence whether people become aware of injustice and how they respond to opportunities to prevent or allow harm to others. For example, potential resisters' links to other people, exposure to role models, or membership in religious communities, or other organizations may offer them sources of information about what is happening. These connections may also offer value frameworks and role models to help potential resisters interpret events, and they may even offer strategies, networks of support, or links to institutions that may assist them in taking effective action. The domestic and international climates, institutions, and rules can empower or weaken potential resisters as well. The combination of domestic networks linked with international organizations, agencies, and actors that focus on shared ideals (often called transnational advocacy networks) can be particularly potent. Transnational advocacy networks can offer ready-made channels for communication with like-minded actors throughout the world and may provide powerful opportunities for action against injustice.

The choices individuals make when they become aware of the occurrence of wrongs depend on who they are, who they know, the nature of the environment, but also on the context of risk—what is likely to happen if a person takes a stance against injustice. These decisions do more than just transform courageous resisters as individuals. An individual's actions can influence the choices other actors make in the future, as that person can help make the environment more or less supportive of courageous resisters, bystanders, or perpetrators. For example, an individual

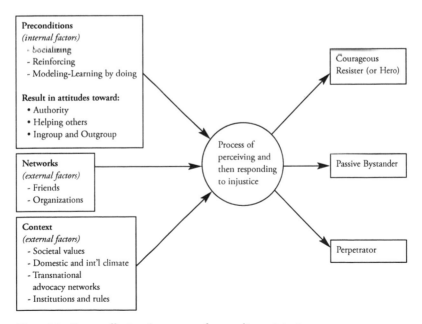

Figure 1.1 Factors affecting the process of responding to injustice

may inspire the creation of international norms to protect human rights that then effect changes in human rights policy at the national level (Risse, Ropp, and Sikkink 1999). One person also may become part of networks of support that help to maintain courageous resistance over time.

Whether courageous resistance is the action of an individual, collective, or institution, it is conscious, voluntary, sustained, other-oriented behavior in a high-risk environment. Even though risks are high, courageous resisters elect to struggle for others' well-being, even as others in the same context choose to remain bystanders or to assist the perpetrators. We understand courageous resistance to be a conscious process of decision making, which is affected not only by who the decision maker is, but where they are and who they know at the particular time they become aware of a grave injustice. This stands in contrast to other work that contends that related behaviors, such as altruism, are relatively stable or even lifelong traits that make selfless responses to others' suffering a virtually automatic response (see Monroe 1996).

This book combines historical examples of courageous resisters with scholarly analysis to examine how and why some individuals, groups, and institutions mobilize to resist policies and actions that harm others. Surprisingly, little previous research has attempted to analyze courageous resisters. Far more energy has been expended to understand what causes human rights abuses and other episodes of injustice rather than to understand those who attempt to end the injustices.

Our work synthesizes existing theory and rich case material to offer a unique analytic framework for understanding courageous resistance. We refine the understanding of courageous resistance to focus on the distinctive preconditions, networks, and contexts that contribute to its development. We also consider how the decision to become a courageous resister affects these actors, their associates, and audiences and their overall context.

THE PLAN OF THE BOOK

As an interdisciplinary group of scholars (historians, social psychologists, political scientists, and sociologists), we have studied numerous cases of courageous resistance across a broad span of time and geography and identified what appear to be crucial commonalities. Chapter 2 expands on the process through which potential actors choose courageous resistance. Chapter 3 uses cases from the Nazi Holocaust and the torture of Iraqi prisoners in Abu Ghraib prison by U.S. soldiers to examine why perpetrators and bystanders make the choices they do. Chapter 4 focuses on several examples of courageous resistance at the individual level. We begin with the stories of a U.S. customs inspector who witnessed African American women being abused by other customs officials, a young army reservist who witnessed the torture of Iraqi prisoners in Abu Ghraib prison, and a U.S. diplomat who worked to save European Jews. The efforts of the first two individuals helped bring about investigations of practices that were later officially banned. For comparative purposes, Chapter 4 also relates the stories of individuals whose actions do not fit quite as easily into our definition of courageous resistance: a German officer who helped the villagers of Le Chambon and a Rwandan woman who testified at the war crimes tribunal following the Rwandan genocide. Chapter 5 examines several cases of collective courageous resistance. The first case profiles efforts by environmental activists to prevent exploitation of the environment and the ethnic people of their small Caribbean island home. The second case is that of people who created groups to publicize and end the Argentine state's policies of kidnapping and torturing in the 1970s, and whose efforts to punish the perpetrators continue to achieve results today. The third case is about the spontaneous public demonstrations on Berlin's Rosenstrasse in the midst of World War II, as non-Jewish German women successfully demanded release of their Jewish husbands, who were slated for shipment to Auschwitz concentration camp for extermination. Chapter 6 considers how organizations and institutions that aim to protect people from harm have come about and influenced ongoing struggles for justice, including the creation of the term genocide and an international regime that recognizes and condemns genocide, but still is weak in offering timely and sufficient intervention. We then consider the creation of the United Nations Universal Declaration of Human Rights and how it changed the context. Finally, Chapter 6 looks at the Convention against Torture and the contribution made by Amnesty International to make it a strong and binding international law. In Chapter 7 we identify patterns across chapters and present our tentative conclusions. We conclude by considering how these findings complement existing research on questions related to courageous resistance. We hope that lessons learned from studying such courageous resistance will inspire and empower even more people to act for justice. The Appendix that follows looks at some ways we can apply the lessons we have learned from studying these courageous resistors. Using the analytical models described in Chapter 2, we provide specific ideas for ways that individuals can strengthen the preconditions and networks that support courageous action. We also identify some of the hurdles that can stop courageous resistance. And so we end this book with an invitation to action. Courageous resistance is the power of ordinary people.

NOTES

1. Collectives can be groups of people who come together spontaneously or who are a sustained community. We define institutions as governments, the laws of governments, intergovernmental entities, nongovernmental organizations, transnational advocacy networks, and agreements such as treaties. Examples within a society can include military, business, political, or social organizations.

2. People who act spontaneously to address injustice, for example, saving a victim from immediate harm, are neither perpetrators nor bystanders. As important as these actions are, however, because they are not sustained, they do not fit into our category of courageous resistance. Rather, such individuals are more accurately characterized as heroes.

3. The type of individual who chooses to act using nonviolent tactics may be motivated by internalized values (sometimes religiously based) that contradict edicts to blindly follow authority. The individual sets a high standard for the treatment of all others that is equally high regardless of who they are, or a high threshold for justifying the use of violence. Also, because courageous resisters learn by doing, prior actions that are prosocial or courageous likely leave them with self-images of people who help rather than harm others. The use of nonviolence radically transforms prospects for success, models positive interactions, opens communications between parties, and may even help create regimes or institutions for addressing contested issues.

4. By the end of World War II, six million Jews and nearly 5 million others— Roma (formerly called gypsies), homosexuals, leftists, artists, and intellectuals—all considered "undesirables" and unworthy of life, would be murdered in Nazi prisons and concentration camps.

5. Africa Watch was added in 1988, and Middle East Watch a year later.

6. For a description of this court, see Chapter 6.

CHAPTER 2

THE PROCESS OF BECOMING A COURAGEOUS RESISTER

> There is no way to peace along the way to safety. For peace must be dared. It is the great venture.
>
> —Dietrich Bonhoeffer

Whether a person becomes a courageous resister depends on how he or she reacts upon becoming aware of grave injustice. People must decide whether to courageously resist the injustice, stand by and do nothing while it occurs, or intentionally participate in the unjust activity. How one responds when facing these crossroads depends on the combination of the individual's preconditions, networks, and the context at the time. This chapter explores how social science research suggests that these factors may work together in influencing people's paths toward courageous resistance.

INDIVIDUAL-LEVEL PRECONDITIONS

The path to becoming a courageous resister begins in formative life experiences through reinforcement and modeling. Psychologists believe that people's early attachments to primary caregivers help lay the foundation for future relationships and are particularly important for empathy and caring. For example, studies on rescuers of Jews from the Nazis showed that rescuers generally had stronger attachments to relatively lenient parents. The rescuers' parents held them to high standards in their treatment of others and modeled this caring and responsibility for others in their own behavior (Oliner and Oliner 1988, 249–50). These early and ongoing experiences interact with our genetic attributes to make us the people we are. They also form people's enduring predispositions, their stable attitude responses. Three predispositions are particularly important in influencing the likelihood of people's courageous resistance: people's attitudes toward authority, their pro-social values, and their perceptions of their relationship to others.

ATTITUDES TOWARD AUTHORITY

A central factor influencing how people react when faced with awareness of injustice is their attitude toward authority. Psychologists Herbert Kelman and V. Lee Hamilton offer a useful framework for understanding these feelings toward authority. They contend that people have three different orientations to laws and authorities: roles, rules, or values (1989, 113). If people feel it is their place in society to obey and support authority by conforming, and that the requirement to follow authority overrides other moral principles, they have what Kelman and Hamilton call a *role orientation* to authority. People with a role orientation are unlikely to challenge injustice perpetrated by figures of authority. If people fear trouble or the costs of not conforming to law and see rules as paramount, they have what Kelman and Hamilton identify as a *rule orientation* toward authority. Few people with a rule orientation to authority are likely to confront injustice by authority figures.

People who have what Kelman and Hamilton call a *value orientation* toward authority are most likely to challenge injustice. Individuals with this approach to authority actively formulate, evaluate, and question all policies in light of their own values. They do not accept any authorities or laws as intrinsically legitimate (113). Rather, these people compare their inner moral code with a law's underlying rationale and may choose to circumvent or challenge a law if they consider it illegitimate. So, if they believe in just or humane treatment of others, they will be motivated to uphold these principles, even if to do so violates a law, involves disobedience to authority, or incurs other risks. Martin Luther King, Jr.'s justification for violating segregationist laws in his famous "Letter from a Birmingham Jail" offers a good example of this orientation to authority: "I submit that an individual who breaks a law that conscience tells him is unjust and who willingly accepts the penalty of imprisonment in order to arouse the conscience of the community over its injustice, is in reality expressing the highest respect for law" (King 1999). Previous research indicates that this value orientation toward authority is characteristic of many who helped rescue Jews in the Holocaust (Tec 1983).

Two of the cases discussed in Chapter 1—Le Chambon and Paul Rusesabagina—show evidence of this orientation toward authority. In Le Chambon, Magda Trocme's response to the need to create fake identity cards seems particularly telling. Although unhappy about the deception, Magda Trocme never wavered from the need to save the Jews: "We had to help them . . . and in order to help them, unfortunately we had to lie" (Hallie 1979, 126–28). Paul Rusesabagina's refusal to join in the killing of Tutsi and moderate Hutus likewise reflected his principles: "I kept telling them, 'I don't agree with what you're doing,' just as openly as I am telling you now. I'm a man who's used to saying no when I have to. That's all I did—what I felt like doing. Because I never agree with killers. I didn't agree with them. I refused, and I told them so" (Gourevitch 1998, 127).

PRO-SOCIAL VALUES

People who have what Ervin Staub calls a pro-social value orientation, "a positive evaluation of human beings, concern about their welfare and a feeling of personal responsibility for their welfare" (Staub 1989, 57), are more likely to respond if and when they become aware of serious injustice. Individuals with this pro-social value orientation view others more positively, give more assistance to those needing help, and are more empathetic in their interactions than others who do not have this orientation (56–57).[1] Scholars who have done extensive research on rescuers report that compared to non-rescuers, individuals who saved Jews from the Nazis show more characteristics consistent with this pro-social approach to life.[2] Despite the many differences amongst them, all rescuers tended to have a greater sense of attachment to others and a feeling of responsibility for people far beyond their immediate familial or communal circles than non-rescuers. For some, this feeling of responsibility extends to all humankind. The rescuers aided victims not because they found them particularly worthy, but because helping behavior reflected "their characteristic ways of determining moral values and actions"(Oliner and Oliner 1988, 249). Holocaust rescuers in general were ordinary people who habitually cared about and for others:

> "They were farmers and teachers, entrepreneurs and factory workers, rich and poor, parents and single people, Protestants and Catholics. Most had done nothing extraordinary before the war nor

have they done much that is extraordinary since. Most were marked neither by exceptional leadership qualities nor by unconventional behavior. They were not heroes cast in larger than life molds. What most distinguished them were their connections with others in relationships of commitment and care" (259–60).

When others face danger, people with pro-social values see their own personal actions to save these others as vitally necessary. As one rescuer of Jews reported, "We helped people who were in need. . . . It wasn't that we were especially fond of Jewish people. We wanted to help everybody who was in trouble" (218). This sense of responsibility seems to appear in Paul Rusesabagina as well. As noted in the introductory chapter, Rusesabagina said he acted because he felt accountable for the other people's well-being: "I really don't know. I felt I was responsible" (Meyer 2005).

How We See Ourselves in Relation to Others

How people see themselves in relation to others also affects how they react when wrongs are committed. Virtually all people categorize others into groups: those who are "more like me" (my in-group) and those who are "less like me" (my out-group). People are more likely to act to protect others whom they see as part of their in-group (that is, primarily family and other close associates for many people) and to devalue those who are outside of it. If others are seen as members of the in-group, their needs, choices, and cultural values are likely to be viewed in a more positive light. People's values and life experiences shape who they consider to be part of their in-groups. The likelihood that one will work to protect a larger number and more diverse set of people increases as that person comes to see more and more diverse kinds of people as part of their in-group.

Courageous resisters envision their in-groups more broadly than others. When the students at the Cevinol school in Le Chambon challenged the Nazi efforts to deport Jews, the justification for their stance was that Jews were no different from anyone else (Hallie 1979, 102). As part of this openness, courageous resisters also appear more likely to accept and embrace a wider range of cultural practices as legitimate. The Chambonnais's respect for the Jewish refugees' cultural practices is illustrative. Rescuers on the French plateau did not try to convert the Jewish people they sheltered; rather, they worked to help the refugees celebrate their holidays and maintain their traditions (Sauvage 1988).

Courageous resisters' perceptions of their in-groups often expand through their experiences, even in some cases through the very practice of challenging injustice. Again, Paul Rusesabagina's actions during the Rwandan genocide appear to fit this pattern. Rusesabagina initially committed himself to help his family members and the neighbors who sought out his aid, but he later accepted responsibility for hiding strangers who sought refuge in his hotel.

The way individuals learn to see themselves in relation to others is likely determined by two factors, which then determine how people respond if and when they become aware of injustice. Some people have a predisposition to extensivity, that is, a strong sense of universal connection with other people (Oliner and Oliner 1988, 249–53).[3] Pastor Trocme's response to the authorities' demands for cooperation in rounding up Jews in Le Chambon certainly suggests he felt this strong universal connection with others: "We do not know Jews. We know only men" (Hallie 1979, 103). We contend that one's propensity for identifying victims as individuals is connected as well. People who see others as differentiated human beings, rather than identify them as members of a particular group, are more likely to be courageous resisters.[4] Paul Rusesabagina's actions during the Rwandan genocide illustrate this tendency. When Tutsi in-laws and associates turned to him for help, he responded to them as individuals, not as Tutsis. Rather than limit who could find sanctuary in the Hotel des Mille Collines, Rusesabagina was willing to shelter everyone—whether Hutu, Tutsi, or other—who came to his hotel for protection.

LEARNING BY DOING

How individuals respond if and when they become aware of injustice develops from formative experiences and also from socialization throughout lifetimes. While all adult behaviors are based to some degree on formative experiences, we argue that people's development of the individual preconditions for courageous resistance—their approaches to authority, pro-social values, and how they see themselves in relation to others—often comes through the process of "learning by doing" (Staub 1989, 80). People's predispositions grow and become internalized when they observe others who model pro-social behavior and when they practice pro-social behavior themselves and feel rewarded. Beginning with minimal steps that aid others, individuals increasingly help others and define themselves as capable of doing so. Once someone engages in one pro-social act or actively defies injustice, that person becomes more likely to take other such actions. Each additional action against injustice further deepens the individual's commitment to courageous resistance (Staub 1989). The story of Le Chambon's resistance began this way. The villagers of Le Chambon gradually became accustomed to disobeying the occupation forces as Trocme and other community leaders refused Vichy orders to ring celebratory bells and salute the flag. Their first actions likely increased their sense of effectiveness and made them see themselves as not only capable of acting for others or against unjust authority, but also as the sort of people who *must do so*.

Courageous resisters' seemingly extraordinary actions to protect others from harm often evolve from virtually continuous orientation to others. For Paul Rusesabagina, a hotelier, offering hospitality to strangers was habitual. Seeing and treating Tutsi compatriots as equals had made it possible for him to marry a Tutsi woman and interact warmly with her family as well as Hutu neighbors. Offering sanctuary to refugees was an extraordinary extension of his ordinary practices. But Rusesabagina had also refused to wear a political button he disagreed with, even when he was repeatedly pressured by the president's office to do so. Similarly, Le Chambon's history as a resort community and refuge for defeated anti-Fascists from the Spanish Civil War likely contributed to the villagers' openness to taking Jewish strangers into their homes and boarding houses, even as the risks of doing so soared.

Over time, people's attitudes toward authority as well as their orientations toward others become habitual and self-reinforcing. Defiance of illegitimate authority and helping others become part of their routine practices. Each action allows people to progress to greater forms of defiance and to increase the amount of help they offer to others. They grow more accustomed to the dangers of courageous resistance in the same way. While people rarely become totally oblivious to the possibilities of harm, they can become habituated to fear and more comfortable with risk (Rachman 1990, 7).[5] If and when this habituation to fear and risk occurs, courageous resisters find that acting against injustice becomes easier.

When people develop the preconditions that are supportive of courageous resistance—value-based orientations toward authority, pro-social values, and an expansive conception of their relationships with others—whether through socialization or through learning by doing, they are more likely to act against injustice. People who do not develop the preconditions for courageous resistance and instead learn differing approaches to authority, values, and ways of relating to others are much less prone to act against injustice. People who embrace values such as aggression, unquestioning obedience to authority, or obedience to the in-group will be especially unlikely to become courageous resisters. When authorities direct these individuals to ostracize or punish subsets of the population, they are more inclined to accept the directives. They are also less prone to see others as individuals distinct from their group identity. People who see their in-group in more narrow terms will likely act to protect fewer people and may even abuse others to champion the cause of their in-group. They will see a much broader segment of the population as their out-group than courageous resisters. They will thus be more vulnerable to propaganda that seeks to devalue or even dehumanize a wide variety of others.[6] A vivid illustration of what can happen if people do not develop the preconditions for courageous resistance occurred in the 1994 Rwandan genocide as many Hutus brutally killed their neighbors. Yet preconditions alone do not determine whether and how a person will courageously resist.

EXTERNAL FACTORS

External forces influence both how preconditions develop throughout a person's life and whether and how a person will courageously resist. Two types of external factors—a person's networks and his context or environment—are particularly significant. When a person faces injustice, his preconditions, existing networks, and context have the potential to strengthen or stifle a choice of courageous resistance. The individual's choices at the series of crossroads arise from the dynamic combination of his networks, environment, and preconditions.

NETWORKS

A person's social and other networks have a crucial influence on whether and how that individual will respond to injustice. Networks affect people's likelihood of becoming courageous resisters in three ways: networks provide necessary knowledge and model alternative interpretations; they create the social capital to support and reaffirm courageous resistance; and they provide crucial resources.

Networks as Models and Sources of Knowledge

Sociologists and political scientists have recently shown increasing interest in networks, especially theories of social networks and transnational advocacy networks. We see the concept of networks as crucial at the individual, collective, and international levels. For the purposes of this book, we consider networks to be social structures of ongoing relationships among individuals, groups, and institutions, which are interactive and result in an exchange of resources. Key resources that might be exchanged include psychological support, information about what is happening or ideas about how to interpret what is occurring, expertise (especially on possible ways to respond to injustice), and physical support ranging from people to technology to financial resources. All of these resources can help counter obstacles to courageous resistance and change calculations as to what is or is not possible. People in the network can offer security by suggesting strategies, diffusing risks, and offering the prospect of eventual success, even if others fail.

People's networks influence how they see and understand themselves in the world.[7] More specifically, people's networks affect their likelihood of learning that something important is occurring, deciding whether they see it as unjust, and deciding whether they view what is happening as their responsibility. The larger the number and variety of people with whom an individual maintains close connections, the greater the likelihood that he or she will be exposed to varying interpretations of the context in which he or she lives. Rescuers of Jews during World War II often got precisely this alternative vision of the world from their associates:

> It is out of such relationships that they became aware of what was occurring around them and mustered their human and material resources to relieve the pain. . . . Their involvement with Jews grew out of the ways in which they ordinarily related to other people—their characteristic ways of feeling; their perception of who should be obeyed; the rules and examples of conduct they learned from parents, friends and religious and political associates and their routine ways of deciding what was wrong and right. (Oliner and Oliner 1988, 259–60)

Having models of alternative behaviors and interpretations coming from networks of associates can also trigger or reinforce preexisting moral codes and inspire people to think that their interpretations are legitimate and shared with others rather than lone aberrations. Research indicates that modeling encourages pro-social behavior far more effectively than reading about helping behaviors or receiving religious or ethical training to care for others.[8] This modeling effect appears to have also occurred on the French plateau of Vivarais-Lignon, albeit on a smaller scale. Virtually all the residents of the area surrounding the village of Le Chambon hid Jews, following the examples of civic and religious leaders such as Trocme and Theis.

People who become courageous resisters open themselves to or seek out relationships with other individuals or networks that offer such alternatives either through the examples of their own actions or through their

writing or teaching. These influential others may present or affirm a reinterpretation of events, or they may make certain goals or values salient,
thus helping the individual toward courageous resistance in both cases.
For example, in contrast to the official rhetoric of the Vichy Government
and Nazi propaganda, members of the Protestant church of Le Chambon
were given an alternative interpretation of events and priorities by their
contact with Pastor Trocme, who, in turn, received ideas, affirmation,
and resources from his membership in a transnational network of peace
and justice advocates.

Positive reinforcement by even one other person can strengthen an
individual's values and understandings of what moral behaviors are and
inspire action.[9] Such support can provide vital encouragement to individuals whose perspectives do not conform to what they perceive to be
majority opinion.[10]

Networks' Social Capital

When people form quality relationships with others, they develop what
is termed social capital: "connections among individuals—social networks and the norms of reciprocity and trustworthiness that arise from
them" (Putnam 2000, 19). The greater people's social capital, the more
likely they are to care about their community and environment and to
trust others. Social capital allows courageous resisters to join with neighbors and friends to reinforce each other's beliefs in the rightness of their
cause. It often enhances their ability to stay together for the "long haul"
to accumulate the necessary evidence and expertise to win public support
in order to press their case. Many resisters depend on the trust and comradeship that develops in their local networks to sustain their motivation
and commitment in the face of fear, frustration, and setbacks.

Social capital is often at the core of courageous resistance, as is the
reliance on others in a network. A strong network of allies and faith that
justice is on one's side are often crucial for courageous resistance. We contend that networks containing those who share one's pro-social values can
have a profound influence on the choices one makes at the crossroads
leading to potential courageous resistance. Courageous resisters generally
seem to have significant social capital and rarely operate in total isolation.
People engaging in courageous resistance may either draw on preexisting
connections, or they may create new networks that yield such benefits.

Social capital appears to be most significant when a person reaches a
crossroads where he or she must decide to act against injustice or not.
Close relationships with others can be crucial in differentiating people

who choose to participate in high-risk movements from others who share the same beliefs, but do not act (McAdam and Paulsen 1993, 648). Courageous resisters often start to take on high-risk pro-social actions because they are asked to help by someone they trust, either a potential victim or someone else who is taking action. The story of Le Chambon suggests how vital these bonds of trust can be for courageous resistance. The villagers and farmers near Le Chambon were often approached by one of the local schoolteachers, who traveled from farm to farm and throughout the village asking virtually every family to take in refugees. Such a widespread call for help was made less risky because of the preexisting bonds of trust among the residents of the region.[11]

Social capital also played a key role in the development of Human Rights Watch presented in Chapter 1. Members of groups such as Charter 77, the Czech resistance movement, and the Moscow Helsinki group would have been much less likely to work together to document human rights abuses had there not been already established relationships based on trust from years of organizing together.[12] Similarly, while the economic capital provided by Robert Bernstein and the Ford Foundation to create Helsinki Watch was important to these activists, if Bernstein and the foundation had lacked social capital with the Eastern bloc activists, the collaboration might have failed.[13] Cases of communal courageous resistance in particular suggest the significance of social capital. As we will see in several of the cases presented in Chapter 5, ongoing and trusting relationships are crucial in bringing some people to activism and in sustaining their efforts through difficult times.

Networks' Material Resources

Networks of friends and associates can give potential resisters other resources that can empower them. Networks help develop connections and norms of trust, but they also provide both material and less tangible support, such as access to information, political power, legal expertise, and strategic tools. Thus, in the case of the Rwandan genocide, Rusesabagina's connections enabled him to feed the Hotel's refugees. He was also alerted to planned raids on the Hotel des Mille Collines by associates cultivated in prior years. In Czechoslovakia, the ratification of the Helsinki Accords created a new resource for activists by inspiring the rise of Charter 77, a domestic political group that criticized the repressive communist regime's violations. This group's persistent calls for the rights guaranteed by the Helsinki Accords kept alive the tradition of dissent until the Czech regime could be brought down more than 20 years later.

People who choose to courageously resist injustice are more likely to do so and better able to sustain their commitment if they are able to rely on some kind of network of support. Even a small, loosely connected circle of trusted confidantes could model behavior and give alternative interpretations of the world, provide social capital, and offer resources to a courageous resister.

Whatever their predispositions, people's likelihood of courageous resistance diminishes if they lack supportive networks. People with very narrow circles of friends and associates and those who expose themselves to few sources of information may be less likely to learn about multiple and varied events, rules, and institutions. If people never hear interpretations that differ from official views or witness demonstrations of alternative responses, they may be more willing to go along with the dominant interpretation and conform in their actions, even if doing so involves severe repression of others. Without the social capital provided by networks of supportive associates, people may also be less likely to take action against injustice. Potential courageous resisters may also lack the other tangible and intangible resources networks provide.

CONTEXTUAL FACTORS

Context, or environment, also influences how people respond when they become aware of injustice. We see three elements of this context as particularly critical in shaping whether a person becomes a courageous resister: societal values, legal institutions, and the domestic and international environment.

Societal Values

Societal values can make it easier or more difficult to act against injustice. Social psychologist Ervin Staub argues that pluralistic societies, in which multiple belief systems are allowed to compete openly, are less likely to allow abuses to happen. Monolithic societies, where there is one strong belief system, are more fertile environments for systemic injustice. Similarly, the degree to which a society prioritizes norms of trust, tolerance, and free expression, as opposed to a culture that emphasizes obedience to state authority, also influences how likely courageous resistance is; societies that emphasize obedience to the state are less likely to support courageous resistance (Staub 1989, 63). For example, the Chambonnais' long-standing distaste for state authority may have made easier their decisions to protect Jews from governmental policies.

Institutions

Legal institutions, the laws that govern a society and the institutional structures that maintain and implement them, are another element of the context. Legal institutions such as a bill of rights, independent judiciary, or laws that provide penalties for bias-related crimes, as well as such international covenants as the Universal Declaration of Human Rights, can empower courageous resisters by providing shared understandings of what is unacceptable, confirmation of values, and tools to fight injustice. The Helsinki Act, which is detailed in Chapter 1, inspired activists across the Eastern bloc to organize against injustice in their countries and armed them with human rights standards to measure their states' performances. Institutions can also constrain people who would like to halt injustice.

Domestic and International Climates

The domestic and international climates are also important elements of the context. A political environment that supports dissent might make it easier to act against injustice. Because all governments need support from the citizenry, even the most repressive regimes must worry about how they are perceived by the populace. Thus, at moments when such regimes are vulnerable or in crisis, courageous resistance may be easier.

For people who choose to act against injustice, an important element of the international context is the presence or absence of transnational advocacy networks. These networks that connect individuals around the world who are dedicated to the same basic principles (e.g., the linkages that exist among international human rights groups and institutions) may offer the potential to address worsening conditions and to educate, inspire, and empower supporters of human dignity (Sikkink 1993, 411).[14] Helsinki Watch, discussed in Chapter 1, offers an example of such a network, albeit more formalized. Helsinki Watch and the groups throughout the world it spawned all now work together as part of Human Rights Watch. Their power is further enhanced by being linked to individuals, governments, and other institutions, both inside and outside of governments, dedicated to defending human rights.

In sum, three elements of the context are particularly critical in shaping whether a person becomes a courageous resister: societal values, legal institutions, and the domestic and international environment. We argue that these contextual factors combine with people's predispositions and networks to shape how individuals respond when they become aware of injustice.

Variation in these aspects of the environment can also constrain people who want to act against injustice. A society that values obedience to authority makes dissent less likely and can lead to a domestic environment of fear, conformity, and acceptance of grave injustice. Situations such as Rwanda's genocide, where the rule of law is under attack or where there are no impartial legal institutions, are less supportive of courageous resistance. Despite the desire to stop wrongs from occurring, if there is no support from institutions, courageous resisters may be virtually impotent. For example, when the Turkish genocide of Armenians in 1915 occurred, because there were no international norms or penalties for a state mistreating its own citizenry, people throughout the world were unable to stop the devastation. The domestic or international climate can also make courageous resistance more difficult. A context seemingly supportive of courageous resistance can change rapidly. For example, terrorist attacks or economic devastation can make a population feel threatened. Staub's research suggests that a context of difficult life conditions within a society can set the stage for a gradually worsening process of human devaluation and brutality and may even undermine value orientations and other factors that would otherwise protect against abuse (Staub 1989, 14). As Chapters 5 and 6 illustrate, lack of transnational advocacy networks can make organizing against injustice much more difficult and less effective. Further, while wars can provide openings for resistance to injustice, they can also create environmental conditions more favorable for injustice.

We argue that people are more likely to become courageous resisters and better able to sustain this commitment if contextual factors are supportive. More specifically, when societal values are pluralistic or value dissent, when legal institutions are equipped to punish injustice, and where transnational advocacy networks around injustice are present, the context is more likely to be supportive of courageous resistance. As with people's networks, however, a supportive context on its own does not guarantee courageous resistance. Instead, how people respond when they face the crossroads of awareness of injustice comes from the dynamic interaction of their individual preconditions with their networks and the context.

The next section of this chapter explores this series of crossroads, when a person decides whether to take action against injustice.

THE CROSSROADS

When people become aware of injustice, they arrive at a series of what we call crossroads. While it may seem that people have only to decide whether to resist the wrongs being committed, we contend that such moments are not that simple. Our conception of this series of crossroads draws heavily on the psychological research of Latane and Darley (1968), but we have added a sixth step to the Latane and Darley model.[15] We posit that there are actually six junctures where people must make decisions:

I.   They must notice that something is happening.
II. They must interpret what they have seen as just or unjust.
III. They must decide whether they should take personal responsibility.
IV. They must consider various responses and decide on a course of action.
V.   They must take their decided course of action.
VI. They must maintain their chosen course of action, reassessing whether to continue.

A person's responses or choices at these junctures determine whether that individual will be a courageous resister, bystander, or perpetrator. Groups (either spontaneously formed collectives or fully formed communities) and institutions also face these decisive crossroads when they learn of wrongs being committed. The junctures of their crossroads are the same as for individuals. Whether individual, group, or institution, some choices made at these crucial points are steps in a larger behavior pattern. Less frequently, the crossroads are the first steps toward becoming a courageous resister, bystander, or perpetrator.[16] (See Figure 2.1)

CROSSROADS I AND II: AWARENESS AND INTERPRETATION

Awareness of injustice is the first critical juncture for the potential courageous resister. This awareness has two elements: recognition that an event is occurring and understanding that the event is unjust. Even if a person appears to have individual preconditions supportive of courageous resistance, networks of support, and a favorable context, failure to either recognize that a wrong is occurring or interpret it as unjust will clearly prevent a person from acting to stop it.

For example, a mother with young children, including a child with serious developmental delays, who lived in Argentina during a period of extreme repression was so immersed in her day-to-day responsibilities and so isolated in her household, that she literally learned of the military regime's horrific human rights violations only after the regime had left power. As a result, she never came to any of the other crossroads that follow from awareness of injustice. A more typical explanation for people's failure to act on the part of Argentines when they did learn of the Dirty War's disappearances was that they assumed that those taken by agents of the state actually were dangerous subversives and that the government's agents had taken them because "they must have done something" (Thalhammer 1995).

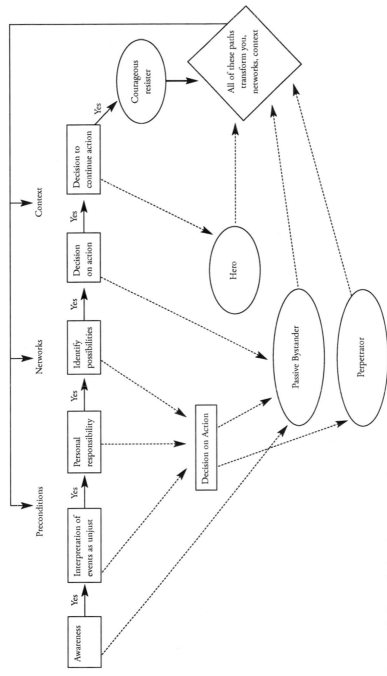

Figure 2.1 The Process of making choices at crossroads

CROSSROAD III: TAKING RESPONSIBILITY

Even if a person recognizes that an event is happening and understands it as harmful, he or she still might not choose to challenge injustice. Courageous resisters decide that what is happening is their responsibility and that it requires attention. Feelings of responsibility may arise from widely varying catalysts (e.g., the arrest, disappearance, or assault of a loved one, seeing photos of abuse, viewing a murder, etc.), as we see in the examples in Chapters 4 and 5.

CROSSROADS IV AND V: DECIDING ON A COURSE OF ACTION AND TAKING IT

Feeling personally responsible for the well-being of victims, courageous resisters decide they must act. The catalysts for these decisions to act vary. They may be triggered by a request for action by a bystander or by a victim, such as the arrival of the first refugee at the Trocme household. They may come about when someone sees another person model an "appropriate" response or reflects on what an admired leader or set of principles would imply in this setting. Feeling a need to respond might also come when someone or something confirms one's interpretation of another's action as noxious and therefore requiring action. Part of this decision to respond to injustice is a choice about how to respond or the course of action to take. All who become aware of injustice and see it as their responsibility face these junctures when they must decide to act or not and how to act.

CROSSROAD VI: MAINTENANCE AND REASSESSMENT

The last crossroads in our model of courageous resistance are the overlapping stages of maintenance and reassessment. If a person confronted with injustice chooses to act to eliminate the injustice and sustains that behavior long enough to assess and accept its costs and risks, she becomes what we have termed a courageous resister (rather than a one-time hero).[17] This stage is included in the model as a way to account for the evolution of commitment to courageous resistance as something intentionally sustained over time. Some courageous actors decide to stop after they have completed an initial courageous task; others decide to dive back in with more commitment or with commitment to an expanded or different goal, such as fighting for human rights or environmental standards more broadly than in their original campaign.

From crossroad VI, a courageous resister can reenter the model at any stage. This stage accounts for some courageous resisters' rapid, seemingly decision-free choice to behave courageously and their protestation that there was nothing to decide, that action was the only option. Staub (1991) presents an argument based on his personal goals theory that supports our assertion that courageous actors can reenter the model and thus short circuit the decision-making process. Staub says that this fast decision making results when a person has a strong motive (e.g., a personal goal), is activated by a powerful stimulus, and has the needed competency or resources to respond. This could represent someone bypassing crossroads I, II, and III and entering the model at crossroad IV: choosing a form of action.

Courageous resisters can exit the model when the variables at a particular stage do not allow for a positive decision. Even courageous actors choose their causes and have days when they cannot respond. Famous rescuer of Holocaust targets Oskar Schindler later expressed remorse that he had not saved more threatened people than he had. As with the previous stages, a person's decision to act and choice of what to do are affected by the interaction of their preconditions, networks, and context. After courageous resisters act against injustice, they are transformed into what Fogelman calls the "rescuer self" (Fogelman 1994, 68). When people behave in even a limited courageous way they come to see themselves as courageous people, as "heroic helpers" (Staub 1993). They are permanently transformed by what they have done. Further, they often transform the context by providing an example or reinterpretation of events for potential courageous resisters and often leave a legacy of networks or institutional change resulting from their actions.

While the focus of this chapter is the path to courageous resistance, the bystander's somewhat parallel journey deserves some brief attention as well. Bystanders have the potential for courageous resistance, and yet they choose not to act against injustice. In order to understand courageous resistance, it is important to understand the individuals, groups, and institutions that stop short and choose to do nothing while others are harmed.[18] The next section of this chapter considers these people whose responses to the critical junctures of the crossroads diverge from the path of courageous resistance.

THE BYSTANDER

Bystanders face the same critical series of crossroads that courageous resisters do, but they respond differently. For some bystanders, their divergence at these crossroads starts at the first juncture (crossroads I and II): awareness of an event and interpretation of it as unjust. A good example of divergence at the first crossroad took place after the end of World War II, when many Germans claimed not to have known what was happening to the Jews after they were removed from their communities. Others believed these victims "must have done something" to deserve imprisonment and so did not identify the police actions as illegitimate. These people failed to recognize the event as unjust, and thus established themselves as bystanders at the first crossroad.

Other bystanders become aware of events, interpret them as unjust, but decide that it is not their responsibility to act (crossroad III). An example of divergence at the second crossroads was the outrage of many U.S. citizens at news of the one hundred–day genocide in Rwanda who felt someone should do something about it. Yet very few citizens even contacted their congressional representatives or the President to call for a response. These people recognized the injustice, but chose the path of bystander when they decided that taking action was not their responsibility.

Still other people may simply choose not to act, even though they do feel responsible for helping address the problem (crossroads IV and V). They may know what harm is being done, disapprove of it, and feel responsible for acting, but they interpret the situation as so overwhelming or risky or hopeless that they dare not resist it. Consider how the context seems to have shaped the decision of one of the numerous bystanders in Rwanda, Catholic Bishop Misago, who remained passive while eighty-two Tutsi schoolchildren were killed. He reportedly said, "When men become like devils and you don't have an army, what can you do? All paths were dangerous. So how could I influence?" (Gourevitch 1998, 139). Misago illustrates crossroad IV when he reported that he considered various responses, but rejected each. His decision to take no action to defend the victims illustrates his choice at crossroad V.

Other bystanders inclined to act against injustice are constrained by institutions within the context. For example, as noted in Chapter 1, General Dallaire wanted to use the UN forces under his control to stop the genocide in Rwanda, but he was ordered by superiors in the UN peacekeeping chain of command not to intervene.

The interaction of predispositions, networks, and contextual factors shapes how an individual responds at each crossroad and makes the difference between a person choosing the role of bystander and a person engaging in courageous resistance. People with the same individual preconditions can respond to the same events quite differently because of variations in their networks or contextual factors. How people approach

each stage of the crossroads, then, depends not only on their predispositions to resist injustice, but also relies greatly on external forces. Is the individual embedded within networks that will support courageous resistance
in one way or another? What are the societal values and legal institutions
present? What is the domestic and international political climate?

LONG-TERM IMPLICATIONS OF PEOPLE'S CHOICES
AT THE CROSSROADS

Whichever path a person chooses when facing injustice, the choice has
such a powerful impact that it fundamentally alters her perspective on the
world and her relation to other people. In such intense circumstances, the
individual redefines how she sees herself, her relationships to others, and
her necessary actions at that moment and in the future.

CHOOSING TO BE A COURAGEOUS RESISTER

When people choose courageous resistance, they change the environment
for bystanders and perpetrators, as well as other potential courageous
resisters. They define what is happening as unjust, thereby redefining the
situation for others. They model behavior that may help transform inac-
tive bystanders into courageous resisters. Courageous resisters' active dissent by criticizing or trying to counteract the actions of perpetrators
offers hope or refuge to victims. The choice of a just, nonviolent form of
resistance can also offer more bystanders an alternative, further challenging a regime's legitimacy. Courageous resisters can also undermine perpetrators' monopoly on the "facts," offering an alternative interpretation
that may bring even some perpetrators to question their own actions.

Just as with individuals, groups' and institutions' responses to the
crossroads can also have a tremendous and long lasting impact on injustice. Spontaneous demonstrations or coordinated collective endeavors
have both forced repressive regimes to reassess policies. The community
of Le Chambon collectively saved thousands of Jewish children targeted
for deportation. Even if the people working together do not know one
another ahead of time, they can have a powerful influence on injustice.
As Chapter 5 shows, even spontaneous protests in which actors do not
coordinate their efforts may be successful.

Governments, intergovernmental and nongovernmental organizations,
and their laws and agreements have all had powerful effects on addressing injustice. Some states, including Tanzania, opened their doors to

refugees in the Rwandan crisis. While UN forces were not allowed to effectively address the genocide in Rwanda, NATO forces did intervene to end the genocide in the former Yugoslavia that also occurred in the 1990s. The United Nations has also played a role in creating international tribunals to punish both Rwandan and Yugoslavian perpetrators after the genocides ended.

CHOOSING TO BE A BYSTANDER

If a person chooses to be a bystander when faced with injustice, the effects are as wide reaching as those of courageous resisters' actions. Bystanders individually decide not to act, but their inaction or lobbying might encourage others in their social, political, or professional circles to acquiesce to the apparent norms or demands of often repressive contexts. While bystanders may see their silence in the face of injustice as having a morally neutral effect, they often actually contribute to the power of those behind the injustice. Perpetrators and their peers often interpret bystanders' inaction as tacit support for the malevolent actions.

Decisions by groups and institutions to stand by and refuse to intervene in the face of injustice can have an equally powerful impact. While the Rwandan genocide was happening, foreign states and the United Nations refused to intervene to even designate the Rwandan tragedy as a genocide, much less put into place timely and effective responses to the killings. In both the Holocaust and the Rwandan genocide, the Catholic hierarchy refused to intervene. In the latter case, clergy acted both as bystanders and active participants in the genocide.

In sum, preconditions, networks, and institutions create conditions that affect how people learn about and interpret events that endanger others. When facing crossroads (deciding whether to join perpetrators, stand passively by, or courageously resist injustice), individuals, groups, and institutions have great potential to do harm or good—their actions are rarely neutral. The choices they make affect not only other potential actors in the present, but future actors as well, who will be influenced by the models they offer and the impact they have on the overall context. As Table 2.1 indicates, people's choices at each crossroads have wide ranging implications. They can contribute to or impede tremendous harm.

Table 2.1 Psychological and sociological effects of decisions at crossroads

What the actor does	Effects on resisters	Effects on perpetrators	Effects on bystanders
Courageously resists injustice	Resisters' pro-social values are reinforced or expanded: *All people should be treated with respect.*	Perpetrators receive feedback that behavior is socially unacceptable.	Bystanders are influenced to model pro-social values and validate existing pro-social values: *Just as I thought, this is unacceptable behavior.*
	Resisters learn by doing, gaining experience in interventions/actions.	Perpetrators may stop that particular anti-social behavior at that moment.	Bystanders may be more likely to join the intervention and thus gain experience in interventions/actions.
	Resister may redefine himself as the sort of person who intervenes when injustice is being committed.	Perpetrators may undermine their anti-social values and behaviors.	May cause bystanders to consider pursuing pro-social values.
	Resisters may be more likely to intervene in the future.	Perpetrators may be less likely to repeat that anti-social behavior in the future.	Bystanders may be more likely to intervene themselves in the future.
Stands by and does nothing	Resisters must justify inaction to themselves: *Why didn't I do something? Perhaps because the behavior is justified, or not as bad as I thought.*	Perpetrators get feedback that the behavior is socially acceptable: *If nobody criticized me, what I am doing must be right.*	May invalidate any latent pro-social values held by the observer: *Maybe this is okay.*
	Unjust action may seem less wrong. The actor's values may change towards those of the perpetrator.	Values supportive of unjust acts may be reinforced.	Values may change towards those of the perpetrator, or existing anti-social values are reinforced.

Table 2.1 *continued*.

Stands by and does nothing	Resisters may be less likely to intervene on behalf of others in the future.	Perpetrators likely will continue unjust behavior and be more likely to repeat it in the future.	Bystanders may be less likely to intervene on behalf of others in the future.
	For actors who stand by and do nothing, the effect of their inaction on themselves will depend in part on how far along the crossroads model they are. For the bystander who just observes the actor's failure to respond, but is not privy to all that was going on in the actor's head, the effects are the same no matter how far along the crossroads model the actor had gone. Inaction on behalf of others can become the norm if bystanders don't intervene. The inaction becomes both socially acceptable and encouraged, and the unjust behavior goes unchecked and is encouraged by the inaction of the bystanders.		

NOTES

1. See also Erkut, Jaquette, and Staub 1981; Staub 1974.
2. For example, research by Monroe and others suggests that the actions of people who act fairly consistently on behalf of others originate in an enduring and wide-ranging altruistic predisposition. Monroe argues that altruists are distinguished from others by their perspective or view of themselves in relation to others, which results from socialization and development of values. She contends that for all the rescuers she interviewed, the "decision to risk their lives to help another person appeared spontaneous and simple. There was no night of anguish spent searching one's soul to find the strength to do the right thing" (Monroe 1996, 214).
3. Some rescuers of Jews during the Holocaust seem to show this tendency (Fogelman 1994; Monroe 1996; Midlarsky, Jones, and Corley 2005).
4. Psychological research supports this connection. Seeing the individualized humanity of victims rather than thinking of them in more abstract terms increases the likelihood that others will aid them (Jenni and Loewenstein 1997; Schelling 1968, Small and Loewenstein 2003). We contend that a propensity to see victims as individuals likely helps courageous resisters resist the temptation to engage in just world thinking (that is, finding reasons to blame the victim for the fate that has befallen him) or in dehumanization (thinking of others as subhuman and therefore outside one's moral code of how to treat others).
5. Psychological research suggests that just as individuals can become habituated to helping others and to maintaining their own moral values, so too can other individuals become habituated to fear. While people rarely become totally oblivious to contexts that may harm them, they may over time come to find that threatening environments do not paralyze them in the same way they do other members of the society. For more on this, see Rachman 1990.
6. See Altemeyer 1996; K. Stenner 2005; Milgram 1965; Zimbardo, Haney, Banks, and Jaffe 1974; M. Haritos Fatorouris 1988; Huggins 2000.
7. According to Bert Klandermans (1987), our ongoing relationships create a collective social identity, which can lead to a "sharedness of beliefs." One of the big challenges for mobilizing is that people need to become aware that there is something wrong and that they share this grievance with others and then determine to act with others. Creating communities of individuals who discuss what is happening and refine their understandings of events, causes, and prospects for change is vital for collective mobilization to take place. Gamson and others concur that people's connections to others offer the context in which they make sense of their world. Bouncing ideas off of those in one's circle of acquaintances allows the individual and his associates to construct meaning and create a collective identity. In other words, it is through our contact with others that we determine what is wrong, who is responsible, and what can be done. See Gamson 1995, 85–106.

8. See Darley and Latane 1970.

9. Experiments by Solomon Asch showed that an individual who is inclined to disagree with peers is much less likely to yield to group pressure to conform, even if only one other person in the group supports the individual (Asch 1956. The source of this potential ally's influence is less clear. It may be that the presence of one like-minded individual is sufficient to confirm an individual's personal assessment of a situation, or it may motivate individuals to act honestly or courageously by promising them at least one social connection as an alternative to total ostracism. Seeing another individual modeling independent behavior may even shake a person out of an "agentic state" and allow him to think clearly, take responsibility for his action, and consider alternatives to obedience and acquiescence. A variety of research on obedience to unjust authority also suggests that it may be very difficult for most individuals to conceive of disobeying those perceived as authorities unless there is a model of dissent. The well-known experiments by Stanley Milgram (in which U.S. volunteers were instructed by researchers to administer a series of painful and potentially harmful electric shocks to others) demonstrate that a majority of ordinary people might be surprisingly obedient to those they perceive as having authority, even when the penalty for refusing orders is quite low. Milgram argues the need to obey those in power is so strong, it not only supersedes the objections of the person apparently receiving the shocks, but also takes precedence over the clear discomfort of those administering the shocks. However, having an ally in resistance makes a large difference. When Milgram's volunteers were paired with others who refused to continue administering shocks, the volunteers' cooperation with the authorities dropped markedly (Milgram 1965; 1974).

10. Research by Elisabeth Noelle-Neumann points out the vital importance of diverse voices within social networks. Noelle-Neumann suggests that, even within a democracy, when the costs and risks of being in the minority may seem insignificant, people fearing ostracism often censor their own expressions of support or criticism of candidates or political parties. Silence in this and more repressive settings can have very negative repercussions because others' silence is interpreted as signaling widespread tacit support for the apparently dominant candidates or positions, inflating their perceived level of dominance in the society. Such interpretations influence citizens' behaviors, encouraging silence by those who believe themselves to be in a smaller minority than they actually are and encouraging some to conform to what they perceive as the majority solution simply because it seems to be the most popular. Breaking this "spiral of silence" by encouraging diverse voices and public dissent deflates the power of the loudest voices within the society and changes the calculus of those who might fear being ostracized for anti-regime opinions or behavior (Noelle-Neumann 1984).

11. The rescuers on the French plateau were also assisted by resistance groups in other countries and by an organization of French women, *Cimade*,

which helped to shepherd refugees across the border into neutral Switzerland. Links between these secret societies of resistance would have been highly risky if not for preexisting social capital that allowed for trust among these organizations and individuals.

12. We're indebted to political science Prof. D. Christopher Brooks of St.Olaf College for this example.

13. Scholars argue that similar bonds explain at least some people's participation in the American Civil Rights Movement's Freedom Summer and other campaigns. For example, Doug McAdam's research on the recruitment of Northerners to join the Freedom Summer campaign in the segregated southern United States examines the applications of those accepted for the dangerous civil rights crusade and those who then chose to participate. All those who applied appeared deeply committed to integration. What seemed to distinguish those who actually participated from those who were accepted but declined to participate were the particular relationships in which the would-be volunteers were enmeshed. A key difference between those who actually took part in the activities and the others who also believed in the cause but didn't participate was that the high-risk activists who took part had received an invitation by others close to them (McAdam and Paulsen 1993, 640–66).

14. For more information on transnational advocacy networks, see Sikkink 1993, or Sikkink and Keck 1998.

15. Latane and Darley examined which factors influence the decision making of bystanders when unpremeditated helpful behavior or intervention is required in a time limited emergency. An example of such intervention would be going to the aid of someone who has collapsed on the street.

16. Previous studies that have focused on rescuers of Jews during World War II have determined that these same variables do not selectively predict what we are calling courageous behavior (Gross 1994; Monroe 1991; Monroe, Barton and Klingemann 1990; Oliner and Oliner 1988; Staub 1993). We contend, however, that by adding consideration of preconditions, networks, and contextual factors, the limitations of the model are addressed.

17. Those who take a spontaneous action to address injustice (that is, saving a victim from immediate harm), but do not sustain such activities are heroes. They fall outside of the definition of courageous resistance considered here. They are obviously also outside the bystander and perpetrator categories presented here as well.

18. Chapter 3 discusses how people become perpetrators.

ORDINARY PERSONS DOING EXTRAORDINARY EVIL

We will have to repent in this generation not merely for the hateful words and actions of the bad people but for the appalling silence of the good people.

—Dr. Martin Luther King Jr.

JEDWABNE

One day in July, 1941, half of the population of the Polish village of Jedwabne murdered the other half. Until Polish-born historian Jan Gross described this, the accepted truth was described on a plaque in Jedwabne as the work of the Gestapo and Nazi occupation police. Gross concluded, however, that the Polish villagers had willingly tortured and murdered some 1,600 Jews of their village. Only a handful of the village's Jews survived (Gross 2001).

In the course of this day of massacre, villagers tortured and humiliated the Jews using kitchen knives and pitchforks to gouge out eyes or dismember children in front of their mothers' eyes. Jews who were not killed in the course of the bludgeoning, beheading, and drowning were rounded up, locked in a barn, and burned. Singing, laugher, and shouts of delight from the murderers accompanied the anguished screams of the victims. How are we to understand these murders, which constitute a part of the Holocaust, especially when we consider the horrible brutality of the murders and the pleasure some took in maiming and killing?

No one forced these villagers to inflict terrible suffering and death on their neighbors, and those who did not participate were not punished. Thus, our efforts to explain extraordinary evil have to clarify why so many are capable of perpetrating serious human rights abuses or "crimes against humanity." The problem of extraordinary evil is studied in seemingly "normal" persons—"ordinary" in the sense that they are part of a majority and are not otherwise criminal (Waller 2002).

In general and with some notable exceptions, scholars who studied the Holocaust during the first decades following World War II saw it as a result of orders from Adolf Hitler or someone else near the top of the dictatorship. Hitler and his closest henchmen developed a system of destruction from plans they thought up in advance and carried out the Holocaust through subordinates who had little choice but to obey.

Gross suggests that rather than a machine Hitler established and controlled from Berlin, the Holocaust was a mosaic of locally accomplished destruction and murders, "discrete episodes, improvised by local decision makers, hinging on unforced behavior" (Gross 2001, 81). He and many other historians have created new viewpoints by examining history not just from the "top down" but through the lives of ordinary people—such as, for example, someone you meet on the street, in school, or in any other ordinary place on any day.

While this book is primarily about courageous resistance, our underlying argument is that ordinary people who become aware of injustice all face crossroads where they must decide how to respond. At such points, people choose whether to become courageous resisters or to take a different path. This chapter examines how ordinary people, such as the Jedwabne villagers, take this different path, either choosing to join in as perpetrators or stand by silently as unjust activities occur.[1] The focus is not on monstrously evil persons such as Dr. Joseph Mengele, the infamous experimenter at Auschwitz, or Idi Amin, dictatorial leader of Uganda from 1971 to 1979, but rather on those who enable such evildoers. Consider, for example, one of the most significant persons on this scale, existential philosopher Martin Heidegger, who was no murderer. But with his great reputation, he lent credibility to the Nazi party and to everything Hitler said when he accepted a top academic position under the Nazis in 1933 and presided over the expulsion of Jewish professors for a year and the abolition of the faculty senate in favor of authoritarian "Fuehrer governance" in the university system.

Many less influential persons have committed atrocities, often when political power holders create circumstances ordering atrocities, or merely licensing or engendering them. In a society founded on decency, the "simple man" is a decent man. However, this same person "goes wild without knowing what he is doing when disorder arises somewhere and the society is no longer holding together" (Vogelin 1999, 105). Those who abuse, torture, or kill within circumstances licensing them to do so, without orders from superiors, probably constitute a clear minority; although the numbers of ordinary persons doing extraordinary evil increases when these persons expect a personal reward. Even fewer, however, will actually resist or even report such crimes. The presence of bystanders looking on often constitutes a pressure for conformity.

The dynamic interactions of people's preconditions, networks, and context shape whether they decide to be perpetrators and bystanders as much as they influence the choice of courageous resistance. Also important for each individual are the risks—what is likely to happen if one does nothing or joins in with the perpetrators of injustice? Similar to the choice to resist injustice, the decision to become a perpetrator or bystander has far-reaching effects. People who choose to become perpetrators and bystanders are transformed just as courageous resisters are. Their actions in turn influence their own preconditions, networks, and context, as well as those of others in the future who will become aware of grave injustice. As such, they influence whether others will be more likely to be courageous resisters, bystanders, or perpetrators.

INDIVIDUAL PRECONDITIONS

People's attitudes toward authority and toward others influence people's likelihood to become perpetrators and bystanders. Someone who has what Kelman and Hamilton identify as a role or rule orientation to authority is more prone to respond to unjust actions by joining in or not intervening to stop them. If an authority encourages these people to fulfill their role in society and participate in unjust activities, they are likely to do so. Similarly, if people see laws or rules as their authority, then following the law, no matter what it says, is paramount. Challenging the authority of the law would be anathema for them. People who have either of these orientations see conformity to authority as their primary goal. Even if they were to become troubled by governing authorities' unjust activities, they would likely stay silent rather than challenge the injustices.[2]

A willingness to obey those who assert authority appears in many ordinary people. Well-known experiments conducted by Stanley Milgram in the 1960s demonstrate that a majority of ordinary people can be surprisingly obedient to those they perceive as having authority, even when the penalty for refusing orders is very low. Milgram recruited volunteers for a study that was ostensibly to determine whether punishment for wrong answers would enhance learning and memory, but really the project was to evaluate people's obedience to authority. Two volunteers would show up simultaneously. One would take the role of teacher and the other of student with the roles allegedly chosen randomly. In fact, however, the student was always a confederate and the teacher was always an unknowing volunteer. Milgram would let the teacher know when the student made "errors," and then the teacher punished the mistakes with an electric shock to the student. The initial shock was fifteen volts, then each successive error met with shocks increasing by fifteen volts each time, up to a maximum of 450 volts, labeled "Danger, High Voltage, XXX." In the end, two-thirds of the "teachers" took the level of shocks all the way up to 450 volts. No one quit before they heard loud objections and screaming. Milgram concluded that the need to obey those in power is so strong, it not only supersedes the objections of the person apparently receiving the shocks, but also takes precedence over the clear discomfort of those administering the shocks. Of the approximately two-thirds who followed the researchers' directions fully, most felt that they were not themselves responsible for any pain or serious harm caused by the shocks they administered (Milgram 1965).[3]

In fact, unless they see a model of dissent, most people may not even imagine disobeying those perceived as authorities. While everyone develops in-group/out-group classifications of others, perpetrators and bystanders seem particularly prone to learn to devalue and dehumanize anyone who is different from them. This suggests that if the targets of injustice are considered to be part of one's out-group, the individual will be less likely to intervene and may even become a perpetrator.

People also often develop the propensity for being a perpetrator or bystander by acting in ways that harm or help others and redefining their own capacities in light of what these actions show they are capable of doing (e.g., being obedient, cruel or fearless) (Staub 1989). This "learning by doing" can begin with minimal steps that injure others, through which individuals may increasingly define themselves as capable of harming others. Once someone does one unjust action toward another or stands by and does nothing while such activity occurs, the person is more likely to take other such actions in the future.[4] A person's predispositions to be a bystander or perpetrator appear to be strengthened by both observing others who model such behavior and are rewarded and by personally engaging in such actions and feeling fulfilled.

NETWORKS

Networks influence people who become perpetrators and bystanders just as they affect those who become courageous resisters. Just as people's networks help them decide whether an action or policy is unjust, an individual's associates may also help one to define others as members of a deservedly devalued out-group. Similarly, if an individual already sees others as members of his out-group, his circle of friends may affirm this judgment. Research on conformity also suggests that people's desires to have the social connections of a group can lead them to participate in unjust activities or to stand by and inactively allow the injustice. If others in an individual's network become perpetrators and bystanders, the individual is more likely to do so, as well (Milgram 1965; Milgram 1974).

Networks appear to be particularly important if a person is bothered by ongoing injustices. Wanting to maintain connection with others and not stand out, the potential dissenter likely will remain silent. Other potential dissenters who share the same concerns might then perceive themselves as an even smaller minority than they actually are, creating further disincentives to resist injustice. This bystander silence appears to give the perpetrators a quiet endorsement and likely suggests to them that their actions are just (Noelle-Neumann 1984).[5] This silent endorsement may then result in the continuation or escalation of the unjust actions.

CONTEXT

Several dimensions of the context of a situation can influence whether people become perpetrators and bystanders to injustice. In Staub's view, the domestic socio-economic political environment and particularly the incidence of difficult life conditions (e.g., living with the destruction of war, long economic hardship, and political violence) is a central dimension. Staub contends that living in such "hard times" is challenging for the individual. The experience appears to increase people's feelings of injustice and powerlessness, their need to blame another group for their problems, their need for a rigid ideology to explain why life has gone so badly, and their desire for a dogmatic blueprint for building a better world. According to Staub, genocide is more likely to occur when these harsh life conditions are especially severe or prolonged (Staub 1989).

Some societal values may also make a person more prone to becoming perpetrators and bystanders. If people see their culture as superior to others, as many Germans did before the Holocaust, the effects of hard times may be intensified. Alternatively, if a culture has a longstanding tradition of hostility toward a group, people who live in that culture may become socialized to see the group as an out-group and devalue its members. Similarly, if a society has "monolithic" values, a single dominant and dogmatic belief system, people in that society may be prone to think that contrary beliefs and those who hold them are threats (Staub 1989).

Institutions also influence whether people become bystanders or perpetrators. Institutions may legitimate injustices by codifying laws that devalue others, as occurred in Nazi Germany regarding Jews. This institutional legitimacy is especially important for people who have a rule-based approach to authority; they likely will follow the law and become perpetrators.

A variation of institutional legitimacy would occur in situations where existing institutions disappear, and the rule of law no longer exists (as occurred in Rwanda's genocide). When no one is in control, other "authorities" have opportunity to arise and condone behaviors otherwise unthinkable for ordinary people when institutional law does exist. Such a complete vacuum of authority can leave hostile attitudes unchecked, giving way to the anarchic behavior. Similarly, when domestic or international institutions fail to intervene to halt injustices, perpetrators may feel emboldened. The silence of "institutional bystanders" (police, national courts, world leaders, the UN, etc.) suggests to perpetrators that there may be no consequences for their actions.[6] Institutional passivity during the occurrence of injustice may also lead some potential resisters to feel that their society's institutions will not support their resistance, which thus encourages their silence.

In the case of Jedwabne, it is clear that anti-Semitism as well as the context of the circumstances motivated the murderers, although certain circumstances triggered them. Gross's explanation of what triggered these murders focuses on the circumstances of World War II. The Jedwabne villagers had been demoralized by ruthless Soviet occupation for almost two years when the front line of World War II moved east, bringing to them the heartless, German "racial" war. The townspeople had heard that German forces were slaughtering Jews all over Poland, and this, together with widespread anti-Semitism, helped the perpetrators to consider their victims less than human, an important element in making mass murder possible. The massacre would have hardly happened without the German occupiers, but it was the Polish villagers who asked the Germans whether "is it permitted to kill the Jews"(Gross 2001, 33).[7] The permission to kill apparently also lent the villagers a sense that they could toy with and mistreat their victims any way they wished. Perhaps some participated in the brutalities due to a sense that general and personal norms were being suspended for just a limited period of time, a temporary bacchanalia outside of the everyday customary constraints. As Gross writes, the Jedwabne murderers were determined to take away their victims' dignity before killing them (Gross 2001, 38, 61).

Nevertheless, it is critical to keep in mind that, just like other instances in the history of atrocities, some of the Jedwabne villagers tried to intervene, or could not bear to look on. Despite the danger of ostracism and perhaps of even sharing the fate of the Jews, some villagers tried to warn Jews before the slaughter. One family, who had to pay the price of severe ostracism after the war, hid Jews. In this family, a Polish woman was the main rescuer, and the fact that perpetrators are overwhelmingly males raises the question about the role of gender in the perpetration of extraordinary evils.[8]

Having a license to harm others does not mean all will use it. Even under circumstances similar to those at Jedwabne, under the worst breakdowns of social norms, mass murder does not always happen. The Jedwabne case brought new scrutiny to the role of the Poles in the atrocities of World War II. Yet, many of the persons honored at the Holocaust memorial in Jerusalem, Yad Vashem, for rescuing Jews are from Poland.

Scholars have tried to isolate the qualities that make some persons tend to perpetrate mass murders and others resist. As circumstances worsen and pressures increase, more "ordinary" persons become perpetrators. Some social psychologists argue that just about every one of us could become a perpetrator under drastic enough circumstances. Others emphasize that perpetrators possess personality traits that make them more likely to behave aggressively and cruelly to begin with. No doubt, some are able to resist authority and mass conformity better than others. Some have a better developed ability for moral reasoning and socially responsible actions than others, as well.[9] Not all U.S. soldiers present at the March 1968 My Lai massacre of civilians during the Vietnam War took part, and, in fact, one soldier intervened to stop the slaughter.[10] The following story of the Abu Ghraib prison abuses in Iraq illustrates the complex dynamics of responsibility for human rights abuses. Importantly, it also illustrates the courage of the very few who resist, even in the face of intense intimidation by superiors and peers.

ABU GHRAIB

In 2004, the story of U.S. military guards at Abu Ghraib who tortured and otherwise abused Iraqi suspects broke into international news. Since then, there has been a steadily mounting number of revelations regarding the abuse of suspects in the United States' "war on terror." These revelations led the human rights organization Amnesty International in its 2005 annual report to accuse the American government of condoning "atrocious violations of human rights" and "thumb[ing] its nose at the rule of law and human rights" (Cowell 2005). There were ringleaders in the Abu Ghraib prison in Iraq who chose roles as perpetrators of humiliation and torture of Iraqi prisoners, but at least one soldier actively resisted.

In early 2004, twenty-five-year-old army reservist Sergeant Joseph Darby discovered that members of his unit, charged with guarding prisoners, had tortured and sexually humiliated inmates of the Abu Ghraib prison near Baghdad. Doing what he thought was right, Darby decided to give investigators hundreds of photographs documenting the scandal at Abu Ghraib. Darby's story will be told in Chapter 4 in more detail, but what matters here are the insights he and the military's official investigative review, the Taguba report, gave into how the abuses at Abu Ghraib happened.[11]

According to Darby, the lack of supervision by superior officers and a pattern of gradually evolving cruelty played a role in his fellow soldiers' increasingly depraved treatment of the prisoners.

> They thought they could do it and get away with it. Because I think what happened is one night they did something small. Because we did have the three that were on the floor and they were being beaten by Graner. Those guys were alleged rapists that had raped a twelve-year-old boy in one of the other tiers. They weren't normal inmates for Tier One. And I knew who those prisoners were when I saw that picture. I mean I wasn't over there and I don't know how it happened, but I've always thought that it probably happened where they took out jailhouse justice on them and beat them. And then slowly thought, "Well, we did this. What else can we do?" And then it slowly progressed up until what it became. (Darby 2006)

Other evidence backs up the significance of higher authorities' support and permission in what occurred at Abu Ghraib. In early 2004, Iraqi suspect Manadel Jamadi died at Abu Ghraib following a CIA interrogation. The government accused Lieutenant Andrew Ledford, a Navy SEAL, whose unit brutally beat Iraqi suspect Jamadi for ten minutes before he died, of dereliction of duty, punching a prisoner, and allowing his platoon to abuse a prisoner. At Ledford's trial, one of his subordinates testified that under the supervision of a CIA interrogator he had roughed up another suspect. He also remembered being told that the Geneva Convention's rules of conduct did not apply to the high value targets they were after because these were "unlawful combatants" (Human Rights Watch 2004).

A document that the American Civil Liberties Union (ACLU) obtained with difficulty and released March 29, 2005, offers support for this claim. Lieutenant General Ricardo Sanchez authorized "twenty-nine interrogation techniques, including Intimidation by Dogs, Stress Positions, and Sensory Deprivation, twelve which far exceeded limits established by the Army's own Field Manual. This authorization was also in violation of the Geneva Convention" (ACLU 2005).

Abu Ghraib also illustrates the powerful pressure toward conformity that people who are lower in an authority structure experience. People may be compelled to be bystanders because of coercion or fear of recrimination from their superiors. For example, an intelligence sergeant in the army accused three fellow soldiers of abusing detainees in Iraq, telling his commander that they had "hit detainees, pulled their hair, tried to asphyxiate them and staged mock executions with pistols pointed at the detainees' heads" (Smith and White 2005, A15). Fearing that one or more of the detainees would die, the sergeant angered his commander with a suggestion that the unit be redeployed elsewhere. His commander, however, considered him the problem, not the abusers. He called the sergeant delusional and ordered him to undergo a psychiatric evaluation, even though a military psychiatrist had made an initial judgment that the sergeant was stable—as indeed his actions as reported in the documents indicate he was (Smith and White 2005, A15).

The pressure of peers was a strong influence in silencing soldiers who did not actively participate in the abuses and torture at Abu Ghraib as well. Darby faced death threats for "ratting out" his fellow soldiers. Related to this is the strength of bystander passivity—the existence of a powerful norm to not intervene—which may have been even stronger than the power of a superior order. Testimony forming part of the basis for the Taguba report indicates that five soldiers, including three noncommissioned officers, looked in on Abu Ghraib, without attempting to intervene, as prisoner suspects were seriously abused. There is evidence of one sergeant who turned his head because he could not bear to watch such disturbing treatment of prisoners.[12] The fact that the abuse was so disturbing and the knowledge that it was this sergeant's duty to actively intervene to stop the abusive behavior were still weaker than the pressure to stand by while his peers were either ignoring the misdeeds or actively engaging in abuse.

As of March 2005, thirty-three military workers at the lower levels of authority had been court-martialed and fifty-five had been reprimanded for mishandling prisoners in Iraq and Afghanistan. A small number of prison guards were also put on trial. Still, the U.S. government asserted that the abuses were the result of a few aberrant prison guards at Abu Ghraib. President Bush himself identified the abuse as strictly the wrong-doing of a clique of a few junior-level enlisted soldiers (Reid 2005, p. A2). Consequently, almost all of the senior officials who were potentially responsible for authorizing or encouraging brutalities against suspects escaped independent investigations.[13]

"MONSTERS OF EVIL" AND ORDINARY PERSONS

Not all evil that ordinary people do is so treacherous and brutal as that committed in Jedwabne. As in other contemporary societies that commit-ted, assented to, or did not stand in the way of great evils, ordinary Germans living under Nazi rule exhibited behaviors ranging from resist-ance to perpetration of evil. There were murderers who killed while sitting at their desks as well as others who pulled the triggers or dumped cyanide-based Zyclon-B into gas chambers. Sebastian Haffner's story, below, illus-trates how an ordinary German was swept into contributing to Nazi domination and acclaim, through a series of compromises that led further and further away from his intention of actually defying Hitler. Having first unwillingly contributed to the isolation of Jews as victims by claim-ing an "Aryan" identity, Haffner, in order to finish his preparation for a legal career, later dons a swastika armband and marches through the streets with his comrades in SA paramilitary-style, intimidating others like him-self who wished to have nothing to do with Nazism. Those in his group committed to acting as Nazi leaders set the tone for the entire group, none of whom wished to step into the painful position of expressing individual differences to group conformity (Haffner 2002, 155, 279ff.).

The role of one infamous Nazi shows the interaction between leader and followers. Adolf Eichmann zealously pursued his job of organizing transport for Jews from all over Europe to their deaths. It is instructive, however, that at his trial in Jerusalem, this mid-level Nazi bureaucrat so important to the Holocaust linked average German citizens to his own actions, pointing out that no one had protested against what he was doing; in fact, his neighbors, friends, and colleagues helped Eichmann to realize that he was relatively well-heeled, influential, and respected. Testimony at Eichmann's trial revealed in fact that the Holocaust would have been impossible without the mass and individual cooperation and compliance of many people who, in better social and political circum-stances, would have been neither villains nor heroes.

During Hitler's dictatorship, many Germans came to think of Hitler as a leader who had succeeded where others had failed. Most Germans looked on passively as Jewish neighbors and colleagues were brutalized, robbed, and deported. Millions of people supported the system in various ways, while knowing at least something about the inhumane persecution of the Jews (the Kristallnacht and deportations, for example, were carried out in public view). Although Germans did not rise up as communities to murder Jews, the aggregate actions of ordinary Germans, under government pressures and encouragement, quickly led to the social isolation of Jewish citizens. This was a prerequisite for stripping them of possessions and deporting them to mass murder.

In short, the Nazi genocide, which we use here as a particularly striking example of twentieth-century crimes against humanity and genocide, would not have been possible without the bystander passivity of the broad masses or the collaboration of ordinary people who were willing to denounce and exploit Jews.[14]

SEBASTIAN HAFFNER'S EXPERIENCE

Sebastian Haffner's recently published memoirs give us a rare view behind the curtain of the everyday life of an ordinary German as Hitler came to power and consolidated his control. As he wrote, "If I were more important I would be less typical . . . in telling my story I am not recounting just my own unimportant experience but what thousands of others also went through." Haffner also grounds the argument for the significance of his memoir by noting that the change in Germany as Hitler came to power in 1933 was taking place primarily "in private. . . . Today the political struggle is expressed by the choice of what a person eats and drinks, whom he loves, what he does in his spare time, whose company he seeks, whether he smiles or frowns, what he reads, what pictures he hangs on the walls" (Haffner 2002, 185–86, 220).

When Hitler became chancellor in January 1933, Haffner was on track to becoming a judge. He soon realized he wouldn't be able to without becoming a Nazi Party member, and by 1939 he had immigrated to England. In the meantime, he took advantage of newly available jobs in journalism that appeared as a result of the firing of Jews and political leftists and discussed the choice of becoming a Nazi "for fear of starvation and destitution" (231). He did not become a Nazi, although his choice to remain in Germany until he had finished taking his assessor exams for his career preparation led him to see himself as someone who enforced Nazi standards and norms and someone who was unwilling to stand up on behalf of any of the Nazis' victims.

Less than a year after Hitler had come to power, Haffner joined about one hundred other men in a training camp, a prerequisite for taking the assessor exam. During the next weeks he spent hours each day marching and singing in formation with the others, under a swastika flag. As his group marched into villages, people would either raise their hands in a stiff-armed Nazi salute or disappear into doorways. Haffner, who himself had fled into house entrances rather than raise his arm, was now part of the Nazi enforcement. "My predicament then," Haffner wrote, "was the Third Reich in a nutshell" (257).

Gathered under an enormous portrait of Hitler, the group listened to Hitler's speeches together. The members of the SA, or so-called "Brownshirts," a Nazi paramilitary organization, quickly assumed roles of leadership and remained aloof when others tried to speak with them. They were the insiders who knew when to laugh and nod. When the national anthem played, the entire group stood at attention with outstretched arms, facing the radio that had just brought them Hitler's voice. "We all sang, or pretended to do so," Haffner wrote, "each one the Gestapo of the others." The event was "dreadfully shaming," although Haffner was able to rationalize at that moment, "This isn't me. It doesn't count." But he knew he was a fellow traveler, someone who participated and conformed in order to make life easier at the moment, or, in Haffner's case, to reach a specific goal—taking the test he had prepared for over the course of several years (267–68).

Haffner asks himself whether he should have refused to take part in this group camp from the beginning. Then he identifies several reasons for going along. First, he wanted to pass the exams, and the "camp report" would play a major role in determining how he did. More important, he writes, was the experience of being "caught completely off guard." The very first day, he might have refused to put on the armband, but he did not know where it would all lead at that point. He considered it better in any case to wear the band in order to maintain his freedom for a "later, greater purpose." Later, when he became more concerned about his compromises, he realized that resistance was impossible since it required organization of others, and each one in the group deeply mistrusted each other. Haffner also blamed what he called a "typically German aspiration" to be proficient just for the sake of being proficient, "the desire to do whatever you are assigned to do as well as it can possibly be done" (272, 281).

Most insidious for Haffner was "the trap of comradeship." Comradeship became a poison to the soul, he wrote, since it relieves persons "of responsibility for their actions, before themselves, before god, before their consciences. Their comrades are their conscience and give absolution for everything, provided they do what everybody else does." By playing by Nazi rules, Haffner and his group "automatically changed, not quite into Nazis, but certainly into usable Nazi material." They were "still not virulently anti-Semitic," he wrote. "But 'we' were not prepared to make an issue of it. . . . We had become a collective entity, and with all the intellectual cowardice and dishonesty of a collective being we instinctively ignored or belittled anything that could disturb our collective self satisfaction." This was "a German Reich in microcosm" (283–88).

In fact, five years later, Reinhard Heydrich, the later executor of the Final Solution, argued successfully against establishing Jewish ghettos within Germany because "today the German population . . . forces the Jew to behave himself. The control of the Jew through the watchful eye of the whole population is better than having him by the thousands in a district where I cannot properly establish a control over his daily life through uniformed agents" (Hilberg 1985, 168).[15]

CONCLUSION

Just as broad socio-political circumstances influence whether people take advantage of a seeming license to brutalize, plunder, and kill, so can they also limit crimes against humanity. An exciting historical development in the twentieth century, which is known as an age of extremes for the breathtaking scale of its crimes against humanity, is the concomitant development in societies around the globe of "bottom up" mass nonviolent actions that curtail these crimes. In communist China, spontaneous collective and nonviolent public protests became the most important form of opposition to the oppressive regime. Germany, the locus of the Holocaust, the most heinous crime in modern history, has become the site of citizen-mobilized protests that are demonstrably responsible for nonviolently curtailing a rise of intolerant and brutal rightwing extremism.

Since the unification of Germany in 1990, protests mobilized by ordinary persons and expressing the will of the majority have peacefully intimidated the will of neo-Nazi and other xenophobic movements. In the first half of the century, Hitler, putting into practice his theory that the fundamental pillar of power derived from mobilizing the masses, stood on the backs of consensus among Germans to stifle dissent. By the end of the century, the masses had learned to turn the tables to some extent, setting and reinforcing tolerance and nonviolence as the norm, also through mobilized mass public demonstrations.

A striking example of this form of people power occurred on the sixtieth anniversary of the end of World War II on May 8, 2005. In Berlin, some three thousand neo-Nazis had planned to demonstrate against what they called "sixty years of liberation lies" and demand the end to

Germany's "cult of guilt." City leaders probably did the right thing by demonstrating the importance of freedom of expression. After considerable debate, they reluctantly agreed to allow the neo-Nazis to march in protest. It was also a brilliant moment for a bottom up expression that the ideals of the extreme right were not the norm and were unwanted. To say "no" to the planned neo-Nazi demonstration, a crowd of more than ten thousand Berliners took to the streets. Their much bigger numbers blocked the planned route of the neo-Nazis. The sense that they were vastly outnumbered led the neo-Nazi leaders to send their supporters back home.[16] Citizen-mobilized crowds had helped establish social norms of tolerance, just as the Nazi-mobilized crowds had done using anti-Semitism in an earlier period.

This recent demonstration against neo-Nazism is not an isolated incident but reflects a trend that German citizens have created. If the government had created the crowds, as dictatorial states often do, the gatherings would be devoid of the meaning that has made them effective—the display of dominant social norms so important that citizens voluntarily take to the streets in numbers to show their determination to sustain them. These citizen actions are no substitute for governmental policies enforcing tolerance, but the 2005 Berlin example indicates how responsible citizens work well together with government.

In 1992 and 1993, hundreds of thousands of Germans took to the streets to express their abhorrence at outbursts of violence aimed at foreign refugees. These demonstrations and candlelight vigils—in contrast to the aggressive torchlight parades of the Nazis—took place throughout Germany in Munich, Berlin, Hamburg, Frankfurt am Main, and Rostock. In Berlin, more than one hundred thousand people, carrying banners with phrases such as "Foreigners need Friends," comprised a "line of light" to express their solidarity with foreign refugees. Former German President Richard von Weizsäcker said this protest showed that Germans today, in contrast to the Germans of the Weimar Republic which collapsed with the rise of Adolph Hitler, are ready to participate in and defend democracy. Ignatz Bubis, former chairman of the Federation of Jewish Communities in Germany, said the protest indicated that most Germans today reject Nazism, unlike those sixty years earlier.[17] As the German case shows, however, constitutional guarantees of civil liberties and limits on governmental power are hardly stronger than the popular will to defend them.

NOTES

1. The Kitty Genovese murder in 1964, where thirty-eight neighbors looked on without helping or calling the police as Genovese was stabbed to death,

compelled Bibb Latane and John Darley to investigate why people who were willing to help others under normal circumstances were reluctant to do so in emergency situations. Latane and Darley show that people find few positive rewards in actively intervening on behalf of victims in an emergency; in fact, intervention might even endanger them.

2. Other research regarding human rights abuses supports the significance of orientation to authority as key for explaining who are prone to become perpetrators or bystanders. Neil Kressel suggests there are four overlapping types of people likely to engage in human rights abuses: "aggressive killers," those who are "fascism-prone," "uneducated killers," and "conformists." Two of the four types—those who are "fascism-prone" and "conformists"—appear to be people who have a role or rule based orientation to authority. People who are, what Kressel labels, "conformist" individuals are simply prone to follow authority uncritically (Kressel 1996).

3. Such agentic behavior declined dramatically in other variations of this experiment. When the "teachers" were paired with others as they administered the shocks, their cooperation with the authorities dropped markedly when their cohort refused to continue administering shocks. Whether seeing someone modeling an alternative helped individuals think of new alternatives or reassured them that their interpretation of events was not isolated, having a potential ally in resistance made a marked difference in levels of resistance to authorities (Milgram 1965; 1974).

4. See Milgram 1965; Zimbardo, Haney, Banks, and Jaffe 1974; Haritos-Fatorouris 1988; Huggins 2000, 27, 57–78.

5. See endnote 10 in Chapter 2 for a further explanation of this phenomenon, which Noelle-Neumann calls the "spiral of silence."

6. According to Staub, a key to preventing genocide is for the rest of the world to strongly and loudly condemn ethnic abuse in its earliest stages, as quickly as the early warning signs of genocide appear. If leaders headed toward genocide know that the world condemns them and will hold them responsible, they will be much less likely to follow that course.

7. Waller summarizes differing scholarly explanations for the origins of extraordinary evil—ideologies, extraordinary group pressures, psychopathologies, a second self, personalities (Waller 2002). One might also turn for explanation to criminological theories such as anomie, opportunity theory, and differential association.

8. Gross gives an example of Jedwabne women who were terribly anti-Semitic and brutal and who called the (male) police rather than take action on their own (Gross 2001, 192).

9. Philip Zimbardo and Mika Haritos-Fatouros emphasize the power of circumstances to influence individuals. See Huggins, Haritos-Fatouros, and Zimbardo 2002. On the other hand, Thomas Carnahan and Sam McFarland emphasize the self-selection and particular personality traits of the perpetrators (Carnahan and McFarland 2007). Sociologists Hirschi and Gottfredson argue that people commit crimes only in environments

in which it is clear that they will be tolerated. Motivational factors need not necessarily be present; although, lack of social controls allows the individual to choose criminal activity without fear of negative consequences (Gottfredson and Hirschi 1990). Kelman and Hamilton (1989) proposed a model of three factors for explaining torture and mass murder: authorization of crime, bureaucratization that lowers individual sense of responsibility within a hierarchy of command, and dehumanization that causes the perpetrator to see the victim as less than human in any case. Christopher Browning's illustrious study (1992) of German mobile killing units also stressed situational factors over ideology to explain why "ordinary men" slaughtered Jews on the eastern front in 1941. He identified the pressure of group behavior and conformity as an important motivation, a factor that Sebastian Haffner also understood to be a major force the Nazis used to their advantage in civilian life in the early years of the Third Reich.

10. In March 1968, members of the U.S. Military massacred hundreds of unarmed civilians, many of them women and children, in the small village of My Lai, Vietnam.

11. The Taguba report, dated June 6, 2003, is available at http://www.public integrity.org/docs/AbuGhraib/Taguba_Report.pdf (accessed May 26, 2005). The Center for Public Integrity has also posted classified documents on which the Taguba report is based, for which see http:// www.publicintegrity.org/docs/AbuGhraib/Tag26.pdf, and http://www .publicintegrity.org/report.aspx?aid=417&sid=100.

12. In background materials from Army Major General Anthony Taguba's investigation, Investigating Officer Chris Ry to Janis Karpinski, June 8, 2003, regarding abuses of military detainees in Iraq, posted by the Center for Public Integrity at http://www.publicintegrity.org/report.aspx?aid= 417&sid=100 and http://www.publicintegrity.org/docs/AbuGhraib/ Tag26.pdf. One soldier made verbal objections to the abuses.

13. One notable exception is the case of Brigadier General Janis Karpinski, the first and only female general officer to lead soldiers in combat. She was eventually demoted to colonel after the abuses that occurred under her leadership came to light (Priest 2005).

14. The Holocaust is a particularly important example for a variety of reasons, including its magnitude, location in the heart of Europe, and reliance on modern advanced technology and bureaucracy. The extensive documentation and study of the Holocaust also make it an unusually apt example.

15. Minutes of the meeting of officials following the Krystallnacht Pogrom, which became Nuremberg Trial Documents, PS-1816, quoted in Hilberg 1985, 168.

16. *The Economist* 2005, http://www.economist.com/cities/briefing.cfm?city _id=BER

17. Peace Media Service, Repr. in *Albert Einstein Institution Newsletter* 4, no. 3 (Winter 1992/1993), http://www.aeinstein.org/organizations.php3 ?action=printContentItem&orgid=88&typeID=16&itemID=171&User _Session=943465fd5f1a4d7d44a33c5ca97dddfe.

CHAPTER 4

THE INDIVIDUAL AS COURAGEOUS RESISTER TO SOCIAL INJUSTICE

> Never doubt that a small group of thoughtful, committed citizens can change the whole world. Indeed, it is the only thing that has.
> —Margaret Mead

INTRODUCTION

In this chapter, we look at individuals who took a courageous stand when they confronted danger and injustice in their workplaces, communities, and wartime situations. We examine several cases of ordinary people called upon to confront authority when harm was being inflicted on others. We begin by exploring the cases of three individuals who clearly fit our definition of courageous resister. The first case involves a whistle-blower in the U.S Customs Service whose situation began in the 1990s when she defied her supervisors after she saw fellow agents abusing travelers. The second case examines the role of a young American soldier who exposed injustices in an Iraqi prison. The third case centers on an American foreign service officer's efforts against the direct orders of superiors to help Jews escape from Europe in the period leading up to World War II. The focus of the chapter then shifts to consider two cases that show some characteristics of courageous resistance but do not fully meet the definitional requirements. We explore the actions of a woman who testified at the post-Rwandan genocide war crimes tribunal in Arusha and the German officer who provided covert assistance to the Chambonais in their efforts to protect Jews from the Nazis. In each of these latter two cases, ordinary people clearly show courage in the face of injustice; yet their actions do not rise to the level of courageous resistance. We conclude this chapter by considering the commonalities and differences among all five cases and the social functions of courageous resistance.

This chapter illustrates the range of ways individual actors may be moved to become courageous resisters. Some of these individuals were themselves victimized earlier and resolved to intervene to prevent others from suffering. Some were moved to action by witnessing oppression, responding to direct requests for assistance, or listening to their own internalized values of how they should act and how the institutions to which they belonged should respond. Previous experiences, value orientations, inclusive views of in-groups that embraced strangers in peril, and learning by doing were all vital in distinguishing the courageous resisters from peers who became bystanders or even perpetrators. For some courageous resisters, preexisting networks of trusted confidantes and strategically placed others helped them to gather information, make sense of what was happening, and confirm that they were obligated to act. Others had to create or transform networks of support to be able to resist injustice. The stories in this chapter demonstrate the significance of changes in contextual forces that also enable courageous resistance.

As Chapter 2 argues, individuals who become aware of injustice come to a number of crossroads, where they must decide whether and how to resist. Their responses at these crossroads spring from the interaction of their preconditions, networks, and context. Variations in these external factors also influence how individuals react to injustice. Let us turn first to the case of U.S. customs inspector Cathy Harris.

CONFRONTING RACIAL PROFILING AND HARASSMENT: CATHY HARRIS AND THE U.S. CUSTOMS SERVICE

Cathy Harris never imagined she would become a courageous resister. Growing up as a poor, African American girl in Bowdon, Georgia, she dreamed of a chance for education and travel.[1] The military offered these opportunities, and when she grew up, she joined. After three and a half years, she received an honorable discharge and continued to work for the federal government, first in the Department of Housing and Urban Development, and then in the Internal Revenue Service before requesting a transfer to the U.S. Customs Service in 1986. At first she worked as a secretary, but a supportive supervisor suggested she apply for a position as a U.S. customs inspector, a job with much greater responsibility and possibilities for advancement. Harris knew becoming a Customs Inspector would require a transfer from her location in Houston, but that seemed reasonable to her.

Things did not work out the way Harris expected. She witnessed problems at her first posting in El Paso, Texas almost from the beginning. She quickly became aware of a disturbing culture of sexually harassing behavior among her colleagues. She herself experienced sexual harassment by a supervisor: "He would constantly comment that 'Black women had the biggest boobs that he had ever seen!' Not only would this supervisor embarrass me by telling me this when I was trapped . . . he would also make this comment and others to me, when I was working in the secondary area with other male coworkers. . . . They all would look at me and laugh" (Harris 2000, 16).

Although troubled by the behavior, Harris focused on preserving her integrity and avoiding the harassment as much as possible. It seemed risky to speak up when she was so new on the job with so little influence. She was a single mother of two children and had to worry about providing for them as well as herself. When she learned that her male supervisor was continuing to harass other women, she filed a sexual harassment charge against him. Eventually a transfer to another location settled her case. Harris later recalled the difficulties of that time and her decision to accept a new posting:

> I had a hard time deciding to file sexual harassment charges against the male supervisor. . . . I was the "seventh female" at the port of El Paso that had undergone this kind of humiliation from this same supervisor. . . . After eighteen months . . . Customs offered to give me a paid transfer. . . . I felt bad leaving and not making sure that the supervisor was punished for what he had done to me and the seven other women. I had made myself a promise that if I was ever sexually harassed again by a Supervisor in my Customs career, that I would see it through. (16–17)

A few years later, after several subsequent transfers that she requested, Harris was promoted to senior U.S. customs inspector and posted in Atlanta, Georgia. Her new position was a prestigious posting for a member of the U.S. Customs Service, and Harris was excited to begin work. As one of the busiest ports in the country, U.S. customs in Atlanta had to search thousands of travelers every day for drugs and other contraband. It was not long until she realized that, as in El Paso, some of her colleagues were abusing their authority in egregious ways: "I sat back and observed the daily abuses against Black travelers. . . . I watched Black women coming out of the search rooms in tears. I watched the Inspectors start verbal and physical confrontations with Black male travelers and wrestle them to the floor and handcuff them" (45). Particularly troubling was the pattern she observed of singling out African American women. These women were subjected to intrusive pat-down searches, forced to take laxatives, and held for hours or even days in nearby hospitals ostensibly to ensure that they had not swallowed drugs. The inspectors earned overtime through the time-consuming searches, and Harris believed that flaunting their power enhanced their feelings of importance.

When a young, pregnant African American woman was exposed to great risk through these invasive search procedures, Harris decided that she had seen enough. Although it meant risking her high-ranking position of senior U.S. customs inspector and the livelihood through which she supported her children, Harris decided that she had to intervene. Following the chain of command, she filed a complaint with the U.S. Customs Service but did not get a satisfactory response. Follow-up complaints to other levels of management led to threats to suspend or dismiss her.

Harris just wanted to ensure that all travelers, including women of color, would be treated fairly when passing through U.S. customs in Atlanta. For her actions, she faced the threat of termination and other forms of hostile retaliation. Harris remembers having two huge male officials standing over her all day as they monitored her activities in an attempt to find some infraction to use against her. The recriminations only made Harris more determined to press on in pursuit of justice. After four years in this hostile workplace, Harris's physical and mental health suffered: "*THIS WAS MY FINAL STRAW!* . . . I had to continue to move forward and inform the public of the atrocities against Black international travelers and Black Customs employees, especially women" (47).

Discouraged by the endless delays and threats, Cathy Harris finally decided in 1997 that she had to take further steps. Feeling she had no other options, Harris went to the U.S. Office of Special Counsel, where she filed for Whistleblower Protection Status. She felt she needed some support for the retaliatory action she was facing for her complaints. The Special Counsel staff told her they could not investigate her claims. Her attempt to work with the Department of Justice was equally ineffectual. "I knew I had to get to the media," Harris said (47).[2]

In the fall of 1998, Harris took her concerns public: "I went to the Black Press, National Newspapers Publishers Association. . . . I formed a non-profit organization, Customs Employees Against Discrimination Association (CEADA). I sought out the help of a media attorney"(49).

The media attorney advised Harris to provide documentation for her serious allegations against her colleagues and superiors. Determined to stop what was happening in Atlanta customs, Harris went back to her office and printed out a six-month history of customs cases. The information documented the pattern of racial profiling that had been leading to strip searches and other humiliations of innocent African American women. In violation of customs service regulations, she shared this information with the attorney who turned it over to several media outlets in Atlanta without consulting her. Drawing on the evidence she supplied and its own follow-up investigation, WAGA TV in Atlanta (Fox News) presented an investigative series that appeared two nights a week on the evening news over a six-week period.

The U.S. Customs Service finally began to pay attention to Harris's charges, but not in the way she had hoped. The agency accused her of sharing confidential records and sent her a notice of termination. Again Harris sought help. Realizing she was only a single individual against a powerful federal agency, Harris secured the services of the Government Accountability Project (GAP), a national organization based in Washington, DC, that assists whistleblowers. Following the advice of the GAP lawyers, Harris used a variety of methods to keep the case on the public agenda. She went on talk shows. She used her newly formed organization CEADA to contact and work with other whistleblowers and supporters in the Customs Service to stage demonstrations at the Atlanta Hartsfield Airport. Harris reached out to local civil rights groups and approached her local congressman.

Working to keep the public eye on the injustices going on at the Customs Service, Harris's personal costs continued to rise. The stress was so severe that she had to extend her unpaid medical leave of absence to eighteen months. With two children in college, she faced financial ruin. She had to file for bankruptcy and was on the brink of losing her house. Contributions from local civil rights groups helped her avoid financial disaster.

When the hearing to determine whether Harris's actions of taking confidential material out of the office warranted dismissal from the customs service occurred, GAP attorneys accompanied her. With their help, Harris argued persuasively that the abuses of authority were so great that she had to release agency files. Her presentation was successful and her dismissal order was reduced to a ten-day suspension.

After spending eighteen months out of work (including the ten-day suspension), Harris returned to work. Despite shock and hostility from her colleagues who never thought she would return to the U.S. Customs

Service in Atlanta, she was able to stay on the job. At the same time, her struggle for justice began to bear fruit. In 2000 Congressman John Lewis and Senator Richard Durbin introduced legislation that gave travelers explicit protections. The U.S. customs commissioner also announced new policies to avoid the violations of travelers' civil rights. Harris was also personally honored numerous times for her courage in standing up against race and gender abuse.[3]

Harris's life was transformed through her campaign to end the injustice in U.S. customs, and her struggle also changed the context faced by future whistleblowers. As Harris grew more comfortable speaking about her experiences, she became a catalyst and role model for others to step forward and report unsavory behavior in government. These other whistleblowers in the U.S. Customs Service and other government agencies began to look to her as a leader, calling her for advice and inspiration. In turn, CEADA, Harris's own organization, as well as other groups such as GAP and Project on Government Oversight (POGO), which had helped Harris, became important elements of support and networks for the new whistleblowers.

How did Cathy Harris become a courageous resister? How did she go from a woman who initially chose to stay silent regarding sexual harassment in 1986 to a woman who risked her career, financial well-being, and physical health to stop abuse of travelers? Harris's struggle against the injustices occurring at the U.S. Customs Service in Atlanta reflects many of the characteristics of courageous resistance outlined in Chapter 2.

PRECONDITIONS

Cathy Harris's case suggests many of the preconditions of courageous resisters. Unlike Harris's colleagues, who felt loyalty and a sense of protectiveness primarily to other inspectors and their practices, Harris had an inclusive view of who deserved her loyalty. From her perspective, all the travelers who passed through customs were part of her in-group and deserving of protection. Harris saw herself as responsible for the well-being of the victims of abuse and refused to define them as unworthy "others" outside her social group. Despite the fact that she wore a U.S. Customs Service uniform, she viewed the travelers as equals and members of her own in-group: "These Black women travelers looked like me. They could have been my mother, sister, aunt, daughter, or niece" (48).

As Harris observed continual victimization of African American women, she came to define the problem at the U.S. Customs Service as a larger pattern of injustice on the part of customs authorities. For Harris, adhering to the values of fairness and equal treatment was more important than following the established customs service practices. Harris's strong sense of her professional role reinforced her sense of disenchantment from an organization that was straying from the values she felt it should champion and a need to oppose the behavior of her colleagues (Glazer and Glazer 1989). She felt a responsibility to perform her duties in a highly competent manner, while protecting the nation's borders and interacting in a respectful way with the country's citizens and visitors. For Harris to betray this responsibility would be to contradict her principles, especially that of treating others as she wished herself and loved ones to be treated. Harris felt her values required that she intervene: "Again who I was would not allow me to be quiet" (Harris 2000, 45).

Harris's previous life experiences were instrumental in her decision to resist. Her time in the military had nurtured her commitment to her principles. Her sensitivity to the plight of the victims was enhanced by her own experiences of marginality in the U.S. Customs Service and as an African American woman in American society. She had also gained first-hand knowledge of abuse of power from the sexual harassment she lived through right after joining the U.S. Customs Service. The legacy of this experience made her keenly aware that unless she spoke up, nothing was likely to change.

Harris's decision to go public was part of her gradual transformation. When Harris first noted the abuses, they troubled her, but she remained silent. After repeated instances, she drew on her earlier experiences of sexual harassment to define the violations as part of a larger pattern of injustice. She first tried to work through the system. Only after the federal government failed to address the situation did Harris broaden her resistance by bringing her charges to an attorney and to the media. As she moved forward with each step, she learned courageous resistance by doing.

NETWORKS

Harris did not originally belong to a network of like-minded potential resisters. She had to call on her own experiences and character to understand the systematic nature of the abuses and how they violated the norms of equal treatment she expected should dominate the culture of her employer and larger society. Once she recognized the injustice and decided to take a public stance, networks became crucial, particularly alliances with congressional personnel, media, civil rights groups, and whistleblower protection organizations. These groups helped in numerous ways. For example, GAP represented Harris in her legal battles. Civil rights groups opened a trust fund for her in a local bank and sought contributions so that she would not lose her home. The broadcast community allowed her to talk about the violations she observed on many radio and television programs. Together these networks also helped enhance her personal credibility and underscored the legitimacy of her claims. While Harris began as an individual resisting the racial profiling and harassment that she witnessed, the support networks she eventually connected with affirmed her values, offered her technical assistance, and contributed resources for the well-being of her family. All of this assistance allowed Harris to continue her fight.

CONTEXT

The context also influenced Harris's fight against the injustices she had observed. Federal policies and laws prohibiting unequal treatment on the basis of race and gender established the clear institutional legitimacy of her concerns. Meanwhile, the failure of the federal government's institutional mechanisms to stop what was happening in Atlanta impelled Harris to go public with the issue. This decision increased the potential risks for Harris. At the same time, other institutions, including nonprofit organizations, did help provide some protection from arbitrary termination. The context mattered in other ways as well. Underlying American political culture and embedded within American legal codes is the value of non-discrimination based on race or gender. At the time Harris began her efforts to require fair treatment of African American women travelers, the battle for racial and gender justice in the United States had been going on for a generation. If Harris had raised concerns about the treatment of women of color travelers thirty years earlier, the response might have been very different. For example, Harris was aided by Congressman John Lewis, who had been a civil right activist in the 1960s and 1970s. As a member of Congress in the 1990s, he was able to take up Harris' cause on the floor of the House. What Harris had discovered in Atlanta's customs office was a clear violation of values shared by the vast majority of Americans in the 1990s. Thus, once the racial profiling was brought to the public eye and framed in terms of these values, the domestic climate of opinion created pressure for change within the U.S. Customs Service.

The issue of how a person handles awareness of injustice is compounded by the individual's membership in any organization. The courageous resister faces the dilemma of whether to be loyal to an organization, such as U.S. customs, or to personal principles. This challenge can be even more daunting in military organizations where soldiers are dependent on their peers for survival.

CHALLENGING PRISONER ABUSE IN IRAQ:
JOSEPH DARBY AND ABU GHRAIB PRISON[4]

Despite longstanding international agreements governing the treatment of enemy prisoners, the context of war can change how these policies are enforced. As soldiers on the ground experience firsthand the narrow margin separating life and death and policy-makers face the heightened threat of war, seemingly clear rules governing the treatment of enemy captives are often ignored. Neither the U.S. policies regarding the treatment of prisoners nor the people who enact them are immune to the constant pressure of making decisions in wartime, when a person's choices can instantaneously mean life or death.

In 2003 the United States invaded Iraq. Although the Iraqi governing regime was relatively quickly deposed, U.S. forces remained in Iraq fighting an ongoing insurgency. Many of the U.S. soldiers stationed in Iraq after the downfall of Saddam Hussein's government spent their time guarding Iraqi prisoners of war. At a prison camp outside of Baghdad called Abu Ghraib, some American soldiers tortured and abused the prisoners over a period of many months. Subsequent investigations of Abu-Ghraib detailed the varieties of physical and sexual abuse that occurred, including the beating of prisoners with broom handles, the threat of rape, dog attacks on the prisoners, and the requirement for prisoners to stand for long periods of time (Hersh 2004). The Taguba report, the military's investigative review, later confirmed that the prisoners had been subjected to "sadistic, blatant, and wanton criminal abuses" (42).

Some of the U.S. soldiers stationed at Abu Ghraib felt uncomfortable with the prisoner abuse and alerted their military superiors to these activities. However, when these initial witnesses to the abuse received little response from their superiors, they dropped the issue, believing they had already done their duty by reporting it.[5]

When Army Specialist Joseph Darby, a twenty-four-year-old reservist in the 372nd Military Police Company, was assigned to Abu Ghraib, he responded to the abuse differently. In January 2004, he asked Specialist Charles Graner, a fellow soldier, for pictures of Hilla, where the unit had been stationed before Abu Ghraib. Specialist Graner gave Darby two CDs containing hundreds of photos of abuse of the prisoners—pictures often featuring humiliatingly posed prisoners with grinning soldiers standing nearby. Darby said he had known that excessive force was sometimes used against prisoners in the heat of the moment and that he himself had even done such things before, but he believed the sexual humiliation of the prisoners in the photos looked premeditated: "When you get into the sexual humiliation and stuff, I mean that's . . . a line you don't cross" (Darby 2006).

Despite his disgust and distress at what he saw, Darby did not decide to act immediately. He thought of the possible repercussions: "No one would trust me in my unit. I'd be labeled a 'rat.' For some . . . if it came down to helping me or getting shot, they'd probably walk away. . . . I didn't know where it would go from there. . . . It was a situation I didn't want to face" (Darby 2006). But then he reasoned that no prisoners should have to face this abuse because he did not have the courage to come forward. Darby decided he had to take responsibility: "I had seen it and ultimately as a soldier and as an MP these guys were doing wrong and breaking the law and it's part of my job to ensure that that doesn't happen. Even if five other people don't come forward I am doing my job" (Darby 2006).

Darby later testified that he agonized over whether to turn in the pictures of his fellow soldiers' brutal acts, but he finally decided to do so because he feared the mistreatment would continue (Inskeep 2004). Darby's mother told ABC News on May 6, 2004, "He said that he could not stand the atrocities that he had stumbled upon. He said he kept thinking, what if it was my mom, my grandmother, my brother or my wife" (Rosin 2004).

Fortunately for Darby, he had a small but trusted network to which he could turn for advice. He went to his roommate and good friend Jeremy McGuire and to Sergeant First Class Keith Colmer, a long-time army man he admired, who had mentored and served with Darby since his enlistment. Without telling them the specifics, he talked through the alternatives and their implications. He considered trying to reason with the soldiers involved, but they mostly outranked him. He had no authority over them. He could not go to the squad leader, Staff Sergeant Ivan "Chip" Frederick, because he was implicated in the pictures. Knowing that Frederick could not afford this scandal, Darby feared a cover-up. Darby discussed options and strategy with his two close friends. He decided he had to go outside the chain of command to the Criminal Investigation Division (CID), which was housed at Abu Ghraib. It took him four days to find the CID. One day in January 2004, Darby slipped an anonymous letter to one of the military investigators whose task it was to evaluate the conditions at the prison. His letter described in detail the torture and abuse of Iraqi prisoners by members of his reserve unit and others. So that his complaint could not be dismissed as one soldier's word against others, Darby included the two CDs filled with hundreds of photos that he had been given by Specialist Charles Graner. Within an hour, one of the investigators came to talk with him and Darby quickly decided he should identify himself to the investigators as the author of the unsigned letter. He then provided a sworn statement.

Darby recalls sleeping with his weapon and away from his fellow soldiers after he blew the whistle but before his identity was revealed: "I had expected them (the soldiers in the photographs) to be charged and taken away, but no, they were going to get new jobs. They'd be walking around with their weapons all day long, knowing that somebody had turned them in and trying to find out who" (Hylton 2006). Three months later, Darby's information about Abu Ghraib was confirmed by another anonymous whistleblower, who released the same photos to the press. The information quickly became available to millions of Americans and to the rest of the world. The actions of Darby and the anonymous source led to official investigations of the torture at Abu Ghraib, the punishment of some key perpetrators, and a public reaffirmation by national leaders that such behavior by U.S. forces was inappropriate.[6] The public outcry triggered subsequent attention to the pattern of alleged abuse of foreign prisoners at comparable military installations in Iraq, Afghanistan, Guantanamo Bay, Cuba, and other sites throughout the world.

In May 2004, President Bush publicly apologized for the "abhorrent" abuse some detainees had suffered. The president indicated that those responsible would be punished. Defense Secretary Donald Rumsfeld praised Darby for his "honorable actions." On October 9, 2004, the House and Senate passed a resolution commending Joseph Darby for exemplary courage "for standing up for what is right. . . . The need to act in accord with one's conscience, risking one's career and even the esteem of one's colleagues by pursuing what is right is especially important today" (Secrecy News 2005). Darby's mother expressed pride in his actions: "This is a man who actually changed history. . . . I think my son is a hero. I think he remained true to himself. . . . I'm so glad that the Iraqi people know that the United States does not allow this kind of stuff (prisoner abuse) and that we do have free speech, we do have freedom of the press" (Zoroya 2004).

Still, Darby's decision to expose the misdeeds in Abu Ghraib came with significant personal costs. By May 2004, he told his mother that both he and his wife were in military protective custody because of the possibility of serious retribution from other soldiers. Their whereabouts were a closely guarded secret from May 2004 until Darby left the army on September 1, 2006. People he had known for years turned their backs on him. Some residents of his hometown believed that he was immoral because he exposed his fellow soldiers. One neighbor told a reporter, "If I were Darby, I'd be sneaking in the back door at midnight" (Rosin

2004). A reporter commented, "Ratting out friends and coworkers, no matter how egregious their behavior, requires a kind of moral courage few of us have, and this story makes it graphically clear why: even when you're revealing the kind of abuse and torture that Darby did, doing so runs the risk of being shunned for life by the entire community of people you respect" (Drum 2004, 1).

Although Darby did not know his identity would be released, he accurately foresaw the costs of becoming a courageous resister. Who was this soldier who defied military hierarchy and became a courageous resister? Why did Darby go outside the military chain of command, while others had reported these acts to their military superiors and thought they had done their duty? Darby's courageous resistance can be explained by examining who he was, who he knew, and the environment or context as he faced crossroads deciding how to respond to the abuse.

PRECONDITIONS

Joseph Darby's background gives some clues as to what enabled him to act so decisively. Growing up, Darby had learned to follow his principles and live up to his values, whatever the consequences. Darby's maternal grandparents, who adopted him when he was three years old and raised him until he was thirteen, taught Joseph to have a clear moral code, to be respectful of adults, and to have old-fashioned manners. The adults who remember him from his teen years describe a boy who had a strong idea about what was proper and who stuck with these beliefs. Darby's wife Bernadette, the high school sweetheart he married soon after graduation, says her husband "stands for what he believes in. . . . His parents had very, very high convictions. They taught him you don't do things that are wrong" (Becker 2004).

Darby identifies himself as a moral person, one who is willing to publicly voice opposition to an unethical act even if voicing those beliefs will get people into trouble. According to Darby, empathy and caring for neighbors are values he was raised with: "We were always the type that helped people. My grandparents helped people if they needed it. . . . It was the way my family was. My uncles will give anybody the shirt off their backs if you ask for it. . . . I was raised that way. I've always been somebody that will help anyone" (Darby 2006).

When Darby was thirteen, he went to live with his mother and stepfather. When Darby was fifteen years old, his family settled in Jenner, a small former mining community in southwestern Pennsylvania. Darby was an outsider among his peers. Gilbert Reffner, a neighbor of the

Darby family in Jenner, remembered that Joseph "didn't fit in with the whole crowd because he didn't have a lot of material things, fancy clothes or a car" (Williamson 2004). In Jenner, Darby was the new kid in a school where everyone had known each other since kindergarten. Working the night shift at Wendy's while in high school to help with the family's income further contributed to Darby's sense of himself as an outsider. This sense of marginalization may have made him more sensitive to the unfair treatment of others.

NETWORKS

The information we have about Joseph Darby's networks of support suggest the networks were limited and mixed:

> I had a roommate who was my counterpart when I was in Iraq . . . and we had gotten to be pretty good friends. . . . I talked to him about it. And then I talked to my mentor . . . who I had served with since my first day in the army. He was an almost 30–year veteran of the Army and I had learned a lot from him and he was basically the man I modeled my career after. . . . I was like, 'What would you do if you were in a situation where you knew something was going on that violated *a lot* of stuff . . . and you knew about it and you had evidence to it? What would you do about it?' And it was just questions like that and talking to them that helped me come to the decision. (Darby 2006)

Talking with these two trusted military buddies helped Darby by reinforcing his interpretation of what was happening as wrong and requiring his response. Darby's friends may also have helped him decide on how to respond by reminding him of his core values: "I'd asked people vaguely, 'What would you do if this happened?' trying to figure it out: 'Okay I know this is wrong. What should I do about it?' and I talked to my mentor who said, 'Well at least I'd be able to sleep at night.' And that's when I got to thinking about everything and made the decision to turn them in and then the question was where and who to turn them in to" (Darby 2006).

On the other side of the dilemma, Darby's decision to report the abuse meant he would become estranged from many others in his military network and some of his family. As a soldier in a military unit at war, Darby felt close connections to his fellow soldiers. The others assigned to work at the prison were not just friends and colleagues; they were people Darby knew from his reserve unit—those who lived near him at home, those with whom he had trained, with whom he had been deployed in Bosnia, and with whom he had shared the dangers of war in Iraq. Losing his fellow soldiers' backing meant that that these and other soldiers might not protect Darby in war. The social and moral support and loyalty that builds among those who face dangerous situations together no longer existed for Darby. Some members of Darby's family also refused to back him. Darby reported that some members of his family thought he was a traitor and that one of his uncles had convinced Darby's only brother not to talk to him anymore (Hylton 2006). Darby also reported that he became afraid for his life: "That was one of the most nervous periods of my life. I was constantly scared. I started getting paranoid. I kept my gun with me at all times. I took it to sleep with me" (Hylton 2006).

In short, Darby's networks played a different role from what we expect. While his relationships with other soldiers provided information about what was happening and the graphic evidence of the crucial photos, Darby's existing networks offered little in the way of other material resources, expertise, or social capital to enable his courageous resistance. Nonetheless, Darby's mentor and his roommate each provided support by validating his worldview and steering him toward a course of action. They affirmed his sense that he needed to stand up for his principles, whatever the cost, even if it meant becoming estranged from the immediate network of his unit and even the military as a whole.

Yet overall, Joseph Darby's courageous resistance cost him dearly in networks of support. Speaking out against the abuses going on in Abu Ghraib eventually led to Darby's ostracism from the camaraderie of his close-knit unit, his isolation from the military as a whole, and the relocation of his family outside of his home community. As of September 2006, Darby had been back to his hometown twice—once for his mother's funeral, and once for a wedding. He doubts he will ever be welcome there again.

CONTEXT

The U.S. public was deeply concerned when it learned of the conditions at Abu Ghraib prison in Iraq in 2004. Although the public understood that the American military would interrogate prisoners of war to aid in its mission to liberate Iraq and help create a democratic and humane society, most Americans did not think torture and humiliation were appropriate tools.

The institutional elements of the context were more ambiguous. The Geneva Convention forbids the use of torture on enemy combatants; yet at the time Darby came forward, ambivalence about the use of torture permeated policy debates in the United States. Despite President Bush and Secretary of Defense Rumsfeld's stated appreciation of Joseph Darby's actions, Bush and Rumsfeld opposed legislation proposed by Senator John McCain, and supported by ninety-two senators, that completely outlawed torture by the United States. Since then, compromise legislation has been passed, which strengthens prohibitions against prisoner abuse and gives the president latitude in determining appropriate interrogation techniques; but this debate continues.

SAVING THOSE MARKED FOR DEATH: HARRY BINGHAM AND THE FOREIGN SERVICE

With Hitler's rise to power in 1933, Nazi policies—including euthanasia and extermination of Jews, gypsies, and others—began to threaten the lives of millions in Europe. By the end of World War II, these policies would result in the murder of six million Jews and nearly five million others, including gypsies, homosexuals, leftists, artists, and intellectuals, all considered "undesirables" and unworthy of life by the Nazi regime. While many ordinary people in occupied Europe complied with the Nazi directives, thousands of people risked their own safety to rescue those threatened by the Nazi policies. Even today, most of these rescuers remain largely unknown.

Hiram (Harry) Bingham IV was one of these largely unknown rescuers. In posthumously recognizing Bingham in 2002 with the U.S. State Department's Constructive Dissent award, U.S. Secretary of State Colin Powell described the career diplomat as having given "his life and his career" to help over 2,500 Jews and others who were on Nazi death lists to leave France for America in 1940 and 1941 (Sleven 2002).[7]

Harry Bingham grew up in a wealthy Connecticut family whose members were well known for being missionaries and explorers. This lineage instilled in Harry Bingham a strong sense of public service and a responsibility to protect others (Rafshoon 2002, 17). When Bingham reached adulthood, he became a career foreign service officer in the U.S. State Department. In 1939, Bingham, who was assigned to Marseilles, France, faced a decision. Jews and other victims of the growing Nazi menace were seeking visas to the United States to escape deportation to Nazi concentration camps, where they would likely face death. Although there were some visas available, Jews were especially unwelcome in the United States, according to the State Department. Bingham's instructions from Washington were to "postpone and postpone and postpone" in responding to Jews' requests for visas.[8] Bingham disagreed with his orders from Washington, and he also knew that willingly violating them would likely cost him his career. However, Bingham believed that his position required him to assist those who needed his professional expertise and compassionate attention to ensure their well-being. Robert "Kim" Bingham, a Justice Department lawyer and Harry Bingham's son, recalls, "My father placed humanity ahead of his career" (Anderson 2002, 1).

Bingham decided he had to disobey his State Department orders. In the summer of 1940, Bingham began to work with Varian Fry to save as many refugees as possible. Fry was an American editor and writer who had come to France representing the Emergency Rescue Committee, a nongovernmental organization that had given Fry the mission of rescuing prominent artists and intellectuals, mainly Jews, from the pro-Nazi Vichy French government established in 1940 after the fall of France to invading German forces. Acting against explicit orders, Bingham issued visas for many refugees whose lives were threatened. Bingham's transgressions even went beyond providing visas. With encouragement and help from Varian Fry, Bingham flaunted the State Department's rules for appropriate diplomatic behavior. At times, Bingham actually hid "wanted" persons in his own home, passed some off as relatives, and disguised others until he could find a way for them to escape. For example, Bingham rescued one critic of Hitler from a concentration camp at Nimms by disguising him in women's clothing and claiming him as his own mother-in-law as they passed through various Nazi checkpoints (Fry 1997). Together, Bingham, Fry and a small circle of friends are estimated to have saved more than one thousand refugees, including such famous persons as the painter Marc Chagall, philosopher Hannah Arendt, and many others.

As word circulated among Jews throughout France about the possibility of obtaining a visa in Marseilles, Nazi officials also learned of Bingham's actions. When they complained to the U.S. State Department about the visas coming out of Marseilles, U.S. Secretary of State Cordell Hull sent a telegram relieving Bingham of his post. Bingham was transferred out of France in April 1941. He was sent to increasingly obscure outposts and was never given another chance for promotion in the Foreign Service. Ultimately, disappointed and dispirited, Bingham quit the Foreign Service. His rescue efforts had cost him his career. Although he went on to live a comfortable private life in the Connecticut countryside, he almost never spoke of his rescue work (Isenberg 2001, 193).[9] His oldest daughter remembers her father referring to it only once: "I remember him saying there were so many more he could have saved and didn't" (Rafshoon 2002, 19).

Bingham's actions eventually helped to change the U.S. State Department. Years later, the State Department recognized the importance of Bingham's actions and his significance as a role model within the institutional culture by posthumously awarding him the "Constructive Dissent" award. This award recognizes that a person of high conscience can disobey his superiors and yet perform humanitarian acts. The State Department also now has a system of reporting that allows Foreign Service officers to bypass the usual layers of bureaucracy to report concerns about critical issues. The actions of Bingham and others like him also provide some solace in the face of abundant evidence that the United States and Great Britain were not interested in the plight of the victims of the Holocaust (Wyman 1984).

What made Harry Bingham decide to risk his career in order to save Jews from Nazi policies? Why did Harry Bingham choose to disobey direct orders from the U.S. State Department regarding visas for Jews?

PRECONDITIONS

Harry Bingham's socialization offers a starting point for understanding why he chose to rescue Jews at the price of his career. Bingham developed pro-social values early in his life. With a family tradition of missionary work and exploration, a sense of responsibility for others and for the public welfare was instilled in Bingham at an early age. These values likely shaped his decision to choose the Foreign Service as a career. He expressed the importance of these pro-social values to his children. Bingham's son recalls, "He always told us, 'Give the best you have to the best that you know'" (Anderson 2002, 1). The Bingham family tradition of missionary work also likely instilled in him a strong belief in his own moral principles and the importance of following them, whatever the consequences. His niece Lucretia Bingham described the Bingham sense of service bluntly: "We are a family of zealots. We believe in causes." (Rafshoon 2002, 17). Having learned this value orientation to authority growing up and believing that the State Department's orders were wrong, Bingham's 's willful disobedience of the orders likely followed fairly naturally.

NETWORKS

Harry Bingham's networks were important in two ways. First, they validated his principles and the importance he attached to them. Varian Fry and other members of the Emergency Rescue Committee affirmed

Bingham's worldview that the Nazi policies were wrong and until they were stopped, Jews needed to escape from Europe. The Emergency Rescue Committee's own state-side efforts to raise awareness of what was going on in Europe offered Bingham a network of people who modeled the importance of following one's principles. Second, Bingham's connections also provided material help; his network in France was crucial in the rescue operation. Friends and associates provided food, clothing, and temporary hiding places for the refugees. The Emergency Rescue Committee and other connections in the United States provided Bingham with the financial resources necessary to run the rescue operation. This U.S.-based network also worked to help the refugees resettle in the United States.

CONTEXT

Bingham's choices as to whether and how to save Jews from the Nazis were likely shaped by certain contextual elements as well. The most important institution for Bingham was the U.S. State Department; its lack of support was highly significant. For Bingham, the State Department's explicit disinterest in helping Jews escape to the United States created a clear crossroads. Obeying his principles required Bingham to make a choice with high risks to his career and even his life. Bingham knew he could not count on support for his efforts and was keenly aware that his Foreign Service future would likely be derailed by the rescue operation. As Bingham's rescue operation became successful and known, the State Department could have chosen to disregard Nazi complaints about it, but instead the State Department transferred him out of Europe. Just as the State Department's institutional policy had crystallized a crossroads for Harry Bingham, its punitive response to his rescue operation demonstrated the costs that courageous resisters can bear for their actions.

Other aspects of the context likely shaped Bingham's actions as well. As in many other countries, there was a strong stream of anti-Semitism in the United States during the 1930s. The American public at the time expressed ambivalence regarding how involved in world problems they wanted their country to be. The combination of this isolationism and anti-Semitism limited the size of Bingham's network in the United States. These societal values also meant that publicly challenging the State Department's policy was not likely to be successful. The international environment also mattered. While the United States would eventually join the war against Germany, at the time that Bingham decided to help

Jews flee Europe, the United States was not yet at war. As a diplomat representing a neutral power in this environment, Bingham did have more leeway to act than he would have if the United States were at war. However, the government's desire to maintain U.S. neutrality and avoid war meant that once Bingham's actions were brought to the State Department's attention, the organization had little choice but to stop him or lose neutral status.

Cathy Harris, Joseph Darby, and Harry Bingham provide clear examples of courageous resistance. Each voluntarily engaged in sustained other-oriented, largely selfless behavior with a significantly high risk or cost to themselves or their associates. Their actions were the result of a conscious decision and continued over time. All could have chosen to minimize their own risks by blending into the ranks of bystanders. Instead, they decided to act against injustice and on behalf of others, despite likely risks. There are other people who oppose grave injustice who do not so neatly fit our definition of courageous resister. Yet, as the next two cases will point out, such individuals are clearly not bystanders to injustice either.

COMPLEX COURAGEOUS RESISTERS

WITNESS JJ TESTIFYING AT THE ARUSHA TRIBUNAL

In Chapter 1, we read about the Rwandan genocide and Paul Rusesabagina's successful effort to save hundreds of innocent Tutsis and moderate Hutus from the killings. Although Rusesabagina was not the only person who helped protect strangers in the genocide, the speed and violence of the Rwandan massacre limited the rescue role that many were able to play. Once the Rwandan genocide ended, however, a different kind of opportunity to stand up against the horrors appeared. States, international institutions, and transnational human rights networks campaigned to hold the perpetrators responsible for their actions by trying them through internationally run tribunals.

Principally because of the pressure from external groups such as these, international war crimes tribunals were established in Arusha, Tanzania to conduct multiple war crimes trials. In order for these trials to succeed, however, Rwandans had to participate as witnesses. The problem was that although the genocide had ended, speaking out about what had happened still carried great risks for Rwandans. There were reported instances of assassinations of prospective witnesses by those who feared their testimony. This intimidation was particularly strong among Tutsi women survivors, who had repeatedly been raped and were struggling to reestablish their lives and overcome the humiliation that accompanied the sexual assaults.

The prosecutors and the women judges were particularly eager to establish the precedent that rape was not simply a by-product of war, but was a war crime and a crime against humanity. Without the Tutsi rape survivors as witnesses, however, the trials were not likely to succeed. Eventually, a number of women overcame their terror to assist in these trials by publicly describing the torture and shame that had accompanied their systematic rape. One such individual was known as Witness JJ.

In her book on Bosnia and Rwanda, journalist Elizabeth Neuffer described the trial of Jean-Paul Akayesu, the mayor of the town of Taba, who had initially opposed the action of the Interahamwe militia, but later went over to their side when it became politically expedient. Women who expected him to protect them were lured to the *Bureau Communale* (municipal center), where they were badly abused. Several years later, when preparing for the trial of Akayesu at Arusha, prosecutors approached a number of peasant women and asked them to testify. Similar to other survivors, Witness JJ was reluctant to relive the horror and shame of her ordeal. She had begun a new life with a man who had lost his wife, and JJ was by then six months pregnant. She was worried about the danger and the impact that testifying would have on her health. Neuffer describes her decision to come forward: "Do I want to talk about those things?" she wondered. "Do I?"

> Then in her mind she heard Akayesu's sneering voice that day at the Bureau Communale: 'Never ask me again what a Tutsi woman tastes like. Tomorrow they will be killed.' Like she was a piece of melon, waiting to be carved, eaten, and thrown away. She had trusted him, and he had betrayed her, and his scorn weighed heavily on her. She could almost feel it, heavy on her heart. . . . Yes, maybe she would testify, and tell of the bad things that had happened in Taba and across Rwanda to the women. If she told her story, maybe the world would listen. (Neuffer 2001, 284)

By the time Witness JJ actually testified, her baby was ten days old. JJ was terribly frightened, but her determination was powerful. Under questioning, JJ explained why she felt she had to testify against Akayesu: "I talked to him directly, face to face so I believe I am responsible, coming to give evidence of his evil deeds in the Taba commune. . . . When someone is leading killers, assassins, he is also a killer, also a murderer, also an assassin. We were exterminated in his presence" (Neuffer 2001, 290).

Witness JJ's decision to testify bolstered the other witnesses who were waiting to be called. "Don't worry," she told the other women who were terrified at the prospect of telling their stories. "You will feel a weight lifted from your heart" (Neuffer 2001, 290).

The type of courage Witness JJ showed, confronting the perpetrators of past horrors, marked a turning point in the trial, which lasted for fifteen months and ultimately resulted in the conviction of the mayor who had led in the abuse of his citizens. Victims who might have remained bystanders in this and other Rwandan war crimes trials were strengthened by the example of Witness JJ. Her choice to speak up encouraged these others to add their testimonies.

COURAGEOUS RESISTANCE OR NOT?

Witness JJ's decision to give testimony in Arusha was her crucial crossroad. Deciding to testify against Akayesu meant JJ was putting her own health, the welfare of her newborn baby, and her new life at risk in order to ensure justice prevailed. Witness JJ's actions also changed the context for others to speak out against the brutalities that had occurred. Her testimony made it easier for other witnesses to come forward regarding Akeyesu and other perpetrators. The presence of international institutions was also crucial when she reached this crossroad. If the Arusha tribunal had been established by the Rwandan government, Witness JJ would likely not have felt safe to participate.

Yet JJ is also distinctive from the other cases so far discussed in this chapter in two ways. First, unlike all the other courageous resisters discussed so far, JJ herself was the victim of extreme human rights abuses. As such, it could be argued that her decision to testify at the trial was not selfless, but rather about revenge. Second, JJ is also the first case where we see courageous resistance by an individual occurring after the injustice has happened. As such, JJ's testimony illustrates how individual witnesses can assist in the institutional struggle against injustice. Chapter 6 further explores how international institutions have been involved in efforts to redress genocide.

COVERT ASSISTANCE FROM AN UNLIKELY SOURCE:
NAZI MAJOR JULIUS SCHMAHLING

In Chapter 1, we read about how the French rescuers in the Le Chambon area were able to save the lives of five thousand men, women, and children who otherwise would have been sent to Nazi concentration camps for extermination. The villagers and refugees were in constant danger as German garrisons were never very far from them. While every effort was made to maintain secrecy on the plateau, the movement of several thousand people under the noses of the German soldiers was well known. Typically, Nazi occupation throughout Europe meant destruction not only for targeted segments of the population, but also for those who were discovered helping to save Jews, Gypsies, homosexuals, or others slated for extermination. Yet although there were some raids and roundups, the Germans never destroyed Le Chambon and neighboring areas as they did other localities suspected of resisting the Nazis and harboring Jews.

Philip Hallie, the author of a major study on Le Chambon, was particularly puzzled by this question of why the Nazis, normally so brutal, allowed Trocme and his villagers to continue their roles as protectors of helpless refugees, especially in the later period when the Germans fully occupied the area. Even after the publication of his book *Less Innocent Blood be Shed*, Hallie returned to the materials for further inquiry. In the autobiographical notes of the late Pastor Andre Trocme, he found reference to covert assistance from an unlikely source, a German officer, Major Julius Schmahling, who had helped save many lives.

Although an officer in the German army, Schmahling would warn the villagers through anonymous phone calls of impending raids so they could hide their vulnerable "guests." Schmahling's close friendship with the highest and most ruthless SS officer in the region also gave him both information and influence. During their many card playing and drinking sessions, Schmahling was able to convince his SS friend that Le Chambon's pacifist beliefs represented no threat to Germany and should not be dealt with by massive violence.

Although Schmahling acted anonymously, many French resisters seemed to know of his sympathies. At the end of the war, as the French resistance fighters regained control of the area, they brought many German officers and officials before their informal court and meted out harsh penalties. In contrast, as Major Schmahling came into the courtroom from his jail, everyone stood up in a sign of respect. People asked if he needed more food or books or anything else. The head of the proceedings, a tough old leader of the Resistance, made a speech of gratitude (Hallie 1986, 114).

Hallie was able to find Schmahling's response in a diary entry that the major wrote just after his reception by the local residents and the resistance leaders. Hallie wrote: "Schmahling described the meeting as '*fast peinlach*,' almost painful: he was glad for their praise and their affection, but didn't they realize decency is the normal thing to do? Didn't they realize that decency needs no rewards, no recognition, that it is done out of the heart, now, immediately, just in order to satisfy the heart now" (114–15)? Hallie concluded that we could learn a great deal from Julius Schmahling, a decent man caught up in an evil cause:

> In studying him [Schmahling] and in learning to admire him, I have learned much about respecting myself and others in an [impure] world. I have learned that ethics is not simply a matter of good and evil, true north and true south. It is a matter of mixtures, like most other points on the compass and like the lives of most of us. We are not called upon to be perfect, but we can make a little, real difference in a mainly cold and indifferent world. We can celebrate human life in a local, intimate celebration, even with the coldness not far away. (115)

COURAGEOUS RESISTER OR NOT?

Major Julius Schmahling has some of the qualities we have come to expect from a courageous resister. Hallie found that Schmahling was an ordinary man, definitely not a religious person, not a member of the resistance or an outspoken critic of the Nazis. Hallie's research suggests that Schmahling had strong pro-social values.

Some of this came from Schmahling's early life experiences. As a young high school teacher in Bavaria before the war, he arrived in class one day to give a lesson on lions. As Schmahling was lecturing his students in the typical authoritarian German style of that period, one timid student in the back of the room kept waving his hand and finally burst out to tell Schmahling, "Yesterday, yes, yesterday I saw a rabbit! Yesterday I really saw a rabbit!" Schmahling was very annoyed to be interrupted and yelled harshly at the boy. The student sat down and never said another word for the rest of the year. Later in his life, Schmahling described that moment as a decisive turning point in his life. He was deeply disturbed by his own lack of compassion for the student: "Teaching and living for him, he vowed, would from that moment forward involve making room for each of his students and each of the people he knew outside of the classroom to speak about the rabbits they had seen" (Hallie 1986, 113).[10]

In Le Chambon, Schmahling used his position to be helpful to others he might have defined as the enemy. His actions suggest he had an extensive view of the world, defining the villagers and the refugees as fellow human beings. Schmahling's covert assistance carried high risk. If he had been caught in the act of alerting the villagers, he could have been judged as a traitor.

Schmahling's relationships with his networks were interesting. His actions, like Darby's in Abu Ghraib, placed him in opposition to the goals of his most immediate network, the German army. Also, clearly Schmahling did not have a network of fellow resisters who helped him in his covert efforts. Schmahling's immediate network was filled with perpetrators. Yet Schmahling probably would not have been able to provide the Chambonnais with much assistance if he had not used these connections in the German army. Although the contacts were ignorant of their role, they were crucial for Schmahling. Hallie describes Schmahling's friendship with Josef Dietrich, a brutal general who had been a close associate of Adolph Hitler in the streets and beer halls of Munich in the 1920s. Schmahling first met and became friends with the general in the north of France when Schmahling was criticizing the cruelty and arrogance of the SS troopers under Dietrich's command. Both were from the same area of Germany, shared similar tastes for food and drink, and enjoyed each other's company both in person and in lengthy phone conversations. They kept their friendship alive when Schmahling was transferred to the south of France. Hallie wrote,

> I have no record of those telephone conversations, but French people who worked in Schmahling's office in France, and Schmahling's children have convinced me that the telephone conversations—and one visit between Dietrich and Schmahling in the south—had much to do with Schmahling's power to protect the region from Klaus Barbie and other Gestapo chiefs in the south. . . . A word from Dietrich on the telephone could . . . prevent Gestapo raids in the Haute-Loire (Hallie 1986, 111).

In other ways, however, it is difficult to see Major Schmahling as a courageous resister. After all, he was an officer in the German occupying army, which was responsible for untold brutality. While Schmahling may have protected Le Chambon wherever possible, he also acted on behalf of his Nazi unit in some situations. While his close association with Dietrich enabled him to stop some killings, it also implicated Schmahling in some of the evil being perpetrated. He certainly never engaged in open resistance.

THE SOCIAL FUNCTIONS OF COURAGEOUS RESISTANCE

Why do we care about courageous resisters? Although many are largely unknown and unsung, these individuals have played a very important role in societies throughout the world. By acting against injustice, people such as Cathy Harris, Joseph Darby, Harry Bingham, Witness JJ, and Julius Schmahling take personal risks to ensure fair and just treatment for others. In the most dramatic situations, such as when Paul Rusesabagina and others in Rwanda protected hundreds, perhaps thousands, of their fellow citizens from horrendous deaths, they save lives. Whether they save lives or engage in other bold, justice-seeking acts as Cathy Harris did, courageous resisters serve as living examples of courage and justice in our world.

In dark times, the rescuers become the pride of their country and the world. In Rwanda, for example, the actions of Rusesabagina and others present an alternative path from the cruelties of genocide. When an African human rights organization took testimonials from victims and rescuers after the Rwandan massacre, they paid homage to the heroes of the genocide and celebrated their ability to see beyond narrow animosities.

These rescuers in Rwanda, like the other courageous resisters, rejected culpability to injustice when they refused to pretend ignorance. They did not accept the common rationale that they were powerless to intervene to save others. They refused to remain bystanders in the face of the imminent death of innocent victims. They put their own safety at risk by their active involvement in protecting others.

Courageous resistance to injustice, whatever form it takes, builds social capital, nourishing the social forces that bind a society together by emphasizing the significance of fairness, trust, and caring for one another. Resisters contribute to social cohesion and morality by refusing to look away when others are victimized. Cathy Harris utilized her position to confront authority when she believed that her superiors were allowing unethical practices to prevail. When Joseph Darby came forward to expose the mistreatment of Iraqi prisoners, he reaffirmed fundamental American values even in the midst of a war. Harry Bingham's story likewise provides some solace in the face of the United States and other countries' studied indifference to the Nazi policies toward Jews.

People like those discussed in this chapter and many others in every country throughout the world provide a beacon for young and old alike. Their importance is encapsulated in historian Howard Zinn's exhortation to study and celebrate them: "Human history is a history not only of cruelty, but also of compassion, sacrifice, courage, kindness. What we choose to emphasize in this complex history will determine our lives. If we see only the worst, it destroys our capacity to do something. If we remember those times and places—and there are so many—when people have behaved magnificently, this gives us the energy to act, and at least the possibility of sending this spinning top of a world in a different direction" (Roby 1998, 2–3).

As we try to understand the circumstances and factors that make resistance possible for individuals caught up in oppressive situations, we also want to understand the ways in which collective resistance operates and the way institutions can promote the structures of a more just society. We now turn to those issues.

NOTES

1. The details of this case are based on presentations at a conference on "Women of Courage: Whistleblowers in the Public Interest," Smith College, February 2003, in addition to the works cited.
2. Whistleblowers are employees who publicly disclose unethical or illegal practices in the workplace, usually after protesting within their organizations and finding no appropriate response. For a fuller description, see Glazer and Glazer 1989.
3. For example, on March 22, 2000, the U.S. House of Representatives passed H.R. 1485, commending Cathy Harris and recommending that the U.S. Customs Service commend rather than terminate her. Glamour magazine saluted Cathy Harris and three other women "who've risked it all to do what they knew was right" (*Glamour* 2000). In the same month, Harris was honored in the Georgia House of Representatives.
4. In addition to the works cited, the details of this case are based on Darby 2006.
5. On April 9, 2004, at the military equivalent of a grand jury in the case of Staff Sergeant Ivan "Chip" Frederick, one of the accused members of the 372nd Military Police Company, Specialist Matthew Wisdom, an MP, reported seeing the abuse of prisoners when he and other soldiers delivered prisoners to Abu Ghraib. He testified that he told his superiors what he had seen and assumed "the issue was taken care of." Frederick himself, in correspondence with his family, said that he had asked his superior officer, Lieutenant Colonel Jerry Phillabaum, the commander of the 320th MP Battalion, about the mistreatment of prisoners and had been told not to worry about it.
6. In December 2005, the U.S. Congress attached an amendment to the Defense Appropriations Bill explicitly stating that U.S. government policies prohibited the use of torture.
7. In recent years, several of these rescuers have come to international prominence. For example, Oskar Schindler was an ethnic German industrialist who saved well over one thousand Jews in his factories by claiming that their labor was essential for the Nazi war effort. Bingham was one of a handful of diplomats from multiple countries who recognized the danger Jews faced and tried to help them. The Swedish Diplomat Raoul Wallenberg, who was sent to Hungary to assist Budapest's Jewish population, far exceeded the expectations or desires of the neutral Swedish government. After the Nazi

takeover of Budapest. Wallenberg worked tirelessly issuing passports, setting up hospitals, and distributing food and medical supplies to the ghettos, and, most importantly, negotiating and bribing Hungarian and Nazi officials in order to save as many Jewish lives as he could. For more on Wallenberg, see Bierman 1981. Japanese diplomat Chiune Sugihara is estimated to have saved ten thousand Jews, risking his career and his and his family's safety to issue Japanese passports from his various posts at consulates in Kovno, Prague, and Konigsberg. Sugihara's lifesaving documents allowed Jews to escape by traveling through the Soviet Union to Japan. Sugihara did this despite being repeatedly refused permission to do so. He was later discharged from the Japanese Foreign Service. Sugihara's story is retold in Levine 1996.

8. "Not only had Congress set low quotas for the number of Central Europeans permitted to immigrate . . . but the State Department had issued a series of internal directives further restricting immigration. . . . A month before Bingham took up his post in Marseille, consuls were ordered to demand that refugees produce certificates from their home country's police about their criminal backgrounds. For the many who had been stripped of their citizenship . . . this was an insurmountable barrier" (Rafshoon 2002, 18).

9. In addition to Isenberg, most of the information for this case comes from Medoff and Fischer 2003; and Ryan 1996, especially chapter 5 on "Rescue and Resistance."

10. Hallie never met Schmahling directly. By the time he began his inquiry, Major Schmahling was dead. But Hallie did spend considerable time with Schmahling's children and probably heard the story about the rabbi from them.

COLLECTIVE RESISTANCE TO INJUSTICE: THE SPECIAL POWER OF PEOPLE WORKING TOGETHER

> The only thing necessary for the triumph of evil is for good men to do nothing.
>
> —attributed to Edmund Burke

INTRODUCTION

Courageous resistance is not solely the province of individuals. The focus of this chapter is collective resistance. Collective resistance occurs when people choose to challenge injustice together. Like the decision of the individual courageous resister, collective resisters' decisions to participate are influenced by the dynamic interaction of their preconditions, networks, and contextual factors. In other words, the choice to respond to injustice as part of a linked, sometimes coordinated, effort depends not only on who the resisters are, but who they know and the nature of the environment. Cooperation with others also uniquely influences both the risks and the available resources of a courageous resister.

The nature of collective resistance, as we use the term here, requires significant interaction with a large and potentially expanding group of activists. In order to qualify as a collective resister, one must work against injustice within a circle broader than his or her family or closest friends and interact and share risks with other people. Collective resistance can be overt or relatively covert—as we saw in the example of the French communities that hid Jewish refugees from Nazi roundups. We differentiate collective resistance according to the degree to which efforts are coordinated, ongoing, and characterized by relationships of mutual trust and support.

One kind of collective resistance is *communal resistance*, in which resisters are either a preexisting community or a newly created community of activists. We use the term communal resistance to refer to those cases where ongoing relationships are established or deepened, and individuals coordinate their efforts to confront injustice. In communal resistance, members' ongoing relationships build social capital and the activists employ networks among themselves to increase their effectiveness and to offer one another support. As we saw in the rescuing communities of the French plateau described in the first chapter, preexisting bonds of trust and reciprocity can offer important foundations that give resisters confidence that others will support their endeavors and not betray them. In some cases, individuals come to activism alone but develop solidarity with those they meet, as they become part of an ongoing effort.

In contrast, some collective resistance is spontaneous. We call this form of collective resistance *joint resistance*. Although such resistance may be relatively short-lived and develops little in the way of networks (especially if the goals are accomplished early on), it illustrates a commitment to ongoing action if necessary.

This chapter presents three cases where people worked together to resist dramatically different forms of injustice, ranging from environmental and cultural threats to severe human rights abuses. The first case focuses on the Caribbean island of Providencia (Old Providence), Colombia, where indigenous locals in the mid-1990s struggled to save the environment and key aspects of their traditional way of life. This case illustrates how elements of the context can significantly influence coordinated efforts against injustice. The second case, the struggle of Argentine human rights groups in the 1970s and 1980s, profiles how relatives of victims worked with others deeply committed to justice to challenge Argentina's brutal military and its policy of kidnapping and murdering civilians. The story of organizing against human rights abuses in Argentina highlights the important role networks play for people who become part of communal efforts to resist injustice. The last case we examine in this chapter, the Rosenstrasse protest in Berlin in 1943, is an example of a more spontaneous joint resistance. Here, non-Jewish German women, who were married to Jews, successfully saved their husbands from deportation to Nazi death camps. The story of the Rosenstrasse protest highlights how individuals who are not formally organized or connected to one another can collectively resist injustice. The Rosenstrasse protests also illustrate how collective courageous resistance can at times transcend immediate institutional barriers without altering other aspects of the context, such as broader societal values or other unjust policies of the same state.

SAVING OLD PROVIDENCE[1]

When today's travelers visit the small Caribbean island of Providencia (Old Providence), they may notice how different it seems from other Caribbean islands. Unlike many of its peer islands, the island of Providence and the reefs surrounding it are clean. Many islanders' lifestyles echo patterns of previous generations, with diets based at least in part on small-scale farming, fishing, or crabbing in a traditional "artisan" way. The cultural celebrations and music festivals on Providence are reminiscent of another century and the islanders' unique heritage, influenced by a combination of English Puritans, their African slaves, and pirates. Most islanders still hold title to the land of their ancestors, and Providence has remained fairly well isolated from problems of the drug trade and related violence that plague nearby islands and mainland Colombia. Providence's healthy ecology and culture is not an accident, but rather the result of island residents who organized to preserve their way of life despite threats and attacks spawned by their efforts.

The struggle to save Providence began one day in 1994. Richard Hawkins V, an Afro-Caribbean islander, overheard loose-lipped drinkers at a local bar talking of secret plans for a massive tourist development, Mount Sinai, which was being misrepresented to the local population as a relatively small-scale, eco-friendly resort. Hawkins, who had traveled throughout the Caribbean region and seen the damage wrought by poorly executed "development," knew immediately that the scale and location of the plan would despoil the delicate environment of the island and the reefs surrounding it. Although he had no children himself, Hawkins was concerned about what the development would mean for future generations' quality of life and for the island's culture. Hawkins discussed the scale of development of the hotel complex and the perceived dangers of the proposed plan with other islanders. Together with Hawkins, these islanders spread the news around the island, calling together other concerned islanders to discuss what could be done (Hawkins 2003).

As the islanders gradually discovered, more than a dozen major projects were on the verge of construction on Providence and the adjoining small island of Santa Catalina. The mayor of these two islands, Alexander Henry Livingston, had secretly signed seventeen documents granting permission for these projects, all without consulting the community.

The islanders had watched the development process transform their sister island of San Andres over the past forty years, and both the process and the outcome had been devastating to residents. The islanders believed the massive scale of the Mount Sinai project and its planned location among the environmentally essential mangroves would similarly damage the environment and destroy the islanders' traditional way of life. These changes and the transfer of beachfront land rights to developers would transform future generations of islanders into second-class citizens, fighting each other for a few low-wage jobs, stripped of their ability to support themselves in traditional ways.

Community leader Josefina Huffington recalled the decision to resist the "megaproject" and the seeming complicity of their elected mayor and his administration: "We had a very, very big fight. . . . A lot of Colombian [mainland] people with money . . . saw the fowl of the golden eggs so they wanted the fowl. They came over to build five-star hotels. That means they were going to steal the economy of the islanders [and] our culture, our habits, also our language. We knew that if that happened we were going to lose our identity as an ethnical [sic] group, so we all got together and decided we were not going to permit it" (Huffington 2003).

Huffington, Hawkins, and the other concerned islanders began to organize. Hawkins shared his concerns about the development with Sandra Gomez, who had migrated to the island from the Colombian metropolis of Cali years earlier. Gomez appreciated Providence's unspoiled nature and was deeply troubled by the development. As she explained later, "I am an islander. . . . I know I'm not [technically], but I felt such affection for the people of the island, I had to do something" (Gomez 2003). Gomez returned to Cali and used her influential family's connections to connect with a Dr. Fabio Londono, a Colombian lawyer affiliated with the Association for Assistance in Social Development, who had expertise in indigenous rights.[2] Londono became interested in the islanders' plight. He accepted the islanders' invitation to visit their island and offered his expertise free of charge.

Londono introduced the islanders to three legal and institutional resources available to them. He explained how recent changes to the new Colombian Constitution (which had gone into effect just three years earlier) gave special protection to indigenous peoples.[3] He also reminded them of international treaties Colombia had signed for protection of the environment and indigenous peoples, which had the same power as Colombia's federal laws.[4] Finally, recalling recent struggles by the residents of San Andres, he suggested the islanders take advantage of new changes in the Colombian Constitution that allowed for greater direct political representation for such former territories as San Andres and Providence.[5]

Huffington recalled,

> We appealed to the national government and Ministry of Development, Ministry of the Environment, the presidency. . . . They held public hearings. The president of the Republic, Gaviria, came here. They had to come here; the governor of the province, Simon Gonzalez [also came]. . . . We let them know, "You are going to comply with the laws. . . . " We told them "These projects . . . must stop because they will have a great impact on this ethnical group. Do what we say or we will sue in International Court." I am not afraid when I get on a tirade. (Huffington 2003)

The islanders developed an alternative development plan to allow only sustainable development on the island, to keep ownership of business and land in the hands of native islanders, and to control the size of the small island's population by pushing for enforcement of restrictions against permanent emigration to the island. Because the resisters saw the megaproject developers as having worked to gain permission for their development in ways that precluded community involvement, resisters' goals evolved to also include making the island's local government more transparent in its decision making. As Huffington recounted, "Our big decision was the government could never take no more steps on this island without the consent of the community. We don't care whatever it may be, the community has to say yes, and no means no" (Huffington 2003).

One strategy the resisters used was a protest demonstration at the main government building in San Isabel, Providencia's largest town. Several hundred islanders converged before the gleaming white government building in their initial protest against the Mount Sinai development. The protestors drew attention on and off the island, garnering media coverage in San Andres and the mainland—including coverage in Bogota's major newspaper, *El Tiempo*. The demonstrators were nonviolent but forceful, making limited, clear, consistent, and united demands. They wanted this specific project stopped immediately and all future projects to be brought before the whole community for consideration, not vetted behind closed doors. The protestors also called for the Colombian people, government, and the world audience to recognize their right to continue to live their traditional lifestyle. After the initial protest, organizers continued to expand the movement's size by reaching out to more members of the community.

Drawing on Londono's advice, the islanders formed study groups to read pertinent parts of the Colombian Constitution, especially as it related to their rights and status as an indigenous people. "The lawyer start[ed] teaching us the Colombian Constitution," Huffington said, gesturing with a maroon, leather-bound book. "The nine leaders formed a bigger group to teach everyone about the constitution." The leaders studied the constitution carefully and discovered a number of articles in the constitution that were directly relevant to their claims. "The first ten articles of the constitution are the column [backbone] of the country. All our key arguments are based on these ten articles," Huffington said. "When big people from government came to Providence they were so surprised [that] the people knew the constitution better than they did" (Huffington 2003).[6]

Knowing that the scope and impact of the projects far exceeded in size and impact what the developers were saying publicly, the islanders also pushed for public meetings with the developers. When the developers would describe their proposal as small-scale and quite eco-friendly, the islanders would confront the developers with documentation that belied their claims.

As the islanders' movement gathered strength, the people most publicly associated with it came under threat. Arsonists burned property belonging to three leaders of the resistance. During one public demonstration, Huffington recalls her cousin saving her from the path of a developer's bulldozer, which appeared to be aiming for her. In fact, after several attempts were made on her life, Huffington left the island for several months until she felt safe enough to return. Other leaders, including Hawkins, stayed.

Despite the threats, the concerted efforts of Providence's citizens bore fruit both regarding the immediate issue and in terms of long-term protection against outside development. By 1995 the islanders managed to stop the large-scale development efforts.[7] In 2000, the island and its reefs were declared a biosphere reserve, which entitled the island to certain protections under international law. In 2001 the islanders' application (filed in conjunction with the Colombian government) to be designated an indigenous people was approved by the United Nations. As an "ethnical people," the islanders' cultural traditions—including their artisan fishing and diving for lobster without using air tanks—were recognized as worthy of protection and investment under international treaties.[8]

More than a decade after their campaign began, the legacy of the island citizens who came together to resist unjust development is a changed

Providence and a supportive situation should the need to resist injustice arise again. Many islanders can still quote relevant passages of the Colombian Constitution. Local grassroots organizations continue to meet monthly to consider what the island needs and how to achieve it. Even as ownership of the archipelago is being contested before the World Court (Nicaragua claims that the archipelago, including San Andres and Providence, should become part of its territory), islanders in Providence adamantly assert that no court or nation can choose to transfer their nationality without their permission. The islanders have been permanently transformed and empowered by their successful activism. How did this group of once politically unsophisticated actors come together and have such clout?

PRECONDITIONS

The islanders who formed the heart of the resistance movement felt a strong sense of connection to other islanders. As Norvel Walter Borwn, a grocer in the village of Bottom House recalled,

> When we were small, [what] was important was relationship. . . . In the two islands, you prepare something to eat, prepare an extra plate, you don't know who's passing and hungry. You have something [for them] to eat, [a] small place where a cousin or niece could come and spend a little time. . . . The churches used to form leaders and had the philosophy that people have to help one another, take care of children and resources because all these were created from God. [We] learned that from our grandparents and from other older persons, because an older person had respect. (Borwn 2003)

A number of the courageous resisters expressed this profound feeling of connection to others. Huffington noted, "Everybody has something to do in life. You must always try to do something to benefit others. . . . Everyone on the island has a good heart. Our feeling is we respect everyone. If you see someone in difficulty you try to help them" (Huffington 2003). Even Gomez, who is not a native islander but claimed to feel like one, revealed that she felt a oneness with the other islanders. Part of the reason for this sense of connectedness likely stems from the island's small size, isolation, and relatively stable population. Virtually all the islanders know one another directly or indirectly, and many are related. Also, until recent decades, virtually all residents belonged to one of the three Christian churches represented on the island: Baptist, Catholic, and Seventh Day Adventist.

Views of authority were also connected to the islanders' history. Individuals felt that acquiescing to the outsiders' development plan without struggle would return islanders to the status of their slave ancestors and reflect a "slave mentality." For example, Huffington recalled that her father Rubin told her, "'It's better to die standing, not to go back and live like slave. If you have to spend every penny I earned, you spend it, because I want you to keep the land because we have received it from our parents.' He always said, 'Never surrender. If you surrender, posterity is going to judge you for it'" (Huffington 2003).

The previous experiences of some of the resisters and the insights they gained were essential in helping them to interpret for themselves and for the other islanders that the developers' promises should be carefully assessed. Despite the relative isolation of the community, many of the community's leaders had spent some time on the Colombian mainland, in the United States, or elsewhere and had become more leery of the promise of rapid change. They had become wary of poorly planned development and grew concerned about the well-being of those who remained on the island, those who might be especially vulnerable to exploitation by outsiders. Time away from the island had also made them appreciate the island's unique qualities. Further, a number of the islanders who had traveled to the Colombian mainland or abroad had also experienced discrimination because of their Afro-Caribbean heritage. This experience generated concern that outsiders' development of the island would create a context in which native islanders would not be treated as equals.[9]

The islanders' awareness of what had happened to San Andres, their sister island, contributed to their decision to resist as well. Until the early 1950s, inhabitants of the idyllic Caribbean islands of Providence and San Andres farmed, fished, and enjoyed close communal ties. In the 1950s, the Colombian government implemented abrupt policies to develop and Hispanicize San Andres. Over the following decades, residents of Providence watched the economic, cultural, and ecological deterioration of their twin island. This rapid and ill-planned "development" irrevocably changed San Andres. Shops, restaurants, and hotels now saturate the northern end of the island and all areas with beach access. But the glittering resorts mask the ugly side of the island's rapid development. Crime, poverty, and pollution are endemic on San Andres. Garbage and sewage processing and other services are hopelessly under capacity for the island's population, which has grown from approximately eight thousand in 1970 to more than one hundred thousand people today. The island's original residents have been pushed out of valuable real estate to less hospitable parts of the island and from self-sufficiency to jobs lacking dignity, job satisfaction, and good wages. Domingo Sanchez said what happened to San Andres was transformative for many of the people of Providence: "Providence saw what was happening with her older sister. They saw her used and thrown aside. . . . When you see your older sisters take a wrong road, I believe you learn from them" (Sanchez 2003).

The people of Providence also learned from watching San Andres that resistance was possible. In the 1950s and 1960s, San Andres islanders lacked the tools to fight the threats to their lives and culture. However, by the 1970s, some Afro-Caribbean islanders on San Andres had created the Sons of the Soil, an organization to fight for their people's rights and resist further encroachment by outsiders. For the Old Providence islanders, the leadership role that Afro-Caribbeans played in the Sons of the Soil was particularly inspirational, as was the legacy of their efforts—especially influencing the Colombian Constitution and domestic law.

In sum, the islanders of Providence appear to have some of the preconditions often associated with courageous resistance. The islanders' sense of connectedness with each other and the island, the legacy of a past shaped by slavery, shared memories of San Andres' development and the influence of the 1970s resistance, and some leaders' personal experiences of discrimination all combined to shape the islanders' response to the injustice they faced. Together, these experiences left the people of Providence well positioned to recognize what was happening, interpret it as a risk to future generations, and see themselves as having to act rapidly to save their island and culture. Strong networks of support and a favorable institutional and political context also shaped their understanding of the options available to them and shaped how Providence's resistance movement unfolded.

NETWORKS

Strong community links across the island helped the Providence protestors in multiple ways. Islanders' contacts with San Andres presented them with a clear and frightening alternative model to counter the developers' perspective. They saw what a poorly planned development would do to Providence and their indigenous cultural traditions. Providence's small size, geographic isolation, and relatively stable population meant that virtually all the islanders knew one another directly or indirectly. The strong church communities reinforced these ties and the islanders' willingness to work together for shared goals when needed. Church and other community organizations offered space and advertised the study and strategizing sessions. Circles of associates outside the island were also vital in providing connections and other resources. Gomez's links to influential mainlanders helped connect her to the indigenous rights lawyer Londono and the Association for Assistance in Social Development.

CONTEXT

Contextual forces also help explain the successful protests that happened in Providence. In the mid 1990s, when developers set their sights on the island, they faced a different domestic and international climate than developers of San Andres had in previous decades. While developers were interested in developing unspoiled Providence as a way to tap the burgeoning eco-tourism market, the people of the island were wary of such claims and sensitive to development's potential impact on the environment and indigenous cultural traditions.

San Andres had been developed before international indigenous rights and ecology networks and institutions existed to make these issues salient and enforceable. Colombia's ratification of important Organization of American States (OAS) and UN treaties on human and indigenous rights and the environment, as well as changes in the Colombian Constitution, government, and bureaucracy, were crucial for the islanders' courageous resistance. The laws the islanders pushed to have enforced were the products of previous struggles by the San Andres–based Sons of the Soil. After what had happened to San Andres, the Sons of the Soil had lobbied the federal government in Bogotá for representation in the National Congress and for protection of their heritage, both of which were incorporated into the 1991 Constitution. In 1993 the national government had also created the Ministry of the Environment and Coralina (the Corporation for Sustainable Development of the Archipelago of San Andres, Providence, and Catalina) to help protect the reefs and environment of the islands.

The people of Providence had other institutional resources as well due to the efforts of Sons of the Soil and other San Andres islanders. Because of the SOS's work, the archipelago was given two seats in the Colombian Congress, became its own region with an independently elected governor, and benefited from special provisions in the 1991 constitution and a federal law (Law 47 passed in 1993) that limited migration to the islands and offered recognition of the rights of ethnic groups within the country to preserve their ways of life. These laws and institutions, in combination with such NGOs as Londono's Association for Assistance in Social Development, the OAS, and UN institutions and transnational networks (associated with ecological and indigenous rights) were vital for Providence's courageous resisters later in the 1990s.

The existence of these new institutional mechanisms and transnational networks supporting indigenous rights and the environment gave the residents of Providence many more resources to defend their island than the people of San Andres had when their island had first attracted "development." Without these outside resources to draw on, the islanders of Providence would have stood little chance in facing the powerful and well-connected would-be developers of the massive project.

THE COMMUNAL NATURE OF THE RESISTANCE

The fact that the islanders' resistance was a collaborative effort of many people was vital. In a community in which everyone knew each other, it was easy for word to spread and for community leaders to persuade many to attend meetings and demonstrations. The creation of a grassroots civic organization allowed the islanders to employ the knowledge and networks of all involved. It also offered them collective support and a sense of collective empowerment. The first public demonstration in San Isabel drew additional protestors, media attention, and new allies in mainland Colombia and abroad. At the same time, however, the collective nature of the movement probably increased the risk for leaders such as Arenas, Huffington, and Hawkins, who were the targets of intimidation efforts.

The next case is another instance of communal courageous resistance. It is a story of how, in the context of fear and repression, a small number of Argentines became aware of human rights abuses by the governing military regime and decided to resist by spreading word of what was happening to the rest of Argentina and the world.

THE STRUGGLE FOR THE "DISAPPEARED": ARGENTINA'S HUMAN RIGHTS GROUPS[10]

In March 1976, after several years of bombings, kidnappings, and firefights by extreme left- and right-wing organizations, Argentina's armed forces removed President Isabel Peron from office. Pledging to rid the society of violence and instability, the military leaders who took over the government instilled their own reign of terror. To silence potential critics of their plans to reorganize the economy and society, the armed forces undertook a brutal campaign of repression in which a key strategy for evoking widespread fear and cooperation was to make civilians "disappear."[11] Troops in civilian attire would enter homes, businesses, and public places without warrants and take away "suspects" (including whole families, infants, and pregnant women) who were never charged, tried, or allowed to prove their innocence. Prisoners were detained in an organized network of more than two hundred highly clandestine prisons. Brutally tortured, they were almost always executed. Some were tortured to death; others were thrown—alive, but drugged—from military aircraft into the Atlantic Ocean. Government officials denied any knowledge of victims' whereabouts. In less than a decade, military personnel permanently "disappeared" between nine thousand and thirty thousand people.[12]

Resistance to this reign of state terror seemed impossible. Public meetings were not permitted, and legal processes were abandoned or subverted. Yet in this context of fear and repression, some people dared to vocalize their opposition to the regime. Eight human rights organizations formed a loose network of resistance against the brutal dictatorship.[13] Despite threats, harassment, and even disappearance and murder of some of their members, the network persistently worked to hold the state accountable for its crimes, gradually gathering both domestic and international attention that helped bring down the brutal military dictatorship. The stories of Anna, a widowed, middle-class mother of three of the "disappeared," and Daniel, a young man who was himself warned to leave the country, demonstrate how this network of resistance formed and evolved over time.

Before her children were kidnapped, Anna had dedicated her energy to providing a home where her children could "maintain the rhythm of their lives." She had shied away from political activity, viewing it with some distaste because of its reputed corruption. Anna described herself before the coup as "very spoiled and pampered and separated from life in the streets," though she reported that her husband's work with the poor taught her something about "how the poor feel" (Anna 1992).

In the first year of military rule, Anna experienced the disappearance of all three of her children. "They were very young [adults]—almost adolescents when the military dictatorship came in 1976," Anna recalled. "All three were kidnapped and disappeared. Not together. First the oldest on August 10 of that year; the other two were taken together three months later. . . . They were very compassionate kids, concerned for others. They were not terrorists, not guerillas." Anna's life was irrevocably transformed: "The disappearance of my children transformed me into an activist, not of a political party but for human rights. I wasn't part of a political party before or after. Human rights is my political party in any case—respect for life and respect for human dignity" (Anna 1992).

Anna's transformation into a courageous resister did not happen immediately. In the days immediately after her children disappeared, Anna tried to work through the system, as did many other mothers and fathers of the missing: "When our children disappeared, we accepted the letter of the law. We presented writs of habeas corpus, knocked on the doors of various jails to learn what they would tell us—where they are, what they had done. They had no answers. Then we went before the judges in the same way" (Anna 1992). Eventually, however, frustrated by an inability to find out from the government what had happened to their disappeared relatives, Anna and others combined forces, gradually coming to a broader understanding of the breadth of the disappearances and adopting a new strategy of action. Anna recalls,

> Then one mother suggested we go. . . . We were already a group in one form or another because we recognized the same faces in the same places, presenting *writs of habeas corpus* or going to the minister of the interior to [get permission to] place an advertisement. At that point, one of the mothers, who was herself later disappeared (and we know was tortured and murdered . . .), she said let's go to the Plaza de Mayo and present this to [Junta leader and President] Videla. We were very naïve then. . . . But we learned to understand a lot at an enormous cost. (Anna 1992)

And so, the relatives of the missing—who came to be known as the Madres (Mothers) of Plaza de Mayo—began to stand in the heart of Buenos Aires's busiest and most symbolic square, demanding to know, "Where are our children?" Initially, Anna recalled, "It was prohibited for more than three people to meet, because they [the military] were sure it was a revolution," so the family members would meet as a tiny group, with women at first walking "in pairs or groups of three" (Anna 1992). Since both unauthorized public meetings and expressions of dissent were banned, deciding to protest publicly and as a group was very dangerous. Wearing white scarves with the names and dates of the disappearances of their family members, the Madres met every Thursday afternoon for a nonviolent vigil in the square across from the presidential palace, demanding that their loved ones be returned to them alive.

Over time, as Anna and other bereaved mothers continued to march in the square, their involvement in the struggle to raise domestic and international awareness of the disappearances grew. Anna was "invited by one of the first founders to join them and then to help write advertisements, seeking information about the missing, and other correspondence to try to document and publicize what was happening to our children and other Argentines." In retrospect, Anna believed that at least part of the reason for her growing involvement was the influence of working as part of a group: "I was converted in a way [by] a discreet pressure: the Madres . . . " (Anna 1992).

Anna maintained her involvement even as dangers intensified. Members of the police, armed with bayonets, attempted to keep the Madres from protesting. Anna also survived an attempt to abduct her. Other early members of the Madres were not as lucky; twelve Madres and two French nuns were abducted in early December 1977 and permanently joined the ranks of the "disappeared" (Fisher 1989, 69). Despite the growing risks and gradually becoming convinced that her children had met the same grisly fate as thousands of other disappeared Argentines, Anna persevered.[14] She continuously searched for information about all of the "disappeared" and remained a regular participant in the Madres' weekly, nonviolent public vigils. Anna and other Madres helped document the involvement of the Argentine military in specific acts of disappearance. Some of them went abroad to seek assistance, approaching such powerful entities as Pope John Paul II, the Organization of American States (OAS) and the U.S. Department of State (Fisher 1989, 76). In addition, the Madres and other human rights advocates tried to empower other Argentines at home; they publicized avenues for filing writs of habeas corpus and affidavits and offered expertise, assistance, and solidarity.

Those resisting the Argentine military's reign of terror also included Daniel and many others like him, who were not as directly affected by the disappearances, but still chose to publicly contest the regime's human rights abuses. At the time of the coup, Daniel was in his early twenties. Unlike Anna, he was involved in political groups (the Peronist Youth and the Agricultural Movement). Growing up, Daniel initially intended to be a famous scientist or cinema artist. However, after being imprisoned at age seventeen under the previous military regime of President Ongania, Daniel decided to dedicate his life to combating dictatorship, which he defined as "the worst thing that could happen to people or a society."[15] Following prison, Daniel saw all his major life choices, including his decision to attend the university and pursue a particular career, as strategic moves that would help him in his "fight for liberty" (Daniel 1992).

After the coup, Daniel watched the political organizations he had worked with gradually being destroyed. Fifty percent of their leaders would be "disappeared."[16] He became active in a nonviolent, ecumenical peace and justice organization (SERPAJ), and through it, grew aware of the scope of disappearances and torture taking place. Daniel made the decision to become active in the fight for the "disappeared" along with his spouse. "When I moved to [work for] the daily movement for human rights, we decided it was the most important thing we could do. The power of a moral force over an immoral force was the only way to fight," Daniel said. "The rest of the world would have to listen. . . . For one not in accord with the violence, it would be immoral not to do anything, but I also couldn't kill. . . . My religious commitment wouldn't allow me not to work for others" (Daniel 1992).

SERPAJ's massive international campaign urged protection of human rights and raised concerns about the impact of assassinations, terrorism, repression, torture, kidnapping, assassinations, and guerrilla actions occurring in Argentina. SERPAJ urged Christians to denounce injustice firmly, but without hatred. Daniel persisted in this campaign even after SERPAJ's founder, Adolfo Perez Esquivel, was imprisoned by the Argentine Armed Forces and then after his own imprisonment in 1980.

When he decided to become active, Daniel had no illusions about the risks associated with fighting a dictatorship. In fact, he recalled the very night of the coup, "they" came looking for him at his home but didn't find him. Aware of the risks but undaunted, for three years he and his wife lived as clandestinely as possible in Argentina. They continued to document the link between the state and the disappearances and to work with religiously based human rights organizations in Argentina and elsewhere to publicize the level of abuses and apply international pressure on the junta.

As the repression grew and many of Daniel's surviving fellow activists fled the country, his friends and associates tried to persuade him to leave. Although leaving the country would have been a relatively easy option for him physically, he decided to remain in Argentina. "If we all left, who would be left to fight?" he remembers asking himself. "If I left I'd die. I couldn't live without my people, their color and smells." Although aware of the risks, Daniel tended to minimize the threat of death, as not being (for him) the sort of "ultimate threat" it appears to be for others, because he so strongly believed in life after death (Daniel 1992).

Over time, the human rights groups worked together to make sure that news of what was happening in Argentina reached the rest of the world. Anna and the other members of the Madres mounted increasingly daring public protests that gained domestic and international attention.[17] As the most visible elements of the small domestic network of human rights advocates, the Madres won celebrity. They also gained additional resources and connections to international networks, which further helped them raise awareness about the thousands of people being disappeared in Argentina. In 1978 and 1979, the now internationally recognized symbols of family loyalty, members of the Madres (Mothers) of Plaza de Mayo delivered a dossier of evidence to Pope John Paul II, seeking his assistance. The Madres' marches attracted international media attention when Argentina hosted the World Cup in 1978. Additional global publicity focused on human rights abuses in Argentina when Perez Esquivel won the 1980 Nobel Peace Prize for founding SERPAJ (Daniel's organization), which conducted cross-national work to address human rights abuse.

The domestic campaign was strengthened by its connections to a transnational network of international human rights activists. Comprised of such nongovernmental organizations as Amnesty International and Human Rights Watch, and by states and intergovernmental organizations such as the OAS, the network disseminated and amplified the concerns of Anna, Daniel, and other Argentine activists. Through the international network, the abuses won greater and greater attention and a variety of outside forces joined the campaign. Individual citizens, politicians, and nongovernmental organizations around the world began to call for investigations and sanctions against the regime. Amnesty International pushed for the release of political prisoners, including the "disappeared."[18]

Meanwhile, world opinion and criticism by various governments, including the United States, which had been sparked by the human rights groups' activities, increasingly pressured the regime to allow an international investigation by the OAS.[19] In 1979, the OAS visited Argentina, and Daniel and Anna's human rights groups were among those that presented their carefully documented eyewitness accounts of state involvement in hundreds of disappearances. The OAS report that followed is widely cited as the turning point in the number of disappearances in Argentina; the report apparently weakened the regime's belief that it could continue its abusive patterns without ramification (Sikkink and Lutz 2000; Weissbrodt and Bartolomei 1991; Brysk 1994). The combination of credible domestic information and international pressure forced the regime to permit space for public demonstration. At the same time, the slogans and demands created by the human rights organizations were the foundations for the broad-based demonstrations that challenged the regime and finally forced its resignation. While the human rights organizations eventually achieved some success in discrediting the regime and ending the disappearances, they did not bring about the safe return of the thousands who had already disappeared and failed to bring most perpetrators to justice.

The organized efforts of Anna, Daniel, and the rest of Argentina's human rights activists changed the activists themselves, their country, and the world. Today, Daniel remains politically active in human rights efforts; Anna remained so until her death of natural causes a few years ago. Thirty years after the coup, the Argentine public remains aware and vigilant regarding human rights. The Argentine courts and elected government have opened new avenues for bringing to justice the torturers and kidnappers who were previously shielded from prosecution or punishment.[20] The strategic decision of the Madres to publicly protest the disappearances has also left a legacy. In other parts of the world—including Central America and the Russian Federation—women protesting state-condoned mistreatment of their loved ones have donned the symbolic white scarves and called for policy change. A new generation of human rights activists calling themselves the Children (Hijos) of Plaza de Mayo now lead campaigns for social justice in Argentina.

PRECONDITIONS

Anna and Daniel's ability to understand and respond to the phenomenon of disappearance was to some degree a reflection of their attitudes and values before the violence began. In addition to feeling grief when her teenaged children were abducted, Anna's outrage regarding the disappearances stemmed from her strong sense of obligation for the welfare of her children and her beliefs that her children were innocent and that the military's actions were morally indefensible. While other relatives of the disappeared accepted that their loved ones had acted in ways that deserved punishment or saw the junta's authority as impenetrable, Anna's confidence in her knowledge of her children, the world and her own central principles were the ultimate authority and determined how she would respond. Years later, when asked to explain why she chose to resist and persist in protesting the disappearances of her children and others, Anna said that the writings of Holocaust survivor and Nobel Prize winner Elie Wiesel greatly affected her: "He made two comments that impressed me very much. He was a small boy in the concentration camps. His family died; he suffered a lot. He said he felt he had to survive and testify. Testify and denounce what had happened. For me the Madres of the Plaza play the same role: to testify and to denounce" (Anna 1992).

The military's transgression of human rights, which was to Anna a sacred value, enabled her to break the law and publicly dissent in the square. Anna, who was Jewish, also saw similarities between the Holocaust and what was happening in her own country. Her knowledge of the Holocaust helped model the need for values of justice and commitment to the vital cause of protecting innocents. She recalled that Wiesel had called for trials of the Nazis and was later asked why he continued to yell even after the last perpetrator had been tried. As Anna recalled, "He said, 'There is always another trial, but even after the last trial one must continue to yell to change others' attitudes.' A young man said to him, 'Well no one is listening.' Wiesel replied, 'I yell so I don't change.' And we—particularly me—but other others sometimes feel that no one is listening to us and nothing is changing, but we continue to yell for ourselves to be able to go on caring. Those two phrases impressed me; they are a model to apply in our lives" (Anna 1992).

For Anna, Wiesel was significant as a model of what it meant to act to uphold one's values. Anna also gradually learned how to resist injustice by engaging in resistance. She did not start off as an activist. Her initial search for answers was regarding her own children, not all the disappeared. As her connection to other families suffering similar tragedies made her aware of the scope of the regime's violence, Anna was gradually transformed into an activist who sought to help not just her own children, but all victims of grave injustice.

Daniel also was motivated by deep-seated principles and learned how to courageously resist the human rights abuses over time, but for him the learning started earlier in his life. Daniel's efforts to stop the disappearances were part of a lifelong campaign against dictatorship. Even more than for Anna, Daniel's early life experiences shaped his response to the military regime. Like Anna, Daniel's resistance to the Argentine state's human rights abuses was not about what the law said. Daniel saw his moral principles as the most important arbiter of what was right or wrong and what should be done. "The power of a moral force over an immoral force was the only way to fight," Daniel said. "The rest of the world would have to listen." These principles also determined how Daniel chose to fight the human rights abuses: "For one not in accord with the violence, it would be immoral not to do anything, but I also couldn't kill. . . . My religious commitment wouldn't allow me not to work for others." Daniel's lifelong values and particular kind of inclusiveness—which extended to all his countrymen and all those he saw as God's children—seem to have shaped not only his sense of what he must do and why, but also his sense of risks and rewards. Daniel displayed broad extensivity (i.e., a feeling of identification with a large number of other people); he felt deeply connected to other Argentines suffering under the military regime. Although he might have left Argentina for safe refuge, he stayed home, working to stop the human rights abuses, unable to leave those he called "[his] people," not only because of his principles and who he was as an individual, but because he felt so strongly attached to Argentines (Daniel 1992).

NETWORKS

The activists' connections and linkages with others were vital to their participation. After her children were taken, Anna and others whose relatives had disappeared came to know each other as they crossed paths fruitlessly searching for answers. Together, they affirmed each other's sense that something was awry with the state's denials and explanations of the disappearances. Hearing one another's stories also helped them confirm not only how widespread the disappearances were, but also that many of the disappeared were not terrorists, as the state implied. Anna recalled, "We all helped each other mutually . . . in different degrees. We all gave each other information as we found it and support, of course." (Anna 1992).

The Madres organization evolved from the connections these women forged as they sought fruitlessly for information about their missing loved ones. From chance meetings they created bonds, then strategies, and gradually became a well-organized human rights group. The members themselves evolved as they became more involved. Over time, each mother "went out looking for one [missing child] and wound up looking for thirty thousand" (Anna 1992). The mothers' collective understandings evolved as to what had happened to their loved ones, who was responsible for the disappearances, and what their own mission as mothers should be; they learned from one another. Each time Anna and the other Madres marched in the weekly protest, these linkages nurtured their resistance. Protesting as part of a group, instead of as individuals, helped the activists to overcome their fears and feel more powerful. After the Madres formed and connected with other human rights groups, Anna found even more support and solidarity.

Similarly, Daniel's religious community strengthened his commitment to the fight against human rights abuses. The other Christians with whom he associated reinforced his deeply internalized values and offered him a perspective on the risks and responsibilities that surmounted official state propaganda: While some people he knew ceased their political activities because they feared the military regime, Daniel reported that he was not afraid of being killed by agents of the Argentine state, because of his faith. "I believe in eternal life; the final word is life, not death" (Daniel 1992).

The networks that sprang up among the Argentine human rights activists also provided tangible help. When the Madres were unable to find any locations to rent, the more established League for the Rights of Man let them use their office. International networks also contributed resources. For example, international women's organizations bought the Madres a house near the capitol building. International experts also shared their legal and scientific expertise, eventually creating a DNA database that employed DNA samples supplied by relatives of the "disappeared" to help identify kidnapped children and potentially reunite them with their biological families.

Context

Many elements of the context were crucial in the struggle against the dictatorship and its abusive strategies." The failure of domestic institutions to protect human rights forced human rights advocates to create new organizations and to turn to international institutions. Further, the lack of public opposition to any regime policy made their protests more risky, but also more noteworthy. Knowing that world opinion would condemn the military's policy of "disappearing" its citizens, the Madres and other human rights organizations worked tirelessly to obtain evidence of what was happening and publicize it. The military regime's law against public dissent and efforts to intimidate the Madres gave the Madres' weekly public vigil additional symbolic power. International publicity and interest shown by such international organizations as the OAS increased the influence within Argentina of the Madres and other human rights groups. Linkages to transnational organizations were clearly central for all the Argentine human rights groups. Later, after the international attention following publication of the OAS report, the Argentine government was forced to provide space for public protest, and human rights became a topic for public debate in Argentina for the first time in years. This public opening contributed significantly to Argentina's successful transition to democracy.[21]

The Communal Nature of the Resistance

The human rights activists' efforts were synergistic, allowing the activists to accomplish much more than they could have as individuals. Being part of organizations allowed Daniel, Anna, and other members to share information and build supportive connections that empowered them with additional resources ranging from financial contributions to legal and organizational expertise, as well as moral support. Their continued work with others helped keep hope alive. These efforts also encouraged more sophisticated understandings of events as the activists gathered and shared their partial information to piece together a picture of large-scale patterns. Working together transformed the activists' understandings of what was going on, the need for them to act, and the range of possible responses. As they took action, their collective endeavors emboldened them and offered them both pragmatic assistance and moral support. They became committed to the other members of their groups, seeing the others' goals and ambitions as on par with their own.

　　As important as these connections are, people who desire to resist injustice do not always have connections to each other. The next case of

Rosenstrasse gives an example of joint resistance, illustrating both the power and limitations of collective resistance without communal ties.

ROSENSTRASSE

For the Nazi regime, Jews who were married to non-Jewish Germans posed a significant problem.[22] The crux of the problem from the regime's view was that intermarried couples united members of the "enemy," "sub-human" population with those of the "master race" in the venerable institution of marriage. Still, the Nuremberg Laws of 1935, which banned all future intermarriages, did not annul existing intermarriages. During the first year of the Third Reich, intermarriage among German Jews fell from 45 to 15 percent, and German leaders seemed to have good reason to hope that intermarriages would dissolve under the increasing pressures of terror. Following complaints from non-Jews on behalf of intermarried Jews who had been brutalized during the Kristallnacht pogrom of 1938, the regime began exempting some intermarried Jews from measures to displace and concentrate German Jews.

By October 1941, however, the majority of intermarried Germans defied Nazi expectations and had not voluntarily sought divorce, despite the pressures of severe discrimination and spiraling persecution. They continued to live in mixed marriages in open disregard for government ideology and laws while bearing untold daily harassment from neighbors and colleagues. When the mass extermination of German Jews began in October 1941, the Nazi leadership, apprehensive about social unrest and the attention drawn to a program they wished to keep secret, "temporarily exempted" intermarried Jews.[23]

On February 27, 1943, during what the Berlin Gestapo called "the Final Roundup," a massive arrest of the last Jews in Berlin, the regime attempted to end this "temporary" exemption. The SS and Gestapo arrested and kidnapped the approximately ten thousand remaining Jews from their homes and workplaces. All those wearing the Star of David were taken without explanation to collecting centers in the heart of Berlin. About eight thousand of the ten thousand Berlin Jews arrested in the Final Roundup were summarily deported to Auschwitz and murdered. The two thousand not immediately shipped off to Auschwitz were Jews married to Aryan Germans. They were held at an administrative center in the heart of Berlin, at Rosenstrasse 2–4, in preparation for deportation as well. Beginning on the first day of these arrests, German partners of the Jews incarcerated at Rosenstrasse gathered together on the street and demanded the return of their loved ones. Intermarried Germans used personal connections and loose existing networks to inform one another of events, and more people increasingly began to gather.[24]

The Aryan spouses, who were mostly women, quickly formed a crowd. A protest broke out as the hundreds of women at the gate began calling out, "Give us our husbands back!" Day and night for a week they staged their protest, and the crowd grew larger. Their decision to protest was extremely dangerous as they risked death or imprisonment. On different occasions, the guards commanded, "Clear the streets or we'll shoot!" This sent the women scrambling into surrounding alleys and courtyards. But within minutes, they began streaming out. Again and again the protest was broken up by threats of gunfire, and each time the protesters advanced once more, massed together, and called out for their husbands who heard them and took hope. At one point, a group as large as six hundred people formed.

These public protests even attracted some non-family members. For example, one intermarried wife brought her brother, a soldier, who in turn brought three other soldiers to the Rosenstrasse protest. The first of these soldiers approached the SS Guards and said that if they did not release his brother-in-law, he would not return to the battlefront.

After a week of protest, the Nazis capitulated and released the women's husbands. Leopold Gutterer, in postwar taped interviews about his time as state secretary to Propaganda Minister Joseph Goebbels, identified some of the characteristics of the protest from the regime's perspective:

> These women were as persons there. Anyone could recognize who they were. They demonstrated openly and risked their existence (*Dasein*). They were very courageous, yes? No doubt about that. If one or the other [of the protesters] had had a pistol along, then the police would have had to shoot. A protest against the system never existed. These women didn't want a revolution. The Jews were released in order to eliminate the protest from the world. That was the simplest solution—to completely eradicate the reason for the protest. Then it wouldn't make sense to protest anymore. So that others didn't take a lesson from [the protest], so that others didn't begin to do the same, the reason [for protest] had to be eliminated. There was unrest, and it could have spread from neighborhood to neighborhood. Of course there was an investigation to find out whether someone was instigating this. But nothing was found. If so, one could have hindered it. [The protest] wasn't organized but spread by word of mouth. It was a spontaneous reaction. Why should Goebbels have had them [the protesters] all arrested? Then he would have only had even more unrest, from the relatives of these newly arrested persons. (Gutterer 1987)

Nevertheless, Gutterer emphasized that "every" option of police state force had been a possibility: "They had to reckon at least with being arrested. It would have been no problem to find out who was there—the police could have gone through, and demanded identification. They could have been sent to jail, at least, or to a concentration camp. All means could have been used against them." Gutterer also said that the threats the SS and police officers made to "clear the streets or we'll shoot" were against the women, not against their family members being held. The protest could have ended in a bloodbath, if even one trigger-happy officer had begun to shoot (Gutterer 1986–87).

The protest was effective because Propaganda Leader and the Nazi regional director for Berlin Joseph Goebbels feared that open resistance, if allowed to continue, would serve as an example and erode public support for the regime and perhaps threaten the whole genocide mission by attracting attention to an effort the regime wanted to hide.[25] Although the Gestapo could have ended the protests with violence, the protesters' demands were met for short-term tactical reasons. The fact that resisters' demands were limited and aimed only at specific initiatives (i.e. release of those taken during this roundup rather than the demise of the regime) helped them achieve success as well.

The Jews married to Aryans were released and remained in Berlin with official status, including food rations through the end of the war. The Rosenstrasse protest caused the regime to use the policy of deporting only those intermarried Jews whose partners died or who had agreed to a divorce. In addition, the Rosenstrasse protest resulted in an exemption from the Final Solution for all other intermarried Jews in Germany and a government decision not to arrest *Mischlinge* (the offspring of intermarriages) because Aryan Germans might also protest their removal. Joseph Goebbels intended to deport the intermarried Jews later.[26] But the end of the war arrived before the regime did this; so 98 percent of German Jews who survived the war without going into hiding were intermarried.[27] Tragically, the policy exemptions stopped at the German border. In the eastern occupied territories, intermarried Jews and Germans and their *Mischlinge* continued to be deported throughout the war years.[28]

Rather than aiming to make a statement for the future, the Rosenstrasse demonstrators actually managed to open up an effective communication with the enemy in the present. In place of conspiracy and arms, they offered a public disclosure of personal beliefs—even though these were anathema to state dogma. The intermarried Germans communicated by their actions that they were willing to put their own "Aryan" lives on the line to prevent the murder of Jewish family members and to impede the Nazi drive to eliminate all traces of Jewish "blood" from Europe, particularly in Germany. One Gestapo officer, who had witnessed the repeated inefficacy of police threats against the women to "clear the streets or draw fire," began to view his unquestioning loyalty to the regime in a new light. "Your relatives are outside protesting for you," he said to one of the imprisoned Jews. "They want you back. That's true German loyalty" (Kuhn 1989). The desire to keep family together was something many Germans could understand; although many also would have found loyalty to Jews over loyalty to the state abominable.

The communication between the regime and the intermarried Germans at Rosenstrasse was effective because it caused the regime to choose between two of its fundamental principles. Had non-Jewish spouses quietly acquiesced to the Final Roundup, the result would undoubtedly have been the "unproblematic" deportations of Jews. However, their protest divided powerful leaders, forcing them to choose between immediate "racial purification" and the principle of maintaining power through sustained popular morale and the appearance of unified popular support. "Hitler and Goebbels wanted to avoid disturbing Berlin's female population at a time when the Propaganda Minister had just called on them to mobilize for 'total war,'" wrote British historian Richard J. Evans. "They even ordered the return of thirty-five [intermarried Jews arrested in the Schlussaktion] who were already in Auschwitz. The women had won. Their husbands survived the war" (Evans 1996).

PRECONDITIONS

The women who demonstrated in Rosenstrasse were in many ways predisposed to make this public statement. Clearly they were people who had a broad enough definition of humanity to see past the pervasive state propaganda that dehumanized Jews and urged them to shun their Jewish friends and relatives, as many other Germans did. As these women resisted official and social pressures to divorce their husbands, they became accustomed to enduring ostracism and resisting conformity. They had gradually learned to live with risks and to handle their fears sufficiently so that they could stand in line for ration cards and other necessary paperwork. Their close relationships to the victims and awareness of the increased level of abuse their loved ones and other Jews had already undergone made it easier for them quickly to recognize these arrests as life threatening and needing immediate response. Their prior experience of looking out for their spouses' well-being (including in some cases remaining married to or marrying a Jewish German specifically to shield him from deportation) made it easier for potential resisters to see them-selves as *the* person who had to take action if the prisoners were to be saved. Elsa Holzer, one of the principal protesters at Rosenstrasse, said, "We had to prove [by risking our lives on the street in protest] whether we really thought it was worth it or not, our love. In my opinion, that can only come from the heart, such a decision. One can't calculate whether it's worth it or not. One is ready, or not. One does it, or not" (Holzer 1989).

For many of these women, their collective public resistance was not so much a conversion to a new kind of behavior, but rather a continuation of courageous resistance. It was one more step on a path already covered with many small courageous steps they had chosen to take since the Nazis had risen to power and begun their campaign to remove all Jews from Germany. Those married to Jews had been under constant pressure for years to divorce their husbands. They had suffered social ostracism and economic hardship for their refusal to do so. They had gradually become accustomed to lives filled with risk, so when their husbands finally were taken away, they were taking just one more step along the same pathway.

Yet, in other ways the Rosenstrasse women's preconditions likely con-strained the actions they took. The women who went out looking for their missing husbands extended their sense of in-group to family mem-bers only. The Rosenstrasse women's sense of their in-group mobilized them as they went searching for their husbands but also established the limits to their activism. Their worldviews likely remained unaltered, and their concern and sense of responsibility apparently remained focused on the limited number of people they were already working to protect. With the decision by Nazi officials to free their husbands, the Rosenstrasse pro-testers ceased protesting and returned to their homes. Their intense con-tact with other women remained largely an isolated episode and did not lead to other activism or a quest to seek the release of other Jews, such as missing in-laws, friends, or acquaintances.

NETWORKS

Networks played a more limited role in what happened at Rosenstrasse than in such cases of collective resistance as Providence or the Argentine human rights struggle. When the Berlin women's husbands were rounded up, the word traveled quickly, and the women acted collectively. However, in the case of the Rosenstrasse protest, it is the absence of net-works that is most telling. Prior to Rosenstrasse, the intermarried Germans likely came to recognize a few others going through the same steps (e.g., waiting for ration cards, and so forth), but apparently they only rarely connected with others in the same situation. Most employed other networks of support.

The Rosenstrasse women worked together only for the limited time necessary to win their spouses' release; they did not go on to form a lasting community. They held no organizational meetings, apparently did not exchange much in the way of information, and when their spouses were returned to them, they returned to relative seclusion, neither keeping in touch with the other protesters nor attempting to change other laws or policies of the Third Reich. Their collective presence had been powerful, but it had not been built upon preexisting social capital, and it did not create social capital. If these women felt transformed by having successfully made the state hierarchy back down from one of its central policies, they did not channel that newfound power into further action, nor did they campaign on behalf of other victims. The women went on using their own, narrow networks of support and looking out for their family members.

CONTEXT

Certain aspects of the context helped the Rosenstrasse protest happen. The Nazi regime needed to avoid social unrest and keep its genocide plans secret. Because Nazi propaganda relied so heavily upon the power of large political gatherings, the fact that the protest took place publicly and nonviolently right in Berlin and at the height of the war effort made it harder for the regime to quell the demonstration violently and forced the Nazis to back down. "A large number of people gathered and in part even took sides with the Jews," complained Goebbels in his diary on March 6. "I ordered the Gestapo not to continue Jewish evacuation."[29] Time was running out for the Nazis, and thus Rosenstrasse possibly stopped what would have become a general inclusion of intermarried Jews in what we now know as the Holocaust.

THE COLLECTIVE NATURE OF THE RESISTANCE

Even if unorganized, only a large public street display of loyalty to Jews such as that at Rosenstrasse could have clearly identified Jews, to the public and even to Gestapo officers, as family members rather than as the subhumans that pervasive official propaganda portrayed. Perhaps the powerful potential of a burgeoning network was understood by the adversaries of the Rosenstrasse women and contributed to the rapid acquiescence of Goebbels and the Gestapo when the women refused to disperse. Of course, Goebbels made the decision to release the Jews at Rosenstrasse, and Hitler agreed with it out of tactical reasons. However, due to the regime's peculiar sensitivity to popular morale within Germany and Hitler's omnipresent fear of revolution, this publicly expressed resistance against a program the regime wished to keep secret exerted a real force.

THE IMPACT OF COLLECTIVE RESISTANCE

Collective resistance is more than the sum of individual actions challenging injustice. The more public the resistance is, the more likely it is to yield change in repressors' behaviors and policies. But public resistance is often highly risky, and its impact is not assured, rapid, or complete. Although some research has suggested that risk to loved ones or the experience of loss can drive potential protesters against injustice to not act, the examples in this chapter show that such very personal experiences and losses can motivate individuals to take action.[30] In addition, while networks of support are helpful for virtually all courageous resisters, particular networks—especially those that offer analytic insight—are especially important for those with minimal experience at resisting authority. Similarly, the context in which resistance takes place matters greatly and varies dramatically from one case to another.

Many of the courageous resisters profiled here, in particular the women of Rosenstrasse and Daniel in Argentina, had already practiced challenging state authority, addressing their fears, and facing social ostracism. Those who previously had defended others who were in need likely saw themselves as able to survive the challenges placed before them and had already developed an understanding of the potential influence that their actions might have. Their networks provided them with sustained opportunities to talk, share, and analyze the situation with many others. Without the networks, they might have missed the opportunity to be even stronger and make more radical changes.

For others, including many of the Argentine and Colombian activists, who were often more politically inexperienced and had been sheltered from danger and exploitation, their prior experiences may not have given them sufficient tools to handle the challenges that would soon face them. For such individuals, however, the communal nature of their resistance came to the fore. Shared knowledge helped make seemingly isolated examples of injustice or abuse part of a larger pattern. It also increased the likelihood of actors learning about the laws, institutions, organizations, and broader networks that might further help them understand what was happening so that they could make a meaningful response and know that their actions were possible—even crucial—in making sure the wrongs were redressed. Tapping into domestic (and even international) networks and learning how to employ institutions also transformed potential activists' perceptions of what was happening and what could be done.

Protecting the endangered rights of others—even those not in one's immediate circle—is the core of collective resistance. Successful advocates of rights seek just treatment not only for themselves, but also for their closest associates (e.g., family members and descendents) and sometimes for whole classes of people, such as all the "disappeared" or all indigenous people. An activist may begin by helping an individual and purposefully or unwittingly may influence the fates of whole classes of people. Once courageous resisters understand the breadth of a problem, define it as injustice, and see that they themselves need to take action, it seems that it is increasingly difficult for them to step away from taking responsibility and action, not only because of the bonds and loyalties they have to their new or deepened community, but because they have been gradually transformed to see themselves as the sort of people who do act and who take responsibility for the well-being of a large circle of people.

The deliberate decision to try to help an entire category of people seems to be most closely associated with communal resistance. The norms of reciprocity and trust developed in collective endeavor can make it difficult for individuals to end their involvement in resistance even after their own limited goals are satisfied. Such courageous resisters rarely return to being passive bystanders while the injustices continue to threaten anyone whom they have come to think of as part of their ingroup.

NOTES

1. The quotations in this section are drawn from forty-eight interviews conducted in Providencia, Colombia, by Kristina Thalhammer in January and February 2003.
2. Londono and his Association for Assistance in Social Development had already won a reputation for helping other Colombian ethnic groups, including the Awa people, to defend their populations against encroachments that threatened their cultures and in preventing unsustainable projects (e.g., a diesel plant near Maipu) that would have devastated the local indigenous culture and wildlife habitat.
3. For example, the 1991 Colombian Constitution, Article 330, states, "The exploitation of the natural resources in indigenous territories will be carried out without any deterioration of the communities' cultural, social, and economical integrity. The government will propitiate the participation

of representatives of the respective communities in the decisions concerning such exploitation." The constitution also declared that the Colombian Federal Government would take responsibility for protecting the environment, biodiversity, and ethnic culture (Articles 63, 68, and 246).

4. The Convention on Biodiversity, which was ratified in 1994 by the Colombian Congress as Law 165, spawned the UN Environment Program and the Global Environment Facility. The UN, in turn, commissioned the Global Biodiversity Assessment (GBA), which was completed in 1996. The GBA repeatedly emphasizes that human use and management cause the main impacts on biodiversity. This study, now a seminal reference on the topic of biodiversity, also emphasizes that in questions of how to protect biodiversity and develop socioeconomic strategies for its sustainable use, people must be seen to be a major part of the solution.

5. The constitution also elevated all *Intendencias* (including the archipelago comprised of San Andres, Old Providence, and several much smaller islands) to the status of departments (states), which could for the first time elect representatives to Colombia's Congress and elect a governor and mayor for each island.

6. For example, Article 2 of the 1991 Colombian Constitution lists among the essential purposes of the government to "serve the community" and "facilitate the participation of all in the decisions that affect them." And Article 3 declares, "Sovereignty lies exclusively with the people." Article 7 declares, "The state recognizes and protects the ethnic and cultural diversity of the Colombian nation" (*Constitucion Politica de Colombia 1996*, 17–18). Translation by Thalhammer.

7. The former mayor of the island, who had given the developers the initial permission, was eventually removed from office and imprisoned for corruption.

8. In June 1989, after four years of preparatory work, the UN's International Labor) Conference adopted a revised version of Convention Number 107 (now Convention Number 169) on Indigenous and Tribal Peoples. Convention Number 169 serves as a basis for International Labor Organization implementation and technical assistance activities for indigenous peoples. Colombia ratified this in 1991.

9. They may also have been inspired by the leadership role Afro-Caribbeans had played in the San Andres–based efforts to resist development.

10. The information and quotations for this section are drawn from seventy-eight interviews conducted by Kristina Thalhammer in Buenos Aires and La Plata, Argentina, between October 1992 and May 1993. All Argentines interviewed are identified by pseudonym on the recommendation of the University of Minnesota Committee on Human Subjects in Research.

11. The military had actually begun to use this tactic even before the 1976 coup officially ended democratic rule. However, after the coup, it became widespread and apparently standard practice. The use of the verb "to disappear," as in "to disappear someone," entered into international use as a result of this tactic in Argentina and elsewhere.

12. The full extent of regime brutality only became clear when the regime left power in 1983; its leaders were put on trial and a truth commission was convened to investigate. *Nunca Mas*, the official report of the Sabato Commission, documents more than eight thousand disappearances. Because of continued secrecy among military and former military personnel, however, the full extent of abuse and the fates of many of the disappeared may never be known. Human rights advocates, including the Madres (Mothers) of Plaza de Mayo, contend that the actual number of regime victims is likely closer to thirty thousand (CONADEP [National Commission on the Disappearance of Persons] 1986).

13. Organizations whose members were generally not related to the regime's victims included The League for the Rights of Man (Liga), the Center for the Study of the Law and Society (CELS), Peace and Justice Service (SERPAJ), the Permanent Assembly for Human Rights (*Asamblea Permanente*), and the Ecumenical Movement for Human Rights (MEDH). In addition, three groups of relatives of regime victims formed part of the human rights network within Argentina: Relatives of the Disappeared and Political Prisoners (*Familiares*), the Madres (Mothers) of Plaza de Mayo (*Madres*), and the Grandmothers of the Plaza (*Abuelas*).

14. For many years, Anna believed that her missing family members could be helped; however, Anna never saw any of her children again.

15. General Juan Carlos Ongania became president via a 1966 military coup. He disbanded Congress and political parties and ruthlessly repressed his opposition until he was himself removed from office by a coup in 1970.

16. The terrorism took a strong personal toll as well. Daniel recalled that shortly after the dictatorship ended, he looked at a photo taken at a close friend's wedding in 1972 and realized that only three of the twelve friends in the photo had survived.

17. The efforts of these domestic human rights advocates allowed for clear, accurate, and convincing evidence to reach the international community of governmental and nongovernmental organizations concerned about human rights. They also humanized the victims, giving those rumored to be terrorists names and faces and arguing that all were innocent since none had ever had a chance to be tried or allowed to defend themselves against any legal charges.

18. Daniel's experience offers a good example of this network's influence. After years of activism, Daniel was himself kidnapped in 1979. Out of the nineteen individuals who disappeared that week, he was the only individual to survive. He attributes his release to an international publicity campaign orchestrated by his colleagues in the human rights network.

19. U.S. President Jimmy Carter ordered economic sanctions against Argentina in 1977.

20. In June 2005, the Argentine Supreme Court struck down sweeping amnesties that shielded hundreds of former officers from prosecution. As of September 2005, Argentina's former President General Jorge Videla

and more than a dozen other officers had been arrested or placed under house arrest for their role in human rights abuses associated with the country's "Dirty War."

21. After the regime fell, the changed context altered the networks. The various communities that had worked very closely during the period of repression splintered after the regime's fall. The change in context relaxed the strong ties that once held together those with a common cause despite divergent social, economic, and political beliefs. The Madres split over a number of issues, including the newly elected regime's attempts to exhume bodies, offering to deliver death certificates for the missing (to allow family members to dispose of property and collect insurance money). The Madres who participated in what came to be known as the *Hebe de Bonafini* line refused any attempts to lay the disappearances to rest. They argued that they would continue to ask for their children to be returned to them alive, and the only acceptable alternative would be that the state fully investigate their murders and punish perpetrators. Some members of the Madres (who came to call themselves Linea Fundadora) and six of the other seven human rights groups rejected this strategy, seeing cooperation and engagement with the fragile democratic regime as more necessary than rigid adherence to their demands against the authoritarian regime.

22. Ursula Büttner makes an estimation of the number of divorces throughout Germany based on statistics from Hamburg and Baden-Württemberg. Büttner identifies many of the laws the Third Reich promulgated to block careers of Germans married to Jews in the introduction to that volume (Büttner 1988, 57).

23. Ironically, of course, intermarried German Jews were the most ideologically offensive to the Nazis. Intermarried members of German "racial" *Volksgemeinschaft* or "Community of the People" meant that the regime would have to forcibly, and thus publicly annul their marriages or else blur the line dividing "racial" Germans from their victims, the Jews, in the forced expulsions and mass murders of the Holocaust.

24. Quotations and details of this case come from interviews and other research conducted by Nathan Stoltzfus. For a richer discussion of this case see Stoltzfus 1992 and Stoltzfus 1996.

25. See also Leugers (2005), especially the articles by Joachim Neander and Antonia Leugers, and Michalczyk (2004), 163–89.

26. Froelich 1993, 487, 514, 528, diary entries for March 6, 9, and 11, 1943. Time was running out for the Nazis, however, and thus Rosenstrasse possibly stopped what would have become a general inclusion of intermarried Jews in what we now know as the Holocaust. Goebbels's State Secretary Leopold Gutterer, who met with him upon his return to Berlin on March 4, said Goebbels would have released the Jews earlier if he had known of the protest earlier. On seeing Goebbels's diary for March 9, 1943, where Goebbels, on a visit to Hitler's *Wolfschanze* bunker, explained the "psychological" problems encountered in deporting the last Jews of Berlin,

Gutterer said the diaries meant Hitler had agreed with Goebbels's decision
to release Jews at Rosenstrasse while reiterating that Berlin would have to
be made *Judenfrei* (an area with no Jewish presence) (Gutterer 1986).

27. Statistics of the Central Organization of Jews in Germany (Reichsvereinigung
der Juden in Deutschland) show that as of September 1944 there were
13,217 officially registered Jews in Germany. All but 230 lived in intermarriage. German National Archives, Potsdam, R 8150, 32. We cannot
deduce from this statistic that the Nazi regime allowed all intermarried
Jews to avoid punishment, because some were in fact murdered. For a history of intermarriage in the Third Reich, see Stoltzfus 1996.

28. Protests in Finland in 1942 against the arrests of Jews and Communists
caused the Germans to discontinue deportations (Stoltzfus 1996, 259).

29. See note 24, above.

30. Repression may seem an efficient tactic for those trying to impose potentially unpopular policies. Exposure to threat can, however, have the reverse
effect, inspiring passive citizens to become the oppressors' most adamant
opponents. In the Argentine case, most of those who were not yet affected
by this military regime's brutality had previous exposure to fear-evoking
episodes, such as Daniel's imprisonment under the previous junta's rule. In
contrast, among those whose families were suddenly faced with a disappeared family member, it was those who had never been truly frightened
before who were more likely to publicly protest the loss of their dear ones.
Terror can immobilize major sectors of a population, but it can also so
enrage those who view it for the first time, as to light in them an intense
need to do something to counter it (Thalhammer 2001, 493–519).

CHAPTER 6

INSTITUTIONS AND
RESISTING INJUSTICE

We have it in our power to pass on to our children a brighter inheritance than that bequeathed to any previous generation. We can halve global poverty and halt the spread of major known diseases in the next 10 years. We can reduce the prevalence of violent conflict and terrorism. We can increase respect for human dignity in every land. And we can forge a set of updated international institutions to help humanity achieve these noble goals. If we act boldly—and if we act together—we can make people everywhere more secure, more prosperous and better able to enjoy their fundamental human rights.

—UN Secretary-General Kofi Annan,
"In Larger Freedom," 2005

INTRODUCTION

As the two previous chapters have shown, courageous resistance takes many forms. The context, including domestic and international laws and norms, shape both when courageous resistance is likely to occur and how successful it will be. Without laws or the threat of punishment to protect human rights, those striving for justice may not be able to end the evils they oppose. This chapter shows how new treaties and mechanisms for enforcing human rights have been created by courageous resistance. In turn, these new laws and mechanisms both shape later resistance and increase the likelihood of future success by those who struggle to protect human rights.

In any context, laws and accepted norms can encourage just behavior. In the international context, strong laws and norms for human rights have pushed nations towards compliance with these goals (Risse, Ropp, and Sikkink 1999). Human rights laws and norms have deepened in recent decades, aided by both courageous individuals and human rights organizations. This chapter will introduce several of the international agreements and mechanisms that have set the standards for how states treat those within their borders. We examine some of the ways that dedicated individuals, groups, and organizations have created and used institutions to resist injustice and to help establish a definition of unacceptable state behavior. In particular, this chapter focuses on how institutions—created by individual, group, and organizational efforts—have changed the context and given greater power to courageous resisters and others who strive to end human rights abuses.

We begin by considering one dedicated individual, Raphael Lemkin, who invented a word to describe the mass killing of a group (and with it, a new way of thinking) and who helped create the 1948 *Convention on the Prevention and Punishment of the Crime of Genocide* to ban genocide. This convention has proven to be a vital, though imperfect, tool for reducing the worst human rights abuses. We then consider an international institution and standards created in the aftermath of the Holocaust. The creation of the United Nations (UN) was crucial in transforming norms and laws regarding human rights. In addition to the Genocide Convention, the United Nations adopted the *Universal Declaration of Human Rights* (UDHR), which defined basic treatment by governments of people in all states. At the founding of the UN, the big powers all envisioned the UN's main function as peacekeeping, but many individuals, groups, and nations (especially the weaker states) all pressed the UN to make human rights a central goal. This led to the creation of both the Genocide Convention and the UDHR. Their actions profoundly changed how the world regards states that engage in human rights abuses.

The UDHR's ideals in turn inspired many states, groups, and individuals to create additional organizations, treaties, and institutions to protect human rights. While some of these were formed through the United Nations, other non-UN treaties and organizations, such as the Helsinki Accord and Human Rights Watch (discussed in Chapter 1), found their inspiration in the UDHR. We next discuss Amnesty International, which was inspired by the UDHR to work on behalf of "prisoners of conscience" and to press for the creation of the *Convention against Torture and Other Cruel, Inhuman or Degrading Treatment or Punishment.*

In addition to the UDHR, we briefly describe a few UN efforts to promote and defend human rights after the cold war and the limitations of
these efforts to date. Pressed by individuals, nongovernmental organizations (NGOs), other intergovernmental organizations (IGOs), and states,
the UN has recently undertaken several major initiatives that could significantly improve human dignity and human rights around the world.
These include a strengthening of the UN's human rights mechanisms, the
new International Criminal Court, a new UN policy that declares that the
UN and its members have a "responsibility to protect" those threatened
by genocide or ethnic cleansing, and the new Human Rights Council. All
these new efforts offer hope, but ongoing human rights abuses, including
the current genocide in Sudan, show an unending need for courageous
resistance at all levels and for further transformations of the context.

BEGINNING THE STRUGGLE TO END GENOCIDE—HOW RAPHAEL LEMKIN MADE GENOCIDE A CRIME

One of the most significant and long-lasting ways that individual actors
have been able to combat human rights abuses has been by establishing
institutions and treaties to protect human rights. The next part of this
chapter tells the story of one such person named Raphael Lemkin and the
treaty he created, the *Convention on the Prevention and Punishment of the
Crime of Genocide.*

Raphael Lemkin's lifelong struggle against genocide began in 1921
when he was a student in Poland. Lemkin's interest was sparked by a murder in Berlin, Germany. Soghomon Tehlirian, a survivor of the 1915
genocide of nearly one million Armenians by Turkish troops, assassinated
Talaat Pasha, the Turkish minister who had overseen the Armenian genocide. After the killing, Tehlirian was put on trial.

During Tehlirian's trial, Lemkin was troubled that the murder of Pasha
was treated as a crime, while Pasha's slaughter of almost one million people was not. When Lemkin asked his professor about this, the professor
explained that there was, in fact, no law under which Talaat Pasha could
be arrested and tried. At the time, international norms regarding national
sovereignty meant that whatever a state did to its own people, no matter
how horrible, was nobody else's business. Reflecting the logic of the
times, the professor said, "Consider the case of a farmer who owns a flock
of chickens. He kills them and this is his business. If you interfere, you
are trespassing" (Power 2002, 17). Thus, while Pasha had helped annihilate Turkey's Armenian population, it was not a crime. In fact, there was
not even a word to describe such mass killings. Lemkin became obsessed

that there was no international law against mass killing, which he knew could soon happen again. This obsession guided the rest of his life.

When Adolf Hitler took power in 1933, Lemkin, now a lawyer, began to warn that the killing of an entire population could happen again. He pleaded for nations to create an international law that would make such killing an international crime. He argued that any leader who tried to kill a whole people, even if the killing took place within that leader's own country, should be subject to prosecution wherever he was caught. Lemkin believed that if world leaders knew that they could face punishment anywhere, they would be far less likely to commit such atrocities.

Lemkin found little support. Part of the reason for this lack of support lay in the nature of the international environment in the early 1930s. Before World War II, most European countries were concerned with their own security and economic problems, and they worried little about such a remote possibility as another mass slaughter, such as that of the Armenians. Certainly no state at the time envisioned such a slaughter within its own borders. If one were to occur, each thought it would be another state's problem. European governments were guarding their own interests. No country wanted to do anything to undermine another country's sovereignty in how it treated its citizens for fear its own sovereignty could also be challenged.

Hitler was very aware of the lack of international concern and took full advantage. Just before invading Poland, he noted the world's silence about the Armenian genocide, "The aim of war is . . . to annihilate the enemy physically. *Who today still speaks of the massacre of the Armenians?*" (Power 2002, 17). For Lemkin, Hitler's plans were not an abstract threat. As a Jew, Lemkin knew that he was personally endangered by Hitler's plans. When no countries stepped in to stop the Holocaust in Poland, Hitler was able to kill 2.5 million of the 2.8 million Jews in Poland. Of Lemkin's forty closest relatives, only he and a brother survived. In 1940, Lemkin, one of the fewer than three hundred thousand Polish Jews to survive the Holocaust, escaped to Sweden, and came to the United States in 1941.

Once in the United States, Lemkin gave hundreds of speeches trying to raise Americans' awareness of the slaughter of the Jews. He pleaded, "If women, children, and old people would be murdered a hundred miles from here, wouldn't you run to help? Then why do you stop this decision in your heart when the distance is 3,000 miles instead of a hundred?" (Power 2002, 27). By December 1941, the United States was absorbed in winning the war; however, Lemkin's appeals to American leaders for an international law garnered as little interest as they had from Europe's leaders before the war.

Eventually, Lemkin realized that if he was to have any hope of making such mass killings an international crime, a word was needed that was simple and easy to remember. Perhaps naming the crime could galvanize support for outlawing it. So, in August 1944, Lemkin published *Axis Rule in Occupied Europe*, a 700-page book describing Nazi oppression. He titled chapter 9 "*Genocide—A New Term and New Conception for Destruction of Nations*." Lemkin wrote, "By 'genocide' we mean the destruction of a nation or of an ethnic group. This new word . . . is made from the ancient Greek word *genos* (race, tribe) and the Latin *cide* (killing)" (Lemkin 1944, 79). The name for mass killings had been born.

The word won quick acceptance from allied governments, journalists, and the public. When the war ended, Lemkin journeyed to Nuremberg where Nazi leaders were being tried for war crimes and persuaded the war crimes prosecutors to adopt the term. When Nazi defendants were charged in November 1945 with "genocide, viz., the extermination of racial and national groups," Lemkin's word had its first legal use.

To Lemkin, the world seemed ready to make genocide an international crime. Lemkin thus began lobbying the new United Nations to outlaw genocide. He was tireless in his efforts, writing personal letters to every delegate. As a result, after much work, Lemkin was asked to helped draft a *convention*, an agreement that ratifying nations are legally bound to uphold, against genocide. On December 9, 1948, the UN adopted by a unanimous vote the Convention on the Prevention and Punishment of the Crime of Genocide that Lemkin had helped to write. Lemkin's efforts had given the horror of mass killings a name and a clear legal definition:

Genocide means any of the following acts committed with intent to destroy, in whole or in part, a national, ethnical, racial or religious group, as such: (a) Killing members of the group; (b) causing serious bodily or mental harm to members of the group; (c) deliberately inflicting on the group conditions of life calculated to bring about its physical destruction in whole or in part; (d) imposing measures intended to prevent births within the group; (e) forcibly transferring children of the group to another group. (United Nations 1948a)

Yet there was still work to do. The Convention needed ratification by twenty member states before it could become recognized as international law. To get nations to ratify the Convention, Lemkin "became a one-man, one-globe, multilingual, single issue lobbying machine" (Power 2002, 61). By the end of 1950, the Genocide Convention had been ratified by twenty countries and became international law. Lemkin said, "This is a day of triumph for mankind and the most beautiful day of my life" (64).

Despite its global importance, the United States was not among those who ratified the Genocide Convention. Although President Truman submitted the convention to the Senate for ratification, the fear of undermining national sovereignty led to strong domestic opposition. Some senators, particularly southern ones, feared that the convention could be used against American mistreatment of Blacks. Even though each objection was carefully answered, the convention was not ratified by the United States until 1986, and then in a watered down form. During the 1970s, however, members of Congress became increasingly concerned about human rights abuses committed by dictatorships with American military aid. Both President Nixon and President Carter submitted the convention for ratification, but each time the Senate failed to ratify it. By the 1980s, some senators urged President Reagan to submit the convention to the Senate again for ratification, which he did, and the convention was ratified in 1986. However, conservative senators managed to pass reservations that effectively turned the passage into a symbolic act. They assured, among other things, that America could never be party to any charge of genocide without its own consent. Legally, that was equivalent to saying that one accused of a horrible crime must consent to being tried. This reservation, in turn, prevents the United States from filing genocide charges against any other state, no matter how egregious (Power 2002, 161–69).

Raphael Lemkin's story illustrates how one person's efforts to combat human rights abuses may have long-lasting effects. Lemkin's word, genocide, created a new way to think about mass killing and made its criminalization possible. And more than any other person, Lemkin helped create an international convention outlawing genocide. The story of Raphael Lemkin and the convention, however, also shows that the development of institutional tools is merely the first step in transforming the context in which struggles for rights might take place. By 2007 the Genocide Convention had been ratified by 140 countries. Unfortunately, more than fifty countries still had not done so.

LARGE AND SMALL STATES AND INTERNATIONAL ORGANIZATIONS: TRANSFORMING THE POST–WORLD WAR II CONTEXT

In August 1944, as victory in World War II seemed more assured, representatives of the "big four"—the United States, Great Britain, Russia, and China—gathered at Dumbarton Oaks, a colonial mansion in Washington D.C., and began preparing to create an organization to replace the failed League of Nations. While the representatives' main purpose for the new organization was to preserve peace, they also discussed human rights. Among the representatives, only Wellington Koo, head of the Chinese delegation, favored granting the new organization a major role in protecting human rights. The other three adamantly opposed the institution doing anything regarding human rights, other than perhaps proclaiming support for human rights principles. The new institution was not to be given any right to interfere in the internal affairs of any nation to protect human rights (Lauren 2003).

The smaller states disagreed with many aspects of the Dumbarton Oaks proposal and were particularly resolute that advancing human rights had to be a central goal of the new organization. In February 1945, twenty Latin-American nations held a conference in Mexico City organized around opposition to the Dumbarton Oaks proposal. They wanted the new organization's charter to contain a universal bill of rights, and they drafted a text, the *Declaration of the International Rights and Duties of Man*, that they hoped would be adopted. While the major powers (primarily the United States, Great Britain, and Russia) continued to oppose adding a bill of human rights to the charter, the pressure from the smaller nations led to far greater emphasis on human rights in the charter than the major powers had wanted. The *Charter of the United Nations*, signed in 1945, was a compromise. It refers seven times to the importance of human rights but also acknowledges the supremacy of national sovereignty.[1]

However, the smaller nations were unable to ensure the UN any enforcement power regarding human rights. Many smaller states, including the Latin-American nations who had met in Mexico City, wanted the UN to have the power to "safeguard and protect," as well as "promote," human rights. When World War II began, most of these states and the U.S. had signed the "Declaration by the United Nations," which stated that the goals for the war were to "defend life, liberty, independence, and religious freedom, and to preserve human rights and justice in their own lands as well as other lands" (Declaration by the United Nations, January 1, 1942). Because the Latin American states had experience American encroachments on their sovereignty in the past, and legitimately thought that such incidents might occur again, they believed that investing the UN with the power to protect human rights would help guard their national sovereignty as well. Mexico and Uruguay each even introduced amendments calling for a permanent human rights unit within the UN with authority to protect human rights. However, the major powers were united against giving the UN any such authority.

The advocates for human rights did not get all they wanted in the new UN charter. However, they made much more progress than human rights advocates at the end of World War I had. The Holocaust had established a new world situation, one in which it was seen as both necessary and possible to make human rights an international priority. As a result, far greater emphasis was placed on human rights in the UN charter than the major powers had wanted. Unlike its failed predecessor, the League of Nations, the new international institution's concerns had become broader than preserving the peace. Its goals now included promoting human rights.

THE UNIVERSAL DECLARATION OF HUMAN RIGHTS

Creating the *Universal Declaration of Human Rights* (UDHR) was the next step, and elements of the context would again be crucial. Shortly after the UN was established, a Commission on Human Rights was created and given the task of developing a universal bill of rights. Eleanor Roosevelt, the widow of President Franklin Roosevelt, was unanimously selected to chair the eighteen-member commission. Her enthusiasm for human rights was well known, and she was widely respected for her humanitarianism, faith in human dignity, energy, intellect, ability to build trusting relationships, and compassion. Roosevelt's wise leadership proved essential in the two years of negotiation over the declaration's content. Getting the UN members, who all came from diverse cultures and religions, to agree on a universal statement of rights ultimately required all of her diplomatic and leadership skills (Glendon 2001).

As with the creation of the UN, the development of the Universal Declaration was shaped by context.[2] The specter of the recent Holocaust had established a consensus that a universal bill of rights was needed. Throughout the two years the commission met and discussed each proposed article, members of the commission often referred to the Nazi horrors and to how each article repudiated Nazi beliefs and deeds. For example, the assertion in Article 2 that rights apply "without distinction of any kind, such as race, color, sex, language, religion, political or other opinion, national or social origin, property, birth or other status" was seen as a repudiation of Nazi racism, which had defined citizenship by "blood" and asserted the rights of Aryans to be the master race. The rights to "life, liberty, and security of person" in Article 3 were noted as condemning both the Nazi genocide and the Nazi practice of killing persons with insanity or mental retardation. In drafting Article 11, which proclaimed the right to a public trial with a presumption of innocence and adequate defense, commission members referred to the Nazis' sham trials of their opponents. When Charles Malik of Lebanon presented the declaration to the UN General Assembly for final vote, he noted that it "was inspired by the barbarous doctrines of Nazism and fascism" (Morsink 1999, 36).

In December 1948, the United Nations General Assembly adopted the *Universal Declaration of Human Rights.*[3] René Cassin, France's representative to the commission, said that the Declaration was "a milestone in the long struggle for human rights" that would offer "a beacon of hope for humanity" (Lauren 2003, 229). Eleanor Roosevelt said that it might become "the Magna Carta of all men everywhere" (230).

THE INFLUENCE OF THE UNIVERSAL DECLARATION OF HUMAN RIGHTS

While the Universal Declaration is a statement of ideals and not of law, its creation fundamentally changed the international environment for human rights. The UDHR created a standard for measuring states' human rights practices and planted the seeds of an international legal system of human rights.[4] This legal system consists of many international conventions, international organizations that monitor compliance, regional human rights systems, and institutions that can punish perpetrators and intervene to stop gross violations of human rights. Further, the shared understanding of human rights embodied in the UDHR provides the foundation for a powerful and growing network of human rights advocates. Individuals, organizations, and states, working both domestically and more and more as an international network, have used these human rights principles to improve human rights practices around the world and to create strong institutions for their enforcement.

By the early 1990s, the Declaration had inspired more than fifty other international human rights covenants and conventions. These agreements include the *International Covenant on Civil and Political Rights* and the *International Covenant on Economic, Social, and Cultural Rights,* which translate the principles of the *Universal Declaration* into binding law for the countries that ratified the agreements. The Declaration has also inspired regional conventions for human rights protection throughout the world. For example, the Declaration led to the *European Convention on Human Rights and Fundamental Freedoms* and the establishment of the European Court on Human Rights, the latter of which has groundbreaking power to *enforce* human rights decisions.

As influential as the Declaration has been, its impact was undermined by the international context of the cold war for almost fifty years. During the cold war, the UN had very limited influence in the face of egregious human rights violations, both in the East and West. Many leaders feared upsetting the delicate balance between the superpowers, and the leaders of the cold war, the United States and the Soviet Union, both held veto power in the UN Security Council.

BUILDING AN INTERNATIONAL HUMAN RIGHTS ORGANIZATION

We have seen how Raphael Lemkin spearheaded new human rights standards. Other individuals have also founded founded non-governmental organizations (NGOs) that have had far-reaching impacts. Through their members' efforts, these organizations have transformed contexts by altering laws, treaties, and other agreements and by influencing the behaviors of governments and other institutions. A key way of doing so has been to create and mobilize networks of people from around the globe.

These networks, now called transnational advocacy networks (TANs), feature fluid and open relationships among committed and knowledgeable individuals and groups working on particular issues. Transnational advocacy networks exist for many causes. They feature voluntary, reciprocal, and horizontal patterns of exchange of information and services. They may include research and advocacy organizations, local social movements, foundations, the media, churches, trade unions, IGOs, and governments (Keck and Sikkink 1998, 8–9). These networks provide a way for millions of citizens in various countries to combine their skills to help define and protect human rights. Further, because the NGOs within these networks rely on a membership base that continues to grow, they can be constantly rejuvenated with new energy and ideas. Finally, because they connect to others with corresponding goals, they benefit from sharing resources, expertise, and personnel. The story of Amnesty International and its successes demonstrates the power of such networks to create institutions and to work through and with these institutions to advance the cause of human rights.

AMNESTY INTERNATIONAL AND THE HUMAN RIGHTS NGOS

During the height of the cold war, the UN and its member nations ignored most human rights violations. In this vacuum of human rights leadership, several human rights NGOs moved beyond the cold war divide to condemn human rights abuses universally, whether they occurred under communist rule, anti-communist dictatorships aligned with the West, or third world regimes. Using the UDHR as their standard by which to call abusers to account, they persistently pushed for the defense of human rights until the issue again moved toward the front of the UN's agenda.

Amnesty International is one of the best known and perhaps most influential human rights NGOs. In 1961, barrister Peter Benenson gathered several other British lawyers and friends, and together they made plans for a yearlong campaign for the release of "prisoners of conscience."[5] They launched the campaign with an article, "The Forgotten Prisoners," in the *London Observer*. It began:

> Open your newspaper any day of the week and you will find a report from somewhere in the world of someone being imprisoned, tortured or executed because his opinions or religion are unacceptable to his government. There are several million such people in prison. . . . That is why we have started Appeal for Amnesty, 1961. . . . We have set up an office in London to collect information about the names, numbers, and conditions of what we have decided to call "Prisoners of Conscience." . . . Our office will from time to time hold press conferences to focus attention on Prisoners of Conscience selected impartially from different parts of the world. (Benenson 1961)[6]

The Appeal for Amnesty was directly based upon the UDHR, which had been created by the prior generation of human rights advocates. Amnesty International focused on Articles 18 and 19 of the Universal Declaration, which held that "everyone has a right to freedom of thought, conscience and religion" and that "everyone has a right to freedom of opinion and expression."[7]

"The Forgotten Prisoners" was quickly reprinted in many countries, and in less than a month, more than a thousand letters arrived, offering either help or information about specific prisoners. In light of this ground swell, the founders created a permanent organization with the name Amnesty International. Central offices gathered information about abuses and distributed them to chapters of Amnesty International through an Urgent Action Network. Local chapters formed to work for the release of specific prisoners by writing letters to the governments holding them and by publicizing the prisoners' plight. Amnesty maintained its "principled neutrality" by targeting right-wing governments, left-wing governments, and third world governments for their human rights abuses (Buchanan 2000, 575–97).

Although working on behalf of political prisoners has remained a key feature of Amnesty International's work, the organization has expanded its mission to embrace the promotion of all human rights and to create new institutions to make this possible. In addition to helping to free thousands of prisoners through letter-writing campaigns, Amnesty has helped create several international human rights conventions.[8] As Clark has noted, "Before Amnesty International became active on the issue, human rights concepts in general—let alone the prohibition on torture—were rarely applied internationally to persuade, criticize, or interpret states' behavior" (2001, 38).

Amnesty's work on the problem of state torture has contributed significantly to the international community's application of human rights standards. Although Article 5 of the UDHR states that "no one shall be subjected to torture or to cruel, inhuman or degrading treatment or punishment," this article has often been ignored. Amnesty has insisted that states be held accountable to Article 5 and, to that end, has conducted persistent campaigns, based on careful research on torture around the world. Amnesty pressed the UN to pass resolutions on torture and, in concert with other NGOs, helped prepare the *Convention against Torture and Other Cruel, Inhuman or Degrading Treatment or Punishment.*

Amnesty began its first campaign for the abolition of torture in 1973. The campaign had many facets, including gathering a petition of one million signatures from eighty-five countries. In the wake of Amnesty's efforts, the UN adopted a resolution in November 1973 restating Article 5 and urging governments to adopt international instruments that outlaw "torture and other inhuman or degrading treatment or punishment" (Clark 2001, 58). Amnesty International also hosted a world conference on torture in Paris in December 1973. In 1974, Amnesty presented to the UN Commission on Human Rights thorough documentation of human rights abuses and torture taking place in Chile under the military regime of General Augusto Pinochet.[9] The brutal detail of the report and Amnesty's testimony led the General Assembly to adopt a second resolution on torture in the fall of 1974. Continued publicity of abuses in Chile led the United Nations to condemn Chile and convinced the United States to withdraw its support for Pinochet's regime at the start of Jimmy Carter's presidency.

Amnesty's efforts were sometimes aided by domestic human rights organizations that focused on a particular country's problems. Amnesty's practice of sharing experiences and expertise with local individuals or groups encouraged others to form their own domestic human rights NGOs (Keck and Sikkink 1998, 89). By uniting with both local and other international human rights organizations, Amnesty helped create the first human rights transnational advocacy network in the 1970s.

Amnesty used its growing influence to vigorously campaign for an international law banning torture. Without this campaign, Clark argues, "it is highly plausible that the Convention would not have been adopted" (2001, 10). From 1979 through 1984, Amnesty leaders worked doggedly with Sweden's UN delegation, members of the UN Commission on Human Rights, and other groups to help draft the *Convention against Torture and Other Cruel, Inhuman or Degrading Treatment or Punishment.* Amnesty International emphasized making the convention as strong as possible, calling also for stronger *enforcement* capabilities for existing standards. Amnesty International repeatedly emphasized that it is not sufficient to have standards unless there were safeguards to prevent abuse and ensure enforcement of the standards.

As soon as the draft was submitted to the General Assembly, Amnesty International began its second campaign to abolish torture. The 1984 Amnesty International report, *Torture in the Eighties,* helped give the convention high visibility. Amnesty used its many chapters and publicity to mobilize support for the convention's adoption. The General Assembly adopted the convention in December 1984, but the convention needed ratification by twenty member states to become law. Amnesty International urged its ratification, despite recognizing remaining weaknesses, and Amnesty members around the world lobbied governments to ratify it. When states complied, they not only gave the document the power of law within those states, but also gave the states themselves the authority and responsibility for enforcing the covenant across state boundaries. The convention finally entered into force in June 1987 and has now been ratified by 141 countries, including the United States in 1994.

In September 1987, even Chile's brutal military regime, which was facing ongoing complaints for its torture and "disappearing" of political opponents, signed the convention. President Pinochet had the convention ratified by the military junta, comprised of four generals, which then ruled Chile. Ironically, it was under this convention that the Spanish government in 1998 sought to try Pinochet on charges that included abduction, torture, disappearance, and execution of thousands of political opponents. Pinochet, who was visiting Great Britain eight years after relinquishing most of his power, was held under house arrest for sixteen months while British courts decided whether he must be extradited to Spain for crimes committed in his own country. Human Rights Watch appealed to the House of Lords, arguing that international law offers no immunity for perpetrators of the gravest human rights crimes, no matter whom or where they are. The British House of Lords eventually found that the United Kingdom, because Britain had ratified the Convention against Torture, was obligated to surrender Pinochet to the Spaniards for all charges of torture occurring after the Torture Convention took effect in Britain. Similarly, Spain justified its pursuit of Pinochet as adherence to its obligations under the same convention. Pinochet narrowly escaped trial when the British foreign secretary accepted medical assessments that Pinochet was unfit to stand trial.

Although Pinochet was allowed to return to Chile, the ruling led to charges filed against Pinochet and his military officers. More importantly, it reopened public debate on human rights in Chile and made progress possible on other human rights cases there.

As mentioned earlier, until recently, respect for national sovereignty shielded states or their agents from external prosecution for crimes against humanity. The Genocide Convention, the Convention against Torture, and the precedents established by various war crimes tribunals and international customary laws have shown that those who commit crimes against humanity can be punished. One year after the death of Amnesty International founder Benenson, Michelle Bachelet, one of those imprisoned and tortured during the Pinochet administration, was sworn into office as the democratically elected president of Chile, and Chile's judicial system stripped Pinochet of immunity from prosecution. Benenson's legacy lives on in the institution he created and in the individuals, networks, and new institutions that Amnesty International helped to create and strengthen.

In the two cases we have just considered, courageous resistance helped change the international context by creating new international institutions and conventions and new standards for how nations are expected to respect human rights. In both cases, the context surrounding these efforts was vital to the outcome that was achieved. Despite his tireless efforts, Lemkin's work to create an international ban on genocide would likely not have succeeded had the United Nations existed and failed to embrace the goal of promoting human rights. Amnesty International employed a network of like-minded individuals and groups and worked with state and intergovernmental agencies to bring about the Convention against Torture. The following section describes how other human rights advocates—especially states and their representatives—changed the international context after the cold war and how the limited power of human rights institutions may be increasing in the post–cold war world.

THE RENEWAL OF HUMAN RIGHTS AT THE UNITED NATIONS FOLLOWING THE COLD WAR

Amnesty International helped free thousands of prisoners and pass several UN human rights conventions, creating stronger international legal standards of human rights. However, its greatest achievement may be that, along with Human Rights Watch and other NGOs in the human rights network, it helped return human rights to the center of the UN's mission in the early 1990s. The renewed UN commitment to human rights required the collapse of communism and the end of the cold war, but once these occurred, promoting and protecting human rights became one of the UN's central goals. This goal likely would not have emerged, however, had not Amnesty and other NGOs campaigned steadily for human rights throughout the 1970s and 1980s.

Beginning in the early 1990s, the UN took several steps to strengthen its promotion of human rights. In 1993, it adopted the *Vienna Declaration and Programme of Action,* which declared that human rights violations are never a matter of a nation's internal jurisdiction alone, but are always a concern for all mankind. This declaration represented a major change from the UN's earlier consensus that the outside world could not interfere in a nation's internal affairs, no matter how horrible that nation's behavior. The *Vienna Declaration* also called for creating the office of High Commissioner for Human Rights, and the UN General Assembly did so later that year. In 2004, the UN also created the office of Special Advisor on the Prevention of Genocide to watch for early warning signs of possible genocide and related crimes and to advise the Security Council on ways to prevent them.

The next section discusses three other UN developments since the cold war that reflect the UN's renewed commitment to human rights: the criminal courts, the policy of "responsibility to protect," and the new Human Rights Council.

THE CRIMINAL COURTS

When Yugoslavia disintegrated in a series of civil wars in the early 1990s, massive war crimes occurred. In 1993, the UN Security Council created the *International Criminal Tribunal for the Former Yugoslavia* (ICTY) to prosecute "persons responsible for serious violations of international humanitarian law" in those civil wars. By mid-2006, the ICTY had rendered verdicts on eighty-five individuals. Slobodan Milosevic, the former President of Serbia, became the first head of state to be tried by an international tribunal, but he died of a heart attack in prison before his trial was completed. Similarly, in 1994, the *International Criminal Tribunal for Rwanda* was established to prosecute those most responsible for the Rwandan genocide. By September 2006, this tribunal had convicted twenty-eight persons, and another twenty-five accused genocide leaders were being tried or were awaiting trial.[10]

The work of these special courts has been painfully slow, but their successes pushed the UN to establish a permanent International Criminal

Court (ICC). While such a court was first proposed after World War II, the cold war so dominated world politics that all effort at creating such a court was blocked for forty years.[11] Efforts were resumed in 1989 as the cold war was ending. For the next nine years, draft statutes for the court were written and revised. Finally, in July 1998, 148 UN members met in Rome, and the *Rome Statute of the International Criminal Court* (ICC) was adopted by a vote of 120 to 7, with 21 abstentions. The ICC came into existence in June 2002, once sixty nations had ratified the statute. As of March 2007, 105 nations had ratified the statute, but none of the three great powers—the United States, China, and Russia—had done so.

There is great reason to hope that the ICC will not only try those guilty of genocide and bring justice to their victims, but that the existence of the ICC will deter future war criminals. Those contemplating genocide, war crimes, or ethnic cleansing know that there is now a standing world court waiting to try them wherever and whenever they are caught.

The ICC issued its first arrest warrants for five Ugandan rebel leaders in October 2005, charging them with crimes against humanity and war crimes. In 2006, the ICC was also investigating genocide related crimes in Darfur and in the Democratic Republic of the Congo.

HUMANITARIAN INTERVENTION AND THE "RESPONSIBILITY TO PROTECT"

When world leaders gathered for the World Millennium Summit in 2005, they undertook two other important initiatives. First, they adopted a new policy called the "responsibility to protect," which obligates the UN to protect populations that are threatened with genocide, ethnic cleansing, or crimes against humanity. This policy obligates the UN, when necessary, to use "humanitarian intervention," that is, to intervene in a country with military force to protect people from genocide and related crimes.

The end of the cold war combined with four catastrophic events in the 1990s to make humanitarian intervention an urgent topic. In the first event, the UN sent troops to Somalia to guard famine relief and to end violence between warlords. But after a number of UN forces were killed, including eighteen Americans (depicted in the film *Black Hawk Down*), the UN withdrew. In the second event, freshly recalling the UN failure in Somalia, the UN failed to intervene to stop the 1994 genocide in Rwanda. Many world leaders and citizens have since felt great guilt over that failure. In the third event, the ethnic cleansing in Bosnia took two hundred thousand lives, but neither the UN nor the North Atlantic Treaty Organization (NATO) intervened for three years. The slaughter of seven thousand men and boys at Srebrenica in Bosnia was Europe's worst mass murder since the Holocaust. Despite promising protection, the UN did not intervene to stop it. Finally, in the fourth event in 1999, Serbian President Slobodan Milosevic tried to expel at gunpoint all ethnic Albanians from the Kosovo province. NATO bombing and a threat of invasion forced an end to that expulsion, and UN peacekeepers then went to Kosovo to keep peace between Serbs and ethnic Albanians.

In each of these cases, civilians within a country needed outside protection. The UN and other international bodies had to decide whether and how to provide it. The governments of these countries were either dysfunctional (as in Somalia) or resisted intervention. The decision to intervene is never an easy one, and the issues are complex. Both national sovereignty and human rights are founding principles of the UN, but humanitarian intervention pits them against each other. Intervention violates national sovereignty in the name of protecting human rights.

Throughout the 1990s, academics and policy makers wrestled with how to weigh these competing concerns and how to establish clear principles that should govern an intervention. In 2000, Secretary-General Annan challenged the UN to find consensus on these issues. The Canadian government then took the lead and created an *International Commission on Intervention and State Sovereignty* (ICISS) to identify core principles to guide decisions and conduct of interventions. After two years of forums held around the world, the commission issued its report, *The Responsibility to Protect*.[12] The ICISS chose the term "responsibility to protect" because it is broader than humanitarian intervention, and asserts that military force should be a last resort, used only after all other options are exhausted. Here, in brief, are its recommendations:

- The ICISS concluded that a state temporarily forfeits sovereignty when it engages in genocide, crimes against humanity, or ethnic cleansing. At this point, "the principle of non-intervention yields to the international responsibility to protect." (International Commission on Intervention and State Sovereignty 2002, xi)
- International responsibility to protect arises, however, only when "a particular state is clearly either unwilling or unable to fulfill its responsibility to protect or is itself the actual perpetrator of crimes or atrocities." (International Commission on Intervention and State Sovereignty 2002, 17)[13]

The international community's first "responsibility to protect" is to prevent. To prevent such crimes, the world must address the root causes of a conflict, such as political disenfranchisement and unjust economic treatment of minority groups. Also, there must be constant efforts to detect early signs of danger, and peacekeeping measures must be started before human rights abuses erupt.[14] If prevention fails, other states must be ready to intervene rapidly and should designate forces, transport, and other strategic resources for a "standby" role to stop a mass killing or ethnic cleansing.

Military intervention should occur only when there is "serious and irreparable harm occurring to human beings, or imminently likely to occur," such as a "large scale loss of life" or "large scale ethnic cleansing" (International Commission on Intervention and State Sovereignty 2002, xii). Military intervention should *not* be used for less violent crimes such as systematic racial discrimination or the imprisonment of political opponents. The UN Security Council, which holds the highest legal responsibility to preserve peace and protect human rights, should ideally authorize interventions. Regional organizations (such as North American Treaty Organization (NATO), Organization of American States (OAS), and African Union (AU)) considering an intervention should always seek the Security Council's approval. If the Security Council fails to protect because one of the five permanent members of the Security Council vetoes a humanitarian intervention, the UN General Assembly may initiate an intervention, or regional organizations may act within their regions. Individual nations should rarely, if ever, intervene alone.[15]

Military interventions must have clear objectives, essential resources, and be conducted in keeping with international law. Saving the civilian population must be an intervention's first responsibility. Finally, an intervention creates a follow-up responsibility to rebuild national institutions and reestablish national sovereignty as soon as possible.[16]

In 2002 through 2003, this ICISS report was endorsed by a UN appointed panel of international experts and passed to Secretary-General Annan. The Secretary-General, in turn, adopted it in his UN renewal plan, *In Larger Freedom: Toward Development, Security, and Human Rights for All,* and placed it on the agenda for the World Summit. All parties knew that, if adopted, the UN would not only recognize a *right* of humanitarian intervention whenever genocide and related crimes were occurring, but would accept a *responsibility* to intervene. Doing so would represent an historic and momentous change for the UN.

The day before the World Summit, Canadian General Romeo Dallaire, who had commanded the UN peacekeeping force in Rwanda, wrote an impassioned plea for the UN to adopt the responsibility to protect:

> Because the United Nations Security Council members demonstrated inexcusable apathy . . . I and my small United Nations peacekeeping

contingent were forced to watch the slaughter up close with no mandate to intervene. . . . Governments of the world have the chance at the United Nations world summit meeting in New York to make "never again" a reality by agreeing to accept their responsibility to protect civilians in the face of mass murder. . . . This would be an historic shift. . . . Having seen what failure to protect means on the ground, I urge the United States to seize the opportunity to show global leadership and help drive this agreement that could save millions of lives. (Dallaire 2005)

Did the World Summit achieve what Dallaire urged? It adopted the responsibility to protect in principle, but the final agreement is only a statement of the general principle. All of the details of the ICISS recommendations and of Kofi Annan's "*In Larger Freedom*" are lacking. Countless procedures and policies must be developed, but as of September 2006, the General Assembly has not scheduled further discussions to negotiate these details that would implement the responsibility to protect policy.

Still, many human rights and humanitarian organizations have hailed this agreement as a giant step forward. Oxfam, for example, called it a "landmark agreement" in which "world leaders agreed to stop future genocides." To Oxfam, "this ground-breaking commitment means that governments can no longer use sovereignty and non-intervention norms as excuses to avoid having to act to protect civilians from mass killings" (2005). Nonetheless, plenty of room remains for the Security Council or individual UN members to wiggle out of this responsibility, and the ability of the five permanent members to veto an intervention remains intact. Only with time will we know whether the UN members will live up to this new commitment they have made.

THE HUMAN RIGHTS COUNCIL

In a second action at the 2005 World Summit, the UN started the process of replacing the failed Commission on Human Rights with a new Human Rights Council. The fifty-three-member commission was the UN body responsible for promoting and protecting human rights. By 2004, however, the failure of the commission was widely recognized. Because its members were elected by the countries from each world region, and regional politics determined who was selected, some commission members had vile human rights records. In the commission's last session, for example, China and Cuba were members, but both imprison political dissidents and do not allow a free press. Saudi Arabia, which suppresses religious freedom and the rights of women, was a member as well. Zimbabwe was a member, although in the summer of 2005, its President Robert Mugabe demolished the homes of up to seven hundred thousand residents in the centers of his political opposition. Most egregiously, Sudan, accused of genocide in Darfur, was a member also. In fact, countries with terrible human rights records often sought seats on the commission to shield themselves from its scrutiny.

Many NGOs, including Amnesty International and Human Rights Watch, urged that the commission be abolished and replaced. In December 2004, Secretary-General Annan recommended that the commission be replaced by a much smaller Human Rights Council that required each nation seeking membership to state its commitment to human rights in writing and to be elected by a two-thirds vote of the General Assembly. With these requirements, countries with appalling human rights records would rarely be elected. And so, in September 2005, the World Summit gave the General Assembly the mandate of establishing a new Human Rights Council during its fall session.

When negotiations began, it was quickly evident that a number of nations hoped to block real reform. Intense negotiations were conducted from October 2005 until February 2006. The most divisive issue was that of council membership. Proponents of a strong council, following the lead of Secretary-General Annan, desired a council of thirty-eight members, with each member elected by two-thirds of the General Assembly and with each state seeking membership required to submit a "letter of commitment" to human rights. Advocates of a strong council wanted to end the practice of regions submitting closed slates for election (e.g., Africa submitting just thirteen nominees for its thirteen allocated slots), as was done for the previous commission, a practice that made it fairly easy for nations with serious human rights abuses to gain seats. These advocates also hoped to bar from membership any nation that was under Security Council sanction for human rights abuses. Finally, advocates of a strong council wanted it to meet much more often than the previous commission's single six-week session each year.

Opponents of reform wanted to retain a fifty-three-member council, election by a simple majority, closed slates, and membership open to all UN members. Human rights NGOs and activists lobbied ambassadors, issued papers in support of a strong council, and watched with both the hope that a strong council would emerge and a fear that abusing nations would kill real reform.

While the aim was to end the negotiations and for the General Assembly to adopt the new Human Rights Council by the beginning of 2006, deadlocked negotiations made that impossible. A series of draft texts, with each one offering alternate wordings to reflect the differing concerns of the UN members, were presented for votes. Finally, in February 2006, General Assembly President Jan Eliasson presented a compromise proposal for final vote. The new Human Rights Council was adopted on March 15, 2006, by a vote of 170 to 4.

There is great hope that the new council will be more effective in promoting and protecting human rights than the commission it replaced. Still, it is a compromise between those who wanted a very strong council and those who wanted the council to be just like the commission under a new name. The council consists of forty-seven members, each one elected by secret ballot by an absolute majority of all UN members (not just those present and voting). Each world region has a specific number of seats, but regions cannot present closed slates. While membership remains open to all UN members, states are required, when they elect members to the council, to consider candidates' contributions to human rights, as well as letters of commitment to human rights, which applicants may voluntarily submit. Any council member found to systematically violate human rights could be expelled from the council by a two-thirds vote of the General Assembly. The council will conduct periodic reviews of the human rights records of all UN members (something the commission did not do), beginning with those elected to the council. The council will meet for three sessions each year, for a minimum of ten weeks (at least four more weeks than did the commission), and it can be called into emergency session.

The United States cast one of the four votes against the compromise council. American Ambassador John Bolton argued that the new council was still too large to be effective and that its election rules were too weak to prevent egregious rights violators from gaining seats. He urged that negotiations be reopened. Secretary-General Annan agreed that the new council was not as strong as he had hoped, but he hailed it as a substantial step forward and urged its adoption—as did all European and Latin nations and most human rights NGOs, including Amnesty International and Human Rights Watch. They all feared that reopening the negotiations would result in a weaker council, not a stronger one, and they believed that the council was enough of an improvement to merit support.

After the council was adopted, Ambassador Bolton pledged full American support. However, the United States decided not to seek a seat on the Council for its first year, or in 2007 for the second year of the council. Some have speculated that if the United States had sought a seat, its maltreatment of Iraqi prisoners and of Al Qaeda and Taliban detainees would have subjected the United States to unwanted international scrutiny.

The discredited Human Rights Commission disbanded on March 27, 2006, and passed its unfinished business to the council. Elections to the new council were held on May 9, 2006. Russia, China, and other countries with dismal human rights records were elected, but the very worst abusers such as Sudan and Zimbabwe, were not. The council held its first regular meeting in June. We will only know how effective the council will be in protecting human rights and ending gross human rights abuses by watching its operations for the next few years. Human Rights Watch, Amnesty International, and other NGOs will be pressing it to be diligent. It is hoped that these organizations will be joined by a new generation of courageous human rights advocates.

DARFUR—A TEST OF THE UN RESOLVE TO END GENOCIDE

Will the strengthened UN machinery, the ICC, the policy of "responsibility to protect," and the new Human Rights Council help end genocide and other human rights abuses in the twenty-first century? We all hope so, of course; however, the gap between the UN's ideals and policies on the one hand and world realities on the other remains massive. Genocide was outlawed by the Genocide Convention in 1948, but genocide has occurred in almost every decade since then, and the UN has done little to stop it. Still, perhaps these new UN initiatives that began after the cold war offer hope for true progress.

During the writing of this book in September 2006, a major genocide has been underway in Darfur, a Texas-size region of Western Sudan, for more than three years. An Arab militia called the *janjaweed* ("evil horsemen"), backed by the Sudanese government, has destroyed about 90 percent of Darfur villages. Whole villages have been slaughtered. Bodies have been dumped in wells to poison the groundwater. Millions have fled to refugee camps. Some reports estimate that up to four hundred thousand have died. The interests of some of the Security Council's five permanent members have hampered the response of the UN to this crisis. France has lucrative oil contracts with Sudan that would be jeopardized by any strong action. China is Sudan's largest trading partner and has invested more than three billion dollars in Sudan's oil production facilities in the last six years. Russia recently sold Sudan a dozen fighter aircraft. The United States has relied on Sudan for information in its war against terrorism. The result has been another long paralysis in the face of another genocide. Thus, despite the commitment to human rights that was central to its inception, the UN has not intervened to stop this genocide. At the UN's urging, the African Union (AU) sent about seven thousand AU peacekeepers to

Sudan, although they have been severely undermanned and undersupplied for their mission. Finally, in late August 2006, the UN Security Council approved sending a peacekeeping force of up to 22,500 personnel to Darfur to replace the AU forces. Sudan has said that it will not accept this UN force, and sending it against Sudan's will would violate its national sovereignty. However, under the "responsibility to protect" policy, a nation's sovereignty is temporarily forfeited when it does not protect its own people from genocide. As of this date (June 2007), the UN force has not been assembled or sent to Sudan, although efforts are underway to mobilize the force.[17]

OUR CHALLENGE

Here, in a nutshell, is the issue. Can we, as world citizens, end horrors such as these? Can we build a world with fewer genocidal Hitlers and Saddam Husseins, fewer Darfurs? This is the challenge we face; and this is certainly among the most serious moral issues of our time. Progress toward ending human rights abuses is torturously slow, and progress will occur only if we all push for it. But if we do, perhaps—just perhaps—our great-grandchildren will be able to look back on a twenty-first century with far fewer genocides, crimes against humanity, and ethnic cleansings than occurred in the twentieth century. We hope this is the case. And this is a legacy we should strive to leave them.

NOTES

1. The preamble proclaims that the nations affirm their "faith in fundamental human rights, in the dignity and worth of the human person, in the equal rights of men and women and of nations large and small." Article 1 declares that a purpose of the UN is the "promoting and encouraging of respect for human rights and for fundamental freedoms for all without distinction as to race, sex, language, or religion." However, the charter also made clear that national sovereignty trumped human rights: Article 2, paragraph 7 states that "nothing contained in the present Charter shall authorize the United Nations to intervene in matters which are essentially within the domestic jurisdiction of any state" (United Nations 1945).
2. An immediate issue for the commission was whether the bill of rights should be a *covenant*, a binding law on all nations that ratify it, or just a *declaration*, a statement of ideals only. Again, many smaller nations wanted a binding covenant, while the major powers wanted only a declaration. Shortly after the Commission on Human Rights began its work, the differing parties reached a compromise. The commission decided to first produce a declaration of human rights principles and postpone the writing of a binding covenant to a later time.

3. The entire Universal Declaration of Human Rights can be read at http://www.un.org/Overview/Rights.html (accessed March 30, 2007). Readers of the declaration will notice that Articles 3 through 21 and Articles 22 through 28 address different kinds of rights. French Jurist Karel Vasak labeled these two kinds of rights "first generation" and "second generation" human rights. The "first generation" rights of Articles 3 to 21 are civil and political rights (rights to life, freedom, fair treatment by the law, etc.), the kinds of rights found in the American Bill of Rights. Articles 22 to 28, the "second generation" rights, cover economic, social, and cultural rights (rights to education, work, subsistence in time of need, and health care). The inclusion of the "second generation" rights was due largely to Latin-American influence, although the rights were certainly consistent with Chairperson Roosevelt's views as well. Many Latin-American constitutions already embraced these rights, and these had been strengthened in their constitutions after the Great Depression. At the time the declaration was written, its writers never distinguished these rights as different in kind. The "second generation" rights were contained in the first draft, and no one tried to expunge them (Morsink 1999, xiv).

4. The UDHR had a tremendous influence in establishing human rights ideals and norms both domestically and internationally. It speeded decolonization and the creation of many new independent countries because its principles implicitly condemned colonial rule. At least twenty-six new countries that emerged post-war used it as the basis for the bills of rights in their new constitutions. Many other countries drew on it as a model (Hannum 1995–96). It also inspired regional commitments to human rights by the European Union, the Organization of American States, and the new African Union. The UNDHR also established the human rights principles that were later incorporated into many binding global treaties.

5. A prisoner of conscience was defined as "any person who is physically restrained (by imprisonment or otherwise) from expressing (in any form of words or symbols) any opinion which he honestly holds and which does not advocate or condone personal violence" (Benenson, 1961).

6. During the cold war, between communist Russia (then the Soviet Union) and its Eastern European allies on the one side against the USA and Western European countries and their allies on the other, each side condemned the abuses of the other but found easy excuses to defend its own abuses and those of its allies. In Britain, leftist political parties campaigned for amnesty for political prisoners under the Franco dictatorship in Spain and under other dictatorships but offered weak excuses for Soviet bloc political prisoners. British conservatives, on the other hand, condemned the treatment of political prisoners under communist regimes but were virtually silent about those under Western dictatorships.

7. Universal Declaration of Human Rights, available at http://www.un.org/Overview/Rights.html (accessed March 3, 2007).

8. Individuals can join Amnesty's letter-writing campaign by going to http://web.amnesty.org/pages/ua-index-eng.
9. General Pinochet overthrew the democratic government of Chile, declaring a "state of siege because of internal or external war." The junta suspended the constitution and basic rights guarantees, and in the "days, weeks, months and years that followed, communists, socialists, trade unionists, progressive church people, students, teachers, singers, lawyers and anyone suspected of sympathy with communism were hunted down, tortured and killed" (Webber 1999, 525, 523–37).
10. Three other special courts were created in this century: one to prosecute the Indonesian army and militias for war crimes committed during East Timor's struggle for independence (2000), a second to try those responsible for war crimes during Sierra Leone's ten-year civil war (2002), and a third to try the Khmer Rouge leaders of the Cambodian genocide (2004).
11. The Nuremberg and Tokyo war crimes tribunals that tried Nazi and Japanese leaders set a precedent for trying individuals for genocide and related crimes. But these courts presented the problem of the war's winners trying the losers. When only winners try losers, courts might seem to be seeking revenge rather than justice and might overlook similar crimes committed by their own side.
12. International Commission on Intervention and State Sovereignty (ICISS), The Responsibility to Protect (Ottawa, International Development Research Centre, 2001).
13. The *Convention on the Prevention and Punishment of the Crime of Genocide* has long been interpreted as establishing a right (but not a duty) for the world to intervene within a country to prevent genocide. The new policy creates a responsibility to do so.
14. In addition to the UN Special Advisor on the Prevention of Genocide, a private organization, the *International Crisis Group* (ICG), watches for early warning signs. Founded in 1995 by American Diplomat Morton Abramowitz and a group of international citizens, the ICG watches for signs of emerging conflicts and human rights abuses, analyzes the causes of the crises, and helps governments and international organizations try to prevent them. The ICG prepares reports on about eighty situations around the world each year, all based on extensive on-site research.
15. The danger of lone nations intervening is that they are more likely to do so for reasons of self-interest or to protect a group with whom they have a special affinity. Historically, interventions by lone nations have usually been to protect their ethnic or religious kin.
16. From state to state, what needs rebuilding may include security, national constitutions and legislatures, respect for human rights, cooperation between former adversaries, protection for returning refugees, educational systems, police forces, an impartial judicial system, and industry and business.
17. For current online information on Darfur, see Darfur Information Center (http://www.darfurinfo.org/), Save Darfur (http://www.savedarfur.org/), and Darfur: A Genocide We Can Stop (http://www.darfurgenocide.org/).

CHAPTER 7

ORDINARY PEOPLE'S EXTRAORDINARY COURAGE, IMPACT, AND HOPE: TENTATIVE CONCLUSIONS

> Society is a very mysterious animal with many faces and hidden potentialities. . . . [I]t is extremely short sighted to believe that the face society happens to be presenting to you at a given moment is its only true face. None of us knows all the potentialities that slumber in the spirit of the population.
>
> —Vaclav Havel

Nazi Germany, Rwanda, Darfur. As anyone familiar with world history knows, humanity's record over the last hundred years is grim. Yet as this book illustrates, even as humanity's collective capacity for good has been overshadowed, there has been hope. The practice of courageous resistance has been just as strong as the record of injustice over the last one hundred years. The inspiring examples of courageous resistance in this book show that ordinary people, often with few resources, can display extraordinary courage and yield impressive results. Courageous resisters have ended or reduced injustice in amazingly varied contexts—from dangerous harassment and environmental degradation to torture, disappearance, and even genocide. These cases show also that voluntary, other-oriented (largely selfless), high-risk, conscious, sustained, and nonviolent resistance to injustice occurs at individual, collective, and institutional levels.

Synthesizing and extending existing theories, our framework combines theories and research from varied disciplines, including social psychology, sociology, and political science, each of which offers partial answers to human evil and to how it can be opposed. Our research counters generalizations that assume we either are or are not altruists by showing that certain contexts can push individuals to choose actions that are much more extreme than their previous actions. Courageous resisters do not simply respond to others in danger instinctively, as work by other researchers (e.g., Monroe 1996) might suggest. Just as some scholars have asserted that certain contexts can increase the likelihood of injustice occurring (see Staub 1989), we assert that both context and networks can lead to increased likelihood of courageous resistance occurring. Our framework also expands on previous research that highlights large-scale nonviolent resistance (see Ackerman and Duvall 2000). We believe that courageous resistance that occurs on a much smaller level, and often times in less dramatic form, can be equally influential in changing the world. Therefore, we have focused on individual and smaller-scale collective nonviolent resistance to injustice and incorporated institutions' roles in achieving justice and transforming prospects for future resistance.

WHAT DIFFERENCE CAN COURAGEOUS RESISTANCE MAKE?

Courageous resisters have successfully opposed injustice in many ways, including blowing the whistle on environmental degradation and harassment; rescuing those targeted for abuse or murder; publicly demonstrating against torture, disappearance, and genocide; and creating new organizations and international standards. They have worked as lone individuals, as groups of individuals in concert spontaneously for short periods of time, and as groups that created or built on long-term relationships of trust, caring, and reciprocity. They have also created and used institutions, including domestic and international organizations, laws, and treaties. These institutions have themselves transformed the context in ways that discourage future abuses and have inspired and empowered courageous resisters that came later or are yet to come.

By choosing to defend others against injustice, despite great risk and personal cost, ordinary people working alone or in concert have improved our world. As we saw in Chapter 1, poor farmers and villagers of the French plateau shared what they had and saved thousands of refugees from Nazi persecution, including more than three thousand Jewish children. A lone hotel manager in Rwanda saved more than a thousand lives during that nation's genocide, as he used his hotel's liquor supplies, fax machine, and telephones and his own networks and wits to keep prowling death squads at bay. As we saw in Chapter 5, unarmed women in Argentina and Berlin held their own against armed soldiers, continuing their protests for loved ones. Through their very public, consistent, and nonviolent protests, the Madres (Mothers) of Plaza de Mayo challenged the repressive Argentine military regime that had "disappeared" their family members, garnered domestic and international attention, and carved out a space for protest in a most unlikely setting. In time, their protests contributed to the collapse of the military regime. Similarly, the German women who on Rosenstrasse protested the arrests of their husbands not only won the release of their spouses, but also changed Nazi policy, ending the deportation of German Jews married to non-Jews. As we saw in Chapter 6, Amnesty International not only helped draft a treaty banning torture, but coordinated members worldwide, who pressured individual governments until this treaty became international law. Since its passage, this law has been used to hold heads of state responsible for engaging in torture, including former Chilean President Augusto Pinochet, a signer of the treaty.

Through their actions, courageous resisters, bystanders, and perpetrators all change themselves, the networks to which they belong, and the general context, making the struggle for a more just society more, or less, likely. Courageous resisters may offer models that redefine for witnesses what is happening and what moral action is required. They may open channels of communication with perpetrators that result in new behaviors or policies. They may create new institutions, such as the International Criminal Court, or laws preventing torture or genocide that make it possible to oppose injustice more effectively in the future. In short, courageous resistance can be successful at the individual, collective, or institutional level and yield important outcomes. It can and often has transformed the world for the better.

In contrast, our cases also show the destructive effects of bystanders who do nothing in the face of injustice. Bystanders to injustice make abuses more acceptable and courageous resistance far more difficult.

WHY DO SOME PEOPLE LOOK OUT FOR THE WELFARE OF OTHERS IN HIGH-COST SETTINGS?

The cases we have profiled and others suggest that courageous resistance results from a series of decisions made at crossroads that are transient and ongoing. While there is no set of necessary and sufficient conditions that predicts courageous resistance, there is a constellation of known factors that encourage it. Various mixtures of certain preconditions, networks, and contextual factors can affect how individuals decide to respond to injustice and be successful at it. We do not claim that the absence of these conditions will encourage individuals, groups, or organizations to become perpetrators or bystanders, nor do we believe that we can predict what any individual will do by looking at these factors. Nonetheless, there is value in identifying these factors and thinking about ways that they can be enhanced to encourage courageous resistance. Finally, we have also identified a number of strategies that may affect the impact of courageous resistance.

THE PROCESS OF CHOOSING TO BE COURAGEOUS

Despite the range of historical and cultural contexts and the different levels at which courageous resistance occurs, some commonalities surface. First, courageous resisters do not simply respond to others in danger instinctively or without thinking. For some courageous resisters—such as the Argentine resister Daniel—the process of assisting others certainly seems to come almost automatically. However, many courageous resisters recalled hesitating in making their decisions about whether or how to act, and some recalled an agonizing process of deciding to take the necessary risks at various crossroads. For example, Joseph Darby seemed to realize that what he saw at Abu Ghraib was wrong and needed to be addressed. However, he consulted with others about how to respond and delayed taking action for several days, altering his plan of action even after he had first signaled authorities about the abuse.

Courageous resisters make conscious choices about whether and how to respond. Before actually beginning resistance and sustaining it, each courageous resister must make a series of positive decisions leading to continuing resistance. For some resisters, this is a slow, deliberative process. A few individuals or groups do appear to become so habituated to helping others that they seem to have reduced their calculus to a point where pro-social action becomes almost automatic, and they see responding to others' danger as unavoidable. For example, some people see themselves as persons who help others or stand up for what they believe, because they remember having acted that way in the past. For people habituated to courageous or principled action, the decision-making process may be much faster than for others, who must consider whether they should take responsibility for victims' welfare, whether they are capable of responding and how they should respond.

The stages of decision making considered here build on theories of altruism presented by Latane and Darley (1970). Courageous resistance, which shares many characteristics with altruistic acts, results from ongoing decisions made at a series of transient crossroads. Many factors can encourage or dissuade people from choosing the pathway that leads to high-risk advocacy. Choices made at each crossroad determine whether potential actors become courageous resisters, bystanders, or perpetrators of injustice. Courageous resisters are those who become aware that something serious is occurring, recognize it as unjust, decide to take responsibility for addressing the injustice, identify possible actions, take action, and then reflect upon the action they have taken and decide to continue with it. Individuals in the same context may have different responses at each crossroad. For example, some Argentines in the Dirty War (discussed in Chapter 5) claimed to be unaware that the state was "disappearing" thousands of citizens, while others believed these victims "must have done something" to deserve imprisonment and so did not identify the state's actions as wrong. This contrasts with the sense of injustice shared by those who would become opponents of a repressive regime. The next step toward courageous resistance is to interpret an action as immoral and therefore requiring action. An excellent illustration of this (from Chapter 6) is the story of Raphael Lemkin, whose discovery that Turkish government officials could not be tried for the mass murder of the Armenians inspired his lifelong campaign to name and confront genocide so that ignoring such killings could never be excused again. Feelings of responsibility for victims may arise in reaction to traumatic crisis (e.g., the arrest, disappearance, or assault of a loved one; witnessing abuse or seeing photos of abuse; viewing a murder, and so forth), as happened with Paul Rusesabagina (profiled in Chapter 1), Joseph Darby and Cathy Harris (profiled in Chapter 4), and many of the Argentine activists and the women of Rosenstrasse (profiled in Chapter 5).

The next stages of the process are considering what action to take and deciding to take it. All who become aware of injustice and decide to defend its victims face this juncture when they must decide whether and how to act. Cathy Harris's decision to oppose the harassment of women travelers and Witness JJ's explanation for why she chose to testify at the Arusha War Crimes Tribunal (both presented in Chapter 4) illustrate indecisiveness at varying crossroads. Both women hesitated before taking action even after they had decided that what was happening was wrong and that they should do something to take responsibility for the victims' fate. JJ recalled, "I talked to him [one of her torturers] directly, face to face so I believe I am responsible, [so I am] coming to give evidence of his evil deeds in the Taba commune"(Neuffer 2001, 290). The story of Sebastian Haffner, the German soldier profiled in Chapter 3, illustrates what happens when a person responds differently at this crossroad of whether or not to take action. Haffner became aware and deeply troubled by what was happening in Germany at the time; however, he never took personal responsibility for the injustices and chose to simply comply with them.

Deciding to take action after considering various responses is common to both heroes and courageous resisters. However, continuing resistance as one reassesses risks and alternatives often distinguishes courageous resisters from heroes. Although some courageous resisters stop their activism after aiding one person or addressing a specific injustice, others decide to continue their commitment and may even expand their activities. The Madres (Mothers) of Plaza de Mayo began protesting the disappearance of their own children. As they continued these demonstrations, many developed a concern for universal human rights. Later, they offered sophisticated political analyses to justify not accepting compensation from the new democratically elected government, to push for information about all the victims, and to demand punishment of all perpetrators (Bouvard 1994).

PRECONDITIONS, NETWORKS, AND CONTEXT AT THE CROSSROADS

While all those facing injustice must face the crossroads explained above, responses to the crossroads vary widely. Why do individuals make such different choices at the crossroads?

The factors that seem to affect these choices are personal preconditions (who the person is and what he has done previously), networks (who the person knows and his ongoing and reciprocal relationships with other individuals, groups, and organizations), and contexts (where the person is relative to important local, national, and international trends and institutions). These factors combine to influence the choices people make at each of the crossroads. Our cases suggest that there are constellations of particular preconditions, networks, and contexts that seem to promote courageous resistance. When these factors converge, individuals are less prone to stand by passively or join the perpetrators of an injustice.

Personal Preconditions

The personal preconditions that we have identified are acquired through a variety of sources. These include early socialization, nurturing relationships, experiences that encourage individuals to act bravely, and pro-social models that help one recognize injustice and consider possible responses. Key values shared by many of the courageous resisters include high levels of extensivity, empathy, and pro-social values; an orientation to authority beyond that of blind obedience, fear of punishment or promise of reward for being obedient; and a sense of oneself, acquired through prior experiences, as one who can and does act on behalf of others, despite high risks.

Pro-social values, especially having an extensive view of common humanity, are integral. Courageous resisters often see their sense of obligation and caring extending beyond themselves to include wider groups of others, whom they feel obligated to respect and protect. Courageous resisters display a range of extensivity. For some, norms of inclusion extend only to close friends and family members; for others, they include people of the same or related religion, all common countrymen, or even all the people of the world. The Rosenstrasse women's decisions to both stay married to their Jewish husbands despite penalties and to resist their husbands' transportation to concentration camps suggest that they looked beyond their own self interests and had an expanded conception of themselves that extended to their spouses. This conceptualization of the in-group was apparently a strong but narrowly defined sense of "us" (i.e., an exclusive form of self-identity one might label "us-ism") more than a fully inclusive sense of "we" that extends to whole groups of others or to all of humanity. Nonetheless, the bond was so strong that the women were willing to risk their own lives for the lives of their spouses. In the story of the struggle to save Old Providence (also told in Chapter 5), a non-native islander chose to work with the islanders in their struggle for justice because she saw their struggle as her problem as well: "I am an islander. . . . I know I'm not [technically], but I felt such affection for the people of the island. I had to do something" (Gomez 2003). The story of the Argentine human rights activists (also presented in Chapter 5) offers another example of "us-ism" but shows how it evolved for some courageous resisters into a more universal understanding of "we." Some of the Argentine activists recall that they initially began their campaign against the regime's human rights abuses to aid a loved one in peril. Over time, however, they gradually expanded their goals to protect all victims of the regime's violence. Their search for one particular individual evolved into an effort to help thousands.

Related to this is a phenomenon we saw in many of our courageous resisters: they tend to see all people as individuals. Thus, while others in the society believed sweeping stereotypes about victims (e.g., viewing "terrorists," "Tutsis," or "Jews" as a group, not as individual persons) or about perpetrators, many courageous resisters were able to continue to see members of both groups as varied, individual humans. In Chapter 4, Cathy Harris's and Joseph Darby's explanations for their actions showed that they not only saw the victims of injustice as individual human beings who could have been members of their own families, but that they believed that some people within the organizations responsible for the abuse could be convinced to break those organizational norms that ignored or condoned the injustices. Interviews with a number of Madres and the autobiography of Paul Rusesabagina suggest that these courageous resisters saw the victims of violence as individuals, while at the same time remembering the humanity of the perpetrators. We believe that doing so allowed them to remain hopeful that their messages might find a sympathetic ear among the perpetrators. As Rusesabagina wrote in his autobiography, "People are never completely good or completely evil. And in order to fight evil, you sometimes have to keep evil people in your orbit. Even the worst of them have their soft side, and if you can find and play with that part of them, you can accomplish a great deal of good. In an era of extremism, you can never afford to be an extremist yourself (Rusesabagina and Zoellner 2006, 223).

Courageous resisters generally have strong values that transcend their obligations to authority or to public opinion. While others may obey authorities blindly or because they seek rewards or want to avoid punishment, courageous resisters are guided by a deep sense of what is right and wrong, just and unjust, that does not depend on popular opinion or authorities. The example of JJ in Chapter 4 illustrates how such a value orientation can shape an individual's decision to respond. While courageous resisters may be embedded within institutions that perpetrate injustice, their personal and professional norms may be so strongly entrenched that when they see the organization with which they are affiliated abusing its power they feel a strong need to defend professional standards and to reform the institution. Joseph Darby and Cathy Harris (profiled in Chapter 4) offer excellent examples of this kind of value orientation. Each refused to allow fellow government employees to abuse power and sought to hold their peers to the standards that they believed the organization should follow, even when their supervisors participated in the abuses. They each expressed both a sense of obligation to care for the rights of victims and a need to uphold the ethical standards of the institutions they served. We believe that in some cases, one's sense of professionalism may create a value orientation that supersedes group conformity and cooperation with injustice within one's organization. Other value orientations can come from religious or humanitarian beliefs such as in the case of Le Chambon.

Another factor important at the crossroads is what courageous resisters know they themselves are capable of doing, based on what they have previously done. This learning by doing often marks a gradual evolution to becoming a courageous resister. Cathy Harris illustrates such a transformation. Harris at first did nothing when she was sexually harassed. Later, however, she refused to remain silent and filed complaints against her harassers. Having learned she had within her the capacity to resist abuse of power, Harris then decided she had to confront the ways her fellow customs officers were mistreating women travelers. Her story illustrates how courageous resisters' actions can help courageous resisters to gradually become more comfortable with risks and to see themselves as capable of effective response. Some of the Argentine human rights activists also appear to have learned resistance by engaging in it. Gradually, as previously apolitical people, like Anna, faced increased risks in their struggle for justice, they changed: "The disappearance of my children transformed me into an activist, not for a political party but for human rights" (Anna 1992).

Networks

Networks offer a second type of influence at decision-making crossroads. In the story of Old Providence (presented in Chapter 5), knowledge of the nature of ecologically devastating developments and what could be done to counter them came from islanders' links to outsiders. Further, the islanders' relationships with residents of a nearby island gave them a graphic view of the dangers development posed for Old Providence.

The story of those organizing to protest the disappeared in Argentina offers another example. Daniel's entrenchment in a community of Christians who were committed to working for peace and justice led him to see the threat of repression posed by the military, not just in terms of himself, but also as a threat to others with whom he shared an obligation. As relatives of the disappeared sought answers regarding family members' whereabouts, they came to know each other. Together, they strengthened each other's understanding that their loved ones were not terrorists and that the regime was responsible for their loved ones' fates.

The story of Joseph Darby, exposing abuse at Abu Ghraib prison, suggests how important powerful links to supportive others can be for a potential courageous resister, even if the links are just with one or two other people. As Darby contemplated what to do about the Abu Ghraib abuses, his mentor's encouragement to trust his own perceptions of what was right or wrong was crucial. This support strengthened Darby's sense that what was happening at the Iraqi prison was wrong and helped him decide to expose the abuse.

Both social networks and larger scale networks, such as transnational issue networks, can increase the likelihood of making the "yes" call at the crossroads leading to courageous resistance and in sustaining the effort. Networks offer opportunities for forming broader and more varied circles of trust and reciprocity, and these can prove especially crucial in settings of high risk. For the Argentine human rights activist Daniel and his wife, connections to other activists within the movement to find the disappeared were crucial in keeping them involved despite the dangers. In the case of Old Providence, the preexisting social links among the islanders helped spread the word about the dangers of the proposed megaprojects. At the same time, through community meetings, local advocates devised strategies of resistance and made long-term plans for the island. Even as the risks grew, the islanders' strong allegiances to others making the same commitment amplified their resolve and made it hard for them not to participate.

Media can also play a role in these networks, either encouraging or discouraging successful resistance. The ability to publicize abuses to a broader audience, which occurred in the cases of Abu Ghraib, the U.S. Customs Service abuses, and in the case of the Madres of the Plaza, can pressure the perpetrators to respond and can activate others to join the resisters' cause. Media exposure does not in itself guarantee that sufficient pressure will be applied to end abuse, however. The genocide in Rwanda and Darfur were and are widely publicized, but this publicity has not yet led to sufficiently large or powerful advocacy networks to end the violence. The use of media power is a tool that can be used by courageous resisters but is not itself a form of courageous resistance.

Finally, networks can also offer very concrete forms of assistance. In Chapter 4, we saw that Harry Bingham's efforts to save Jews drew heavily on the resources offered by his network of connections (funds, hiding places for Jews as they awaited escape, help with refugees' resettlement in the United States, etc.). International funding also helped support the French rescuers in and around Le Chambon. Similarly, after having great trouble in finding venues for meeting, the Madres of the Plaza were able to purchase a spacious apartment with support from European women's and human rights groups.

Context

The cases we have considered also illustrate how important the context can be for promoting action against injustice. In societies where free exchange of ideas does not bring great fear of physical punishment, there is still self-censorship, as many people fear criticism or ostracism for taking an unpopular stand. In such settings, the existence of models of opposition and networks of support are important, even if the risks one confronts are relatively small. A context in which free expression and association are discouraged or punished creates tough challenges for discovering what is happening, moving past official explanations or silence to discern whether injustice is really underway, and figuring out how to respond to injustice in a context where organizational or political channels may be closed or ineffectual.

Context matters. For example, the power of the Rosenstrasse women's protests regarding their husbands' imprisonment seems impossible in the repressive setting of fascist Germany. How did it succeed? Prospects for success were likely enhanced by the domestic climate within Germany at the time of the arrests and subsequent protests. High-ranking officials could not allow a public protest to undermine the regime's power or inspire other resistance when the war was going badly and additional sacrifices were being asked for on the home front. Even in democratically elected countries, there are certain domestic political opportunities, such as elections, that offer better openings for courageous resistance than do others.

As Lemkin discovered when he watched the world's silence after the Turkish slaughter of Armenians, knowing that something serious occurs, seeing it as wrong, and being able to stop or punish the perpetrators can be completely different things. In a context in which the truth can be discovered and disclosed, organizations are able to form to challenge the injustice. Individuals are able to voice their outrage, and laws and punishments to enforce the rights of victims can go a long way toward addressing injustice. When these optimal conditions are not available, however, we have seen courageous resisters adapt to the context and either make the most of those circumstances to help their efforts or—as Lemkin and others did—attempt to transform the settings to make the pursuit of justice more likely to succeed. The Madres of the Plaza and women of Rosenstrasse created public space to communicate their concern, grief, and outrage at the state's role in their loved ones' captivity and managed to communicate with military regimes that had closed all official avenues for criticism. The creators of Amnesty International and Human Rights Watch transformed the context for challenging human rights abuses by creating the means for gathering and circulating information about human rights offenses and by working to create and strengthen international law and courts capable of punishing perpetrators.

Clearly, risks associated with all kinds of resistance are affected by the context of the situation. But context also affects the prospects for understanding and evaluating what events mean, who is responsible, and weighing options for taking action. We have seen that courageous resisters are better able to resist injustice at some times rather than others. For example, contextual factors that increase perpetrators' needs for approval, resources, and stability may yield policies aimed at courting public opinion, or at least not inflaming it. This can make it difficult for the perpetrators to use violence to silence protests, especially peaceful ones that resonate with popular sentiment, such as a call to reunite family members. Societal or international networks, norms, and pressures can also affect the impact of struggles for courageous resistance. Those attempting public protests within Nazi Germany could not rely on international networks for support or the international media to spread their message because these options did not exist. In contrast, the Madres of the Plaza were well served by their connection with transnational advocacy networks. Finally, strategies of resistance can be vital: nonviolence, consistency, limited demands, and appearing not to be self-interested can improve the likelihood that a small group will effectively challenge the official view of events and create an awareness of injustice.

Strategically assessing what is possible despite possible risks characterizes many courageous resisters we have seen. U.S. Diplomat Harry Bingham took advantage of the neutral status of the United States to issue passports to European Jews fleeing to the United States. The villagers in and around Le Chambon took advantage of their remote location to hide refugees from the Nazis and work with other underground organizations that helped the hunted escape to Switzerland. Witness JJ's decision to testify at the Rwandan war crimes tribunal was possible only because those international institutions existed to conduct trials and hold the *genocidaires* accountable for violating international law. Colombian NGOs, constitutional changes, and international institutions regarding the environment and indigenous rights were vital for the islanders of Old Providence. International laws regarding torture and human rights were essential for seeking prosecution of Augusto Pinochet. The transnational issue networks, which were inspired by such institutions as the Universal Declaration of Human Rights, played a key role in creating other institutions, including the International Criminal Court, which will someday prosecute those abetting the ongoing genocide in Sudan.

But even institutions whose mission is to defend rights are not always capable of resistance. The story of General Romeo Dallaire (presented in Chapter 1) illustrates the limitations that can also be imposed by the international context and by institutions. While Dallaire wanted to stop the slaughter in Rwanda, as a UN peacekeeper, he was blocked by the lack of international support for UN intervention. At other times, as the story of Raphael Lemkin points out, resistance to injustice is constrained by a lack of institutions, which courageous resisters eventually may be able to create.

Institutions are crucial components of the context. Courageous resistance at the individual, collective, and institutional levels can build new institutions. Lemkin's coining of the term "genocide" became the core of a number of powerful institutions and international treaties. In Chapters 1 and 6, we saw how individuals, groups, and institutions can create lasting legacies by changing the world's knowledge of and ability to respond to human rights abuses. The work of such citizen groups as Czechoslovakia's Charter 77 and of individuals and institutions such as Robert Bernstein and the Ford Foundation helped bring real power to the Helsinki Accords and established ongoing monitoring organizations, including *Helsinki Watch* and *Human Rights Watch*. This and other cases show how the international regimes and transnational issue networks associated with environmental and human rights protection can exert powerful muscle to help pass laws, create international treaties, and initiate institutional reform that can transform the context. The very existence of these norms can make future courageous resistance more likely to occur and succeed as they establish precedents to which potential actors can refer. Yet these cases also show that institutions alone are insufficient to secure justice. Institutions need ongoing human effort to be effective as well. Despite the Genocide Convention, genocide still occurs, and more effort is needed to end it.

COURAGEOUS RESISTANCE IS MULTIFACETED AND COMPLICATED

Courageous resistance is a complex category. There is no single archetype that describes courageous resistance, athough a number of factors separate courageous resisters from other moral actors. For example, we distinguish courageous resisters from heroes by emphasizing the sustained nature of their efforts. We believe this distinction is vital because the process of reassessing and maintaining action (rather than acting spontaneously for a short period of time) has a more profound impact not only on the courageous resisters themselves, but on those who learn of their activities, on prospects for changing institutions, and on the general context for justice. Some courageous resisters' actions reflect their lifelong attitudes and behaviors. However, our research counters generalizations that we either are or are not altruists by showing that certain contexts can push individuals to choose actions that are much more extreme than their previous actions. The incremental practice of other-orientedness and an ethics of courage can make bolder and more courageous actions more likely. So can a traumatic witnessing of injustice or suffering, even for those who had rarely or never practiced pro-social behavior in the earlier phases of their lives.

Understanding courageous resistance is also complicated because those who act altruistically or courageously at certain moments may play different roles at the same or different times in their lives as well. For example, Julius Schmahling simultaneously participated in unjust Nazi functions—including the round up of Jews—and helped French rescuers to keep safe their hidden guests by alerting them before upcoming raids. In the Rwandan case, JJ was a victim during the genocide but became a courageous resister afterward. Courageous resisters' actions may not be completely selfless. JJ, for example, wanted to see her own and others' torturers punished. The Argentine Madres of the Plaza and the women who won their husbands' release from the Rosenstrasse detention center in Berlin were originally motivated by concern for members of their own families.

We contend that while certain changes in context can encourage and permit ordinary people to act unjustly (e.g., Staub's theory that a context of difficult life conditions may reorder goal priorities), other changes can lead to increased likelihood of courageous resistance occurring and being successful (e.g., individuals or states may stand up for human rights to maintain or improve their domestic or international reputation or stability). People with similar individual preconditions can respond to the same events quite differently because of variations in their personal preconditions or in their networks or contextual factors. As Chapter 5 points out, for example, while the kidnapping of a family member by Argentine forces pushed some people out of the political sphere, it mobilized others for the first time. Similarly, difficult life conditions and other contextual forces can also lead individuals with very different preconditions to take the same actions against injustice. Anna and Daniel came to the Argentine human rights movement from very different preconditions—one had never been politically active, while the other had been highly engaged in political organizing—and yet they both became courageous resisters.

DECISIONS TRANSFORM PROSPECTS FOR JUSTICE

All actions resulting from the multistage decision-making process we have introduced transform the decision makers, the networks to which they belong, and the general context to increase or decrease the likelihood of a more just society. Courageous resisters and heroes, bystanders and perpetrators all have an impact on their surroundings. They offer models that may redefine for those who witness them what is happening and what an appropriate response should be. They may open channels of communication with perpetrators that result in new behaviors or policies. They may create new institutions, such as the International Criminal Court or laws against torture or genocide, that may create more effective remedies for injustices in the future. Courageous resisters, former bystanders, and survivors of injustice may all play an important role after an injustice occurs by bearing witness to abuses and bringing perpetrators to justice or by creating new institutions that will be able to more effectively deal with future episodes.

WHAT MAKES COURAGEOUS RESISTANCE SUCCESSFUL?

Despite a range of resources, locations, and time periods, the cases we have presented were all successful to some degree. However, not all attempts at courageous resistance are successful. Similar efforts in the same time frames and contexts may have been unsuccessful, but have generally escaped our notice—perhaps because those attempting them were so thoroughly silenced. We cannot claim to present a list of strategies that will guarantee success of courageous resistance, but we have found that certain patterns do emerge from these cases.

Nonviolent strategies can prevent a spiraling of violence, set a model for future problem resolution, and deepen courageous resisters' credibility and support among bystanders. They also rob authorities of justification for brutally repressing their critics. It is far easier to execute armed insurrectionists than to attack peaceful demonstrators seeking to aid their family members. While both public and private action can both save lives and transform resisters, public protest seems to have a greater likelihood of transforming the context in the long term and inspiring many more bystanders to support the quest for justice. Collective efforts that create or build upon existing social capital can evolve over time to address broader forms of injustice. Courageous resistance at the individual, collective, and institutional level can raise the costs for perpetrators and may cause them to reevaluate and reduce or end their crimes. Courageous resisters can serve as a model for others, influencing bystanders to become courageous resisters themselves or to at least reconsider the validity of perpetrators' interpretations of what is occurring and its fairness. Courageous resisters can act collectively, either in impromptu (joint) public forms or longer term, organized, and social capital–building (communal) public forms. *Public* forms are especially powerful because they open channels of communication with perpetrators or the public or both, forcing consideration of demands for justice. Although both are potentially potent, the longer-term efforts are more likely to transform society and individuals than are short, impromptu efforts.

We wish that we could envision a world of perfect justice, a world where courageous resisters are no longer needed. Sadly, that world has not yet arrived. In the meantime, however, we admire the resistance and contributions of all the courageous people who have enlarged the context of justice. We appreciate the institutions, both domestic and international, that have been created to fight injustice. We hope that by telling these stories and distilling their lessons of courageous resistance, we are all more prepared to oppose injustice and to help create a world of justice and human rights for all. We are now closing the first decade of yet another century. In another one hundred years, we hope the need for courageous resistance and the lessons of this book will have become obsolete.

APPLYING WHAT
WE HAVE LEARNED

> Always hold firmly to the thought that each one of us can do something to bring some portion of misery to an end.
> —Syracuse Cultural Workers[1]

Shortly after the September 11, 2001, tragedy, one of the authors of this book heard a moral tale about a child who came to her grandfather indignant over an injustice she had experienced. "What shall I do, grandfather?" she asked. Her grandfather replied, "I have two wolves inside me. One gets very angry when I have been treated unfairly and it wants to hit back, to hurt the one who hurt me. The other wolf also gets angry when I have been unfairly treated, but it wants justice and peace more than anything, and it wants to heal the rift between me and my aggressor." "Which wolf wins, grandfather?" the little girl asked. "The one I feed," he replied.

If by reading this book you have been inspired by the stories of the courageous individuals and groups, but you have wondered if you could ever have that kind of courage, you are not alone. We wonder also. We cannot help but be appalled at the perpetrators of evil we have read about in this book, nor can we help admiring the courageous resistors about whom we have learned. But it is easy to separate ourselves from both groups. We may say to ourselves, "Surely I would never kill children as did the Nazis, or force pregnant women to take dangerous drugs just to boost my overtime pay," as some U.S. Customs Service officials were alleged to have done. And while we hope that we would have the courage of Cathy Harris, the whistleblower from the U.S. customs, or that we, too, would shelter someone who was being targeted for death by a powerful group, it is hard to believe that people who stand up for others at such cost and risk to themselves are not exceptional.

However, this book shows that both the courageous resisters to evil and the evildoers themselves are ordinary people like us. The courageous resisters have fed within themselves the wolf that wants justice. The choices they have made, the networks they have joined, and their circumstances have all shaped their ability to seek justice. Other researchers have investigated the factors that lead ordinary people to destructive human rights abuses (see Staub 1989; Waller 2002). Our emphasis, and the motivation for this book, is ordinary people's capacity for courageous resistance on behalf of others when they are in danger.

We are all born with the capacity to develop the kind of courage we have read about in this book—from Joseph Darby blowing the whistle on the abuse of prisoners at Abu Ghraib, to Anna and the Madres (Mothers) of Plaza de Mayo protesting the disappearance of their children, to the entire village of Le Chambon rescuing thousands of Jews. Evidence of this capacity for extraordinary courage comes from a wide range of scholarly research, some of which you have read about in this book. Psychological and sociological literature that describes the factors influencing individual and collective behavior suggests ordinary people's capacity for extraordinary courage. Work by political scientists and historians who have examined cases of courageous resistance over time provides support for this premise as well. Evidence comes from biology and evolutionary biology, which offer evidence for the complex adaptive function of empathy and mutual care in social animals such as humans. It also comes from compelling cultural messages over thousands of years. People have taught that we not only are capable of such courage on behalf of others, but that we are called to it as the finest realization of our humanity.

One source of these widespread cultural messages is religious literature. The Talmud teaches that every decision we make either adds to the good in the world, or to the bad. Thomas Aquinas, a thirteenth-century Christian philosopher, wrote in his classic work, *Summa Theologica,* that every human act is a moral act, a choice. Islam teaches that no one is a believer until you desire for another that which you desire for yourself, and Buddhism, in the Udana-Varqa, says hurt not others in ways that you yourself would find hurtful. All major religions teach that we are called to care for others. This convergence of religious messages over time is part of the support cultures offer for the other-oriented behavior they encourage. This is part of the cultural environment that reinforces laws protecting human rights and that makes courageous resistance possible.

In the most extensive psychological study of such altruistic behaviors, which you read about in chapter 2, Pearl and Samuel Oliner interviewed and tested 406 people who rescued Jews during the Holocaust (Oliner and Oliner 1988). They compared them to 126 non-rescuers, matched to the rescuers by age, sex, education, and geographic location during the war. The study revealed a remarkable similarity between the rescuers and non-rescuers on factors that one might think would be different. For example, both groups had equal knowledge of the dangers the Jews faced, and they had equal access to resources that would help them were they to decide to come to the rescue. What did differentiate the rescuers from the non-rescuers was a greater attachment to people and a greater sense of responsibility for them, a greater comprehension of the need for their help, more empathy for the pain and helplessness of others, and a willingness to act despite the obvious risk. The most striking characteristic of the rescuers was their sense of inclusiveness, the willingness to see all people as similar to themselves and the tendency to befriend others on that basis. The rescuers were not born with these characteristics.

What distinguish rescuers from non-rescuers, according to the Oliners, are traits that are learned, ones that come from specific kinds of experiences that are chosen, from communities that one can help to form. There is not a magic formula or algorithm that will guarantee a courageous decision in every situation, but we can apply what we have learned to suggest a set of guidelines that will feed the wolf that wants justice and peace, the wolf that chooses life over death, justice over abuse. The news is filled with stories of oppression, inequity, misuse of power, degradation of the environment—all situations that cry out for action. Perhaps we, each of us individually and all of us collectively, are facing situations that call for courageous resistance.

What might we do to increase the likelihood that we will respond to the needs of those around us and in doing so, create the very caring communities in which we would like to live? The answer lies in the deliberate cultivation of the individual level *preconditions* that undergird courageous resistance—empathy and other-oriented behavior, the sense of connection to individuals and groups beyond ourselves, and in practicing the skills necessary for effective action. It also involves being connected to other people who share our values and vision for a more just world, people from whom we can learn valuable skills, and with whom we can share resources and insights—our *networks*. And we have learned how all of this is facilitated in an environment, a cultural *context*, in which human rights are valued and nations and institutions such as the United Nations codify human rights in their laws and then enforce them.

IS REAL ALTRUISM POSSIBLE?

When Kristin Monroe interviewed a number of those who, often at great personal risk, rescued Jews during the Holocaust, she concluded that their most important shared quality was that they viewed all humanity as "belonging to one human family" (Monroe 1996, 205). These rescuers' perspectives made distinctions based on race, religion, or nationality seem meaningless.

Two American psychologists were among those who offered theories of personality development several decades ago that specifically included this broad concern for others. Alfred Adler believed every human is born with the potential for a general concern for the welfare of others, but this potential must be nurtured to develop fully. As one matures psychologically, the range of those one cares about expands. When a person is psychologically immature, their concern for others, though genuine, may be limited to their family, community, ethnic group, or nation. Many adults never develop beyond this immaturity. But if one becomes fully mature, psychologically speaking, their concern embraces the whole human community, regardless of race, nationality, or any other distinction; one has a sense of "oneness with humanity" (Adler 1954, 38). A person with mature social interest acts "in the interests of mankind generally," and engages in activities that are aimed at "helpfulness to all mankind, present and future" (Adler 1964, 78). Abraham Maslow expressed a similar idea when he described those who reach full psychological maturity as "self-actualized" (Maslow 1954). One of the main qualities self-actualized individuals were found to possess is "human kinship." Individuals with this quality "have a deep feeling of identification, sympathy, and affection for human beings in general . . . [a] feeling of identification with mankind . . . a genuine desire to help the human race" (138).[2] This book tells the stories of a number of people who did just that. Although not all the courageous resisters we have profiled demonstrate this level of extensivity, each has demonstrated such concern for some others.

Many researchers have made the point that feeling attached to or connected to other people is what allows us to feel empathy for them. According to this thinking, the closer you feel to someone, the more empathy you will feel and the more you will want to help them. Attachment to family and close friends seems primary, but it is not the only kind of attachment we can feel. It was empathy for their Jewish husbands that brought the Aryan women to Rosenstrasse to face the guns of the Nazis, and it was the need to find her three children, who had all been kidnapped by special forces sponsored by the Argentinean government, that moved Anna to join the Madres (Mothers) of Plaza de Mayo. But the villagers of Le Chambon did not know the people they rescued. Their connection simply was to other human beings in distress. Joseph Darby did not know the Iraqi detainees who were being tortured, but he saw in them his mother, his grandmother, his little brother, and he felt responsible for them.

A Personality Theory

Throughout this book we have talked about the role of preconditions, networks, and context in courageous resistance. A personality theory proposed by Ervin Staub uses these concepts in slightly different language. He calls the concern for others and for the world a pro-social goal orientation. He explains this as individuals having a positive disposition towards others, placing a value on the welfare of others, and feeling personally responsible for others' welfare. This concept is part of his Personal Goal Theory, which states that we have individual potential motivators that vary in importance to us at different times and under different circumstances (Staub 2003). We may have a motivation for comfort and relaxation that can be very important to us when we think of a sunny day at the beach, but this motivator is suppressed when a different motivator of ours—working for justice—has been activated by a request from friends to join them in working on a Habitat for Humanity house. Whether a goal is activated and the strength of that goal will depend on the interaction of the situation (the environment) and the importance of that goal to the individual. When goals are in conflict, as when pro-social goals conflict with self-interest, the goal that wins will depend on the relative strength of the competing personal variables and on what is happening in the environment. The personal variables may include which goal is more important to us—we may think of ourselves as generous persons who respond to emergencies, but certain circumstances may make other goals more important. Our decision may be influenced by how recently we were engaged in similar behavior as well.[3] If, like Cathy Harris and Joseph Darby, we have experienced harassment or discrimination ourselves, these personal variables might move other-oriented goals higher in the hierarchy of our motivations, making them more likely to be a first response or a close second.

The environment may also include cues that indicate how vivid the need for our action is—is a disaster constantly in the news with poignant pictures of injured children, or is the news item tucked at the end of the second section of the newspaper and rarely shown on TV? In December 2004, people around the world responded with great compassion and generosity to the victims of the tsunami in Southeast Asia—so much so that some aid agencies stopped taking donations. Pictures of victims and destruction were on the news and on the front pages of newspapers for weeks. At the same time, the world virtually ignored the genocide happening in the Darfur region of Sudan, where an estimated minimum of two hundred thousand people had been murdered in the two previous years, and the murders and rapes were happening daily. But this was rarely mentioned in the news. In all of 2004, the major U.S. television networks, ABC, NBC, and CBS, together spent a total of twenty-six minutes televising the genocide in their evening newscasts. In 2005, as the killing continued, the three networks combined devoted just eighteen minutes to the story over the course of the whole year (Kristof 2006). When stories of Darfur were in the paper at all, they appeared in the back pages.

Another potentially important issue is the degree of need of the victims. Interestingly, we are more likely to respond if people need a significant amount of help, than if their need is minimal. Finally, it is more likely that specific forces that motivate us will be activated when the goals associated with those forces can be achieved by skills we have learned through our connections with others. Harry Bingham, who helped rescue prominent European Jews and bring them to the United States, was a career foreign service officer who had the critical skills to move applications for visas through the system. His connection to Varian Fry and the Emergency Rescue Committee provided him with resources and linkages to other concerned people working against the Nazis.

In essence, if we want to become the kind of person who is more likely to make courageous decisions, we must deliberately cultivate our pro-social goals, develop skills that support those goals, associate with people who share those goals, and put ourselves in situations that call on those goals. In their 1995 book, *Toward a Caring Society*, the Oliners suggest we need to deliberately cultivate our attachments, our empathy for other people, and our senses of inclusivity, connection and responsibility for others. Strong attachments will encourage our empathy and thus our other-oriented motivations and our pro-social goals, and increasing inclusivity will help us to apply these goals to a wider and wider circle of people.

SIX STEPS TO TRANSFORMING OURSELVES[4]

Anyone who has taken a psychology course will recognize the concept of attachment as it refers to infant-caregiver relationships. John Bowlby

(1969) emphasized that a sustained connection to a secure and stable adult is critical to healthy development in children. More recent work has proposed that attachment and interconnectedness to others is fundamental to us throughout our lives. We are social animals, and we thrive in part to the degree we foster those relationships. The way we use the term "attachment" in everyday language usually refers to a few special persons in our life. Oliner and others (1992), in *Embracing the Other*, conceive of attachment as a dimension, "a sense of interpersonal connectedness that ranges in intensities, from love at one pole to alienation (extreme detachment) at the other. In between is a broad continuum reflecting varying intensities of attachment and detachment" (371).[5]

In this context, the more we can increase our genuine attachment to others, the greater the potential development of our empathy for them. The more empathy we feel for others, the greater our other-oriented motivation. Then, if we use Staub's Personal Goal Theory, concern for others will be a more dominant goal in our hierarchy—it will be more important to us, and it will be easier for us to access it. This motivation underlies the first three steps in transforming ourselves into more other-oriented persons.

STEP 1: BONDING

We form bonds with other people, places, jobs, and even pets that are so strong that if something happened to them we would feel a wrenching loss. Opening ourselves up to loving something or someone so much is risky, rewarding, and it makes us more caring people. One way, then, to become more other-oriented is to be willing to take the risk to care. It can start as simply as loving a pet and being willing to be a responsible caregiver to it, to be willing to inconvenience ourselves for it, to practice faithfulness. If we allow ourselves to care deeply for our friends, we will open ourselves to become more other-oriented overall. If we love some particular bit of landscape, a favorite walk, a beach, a beautiful tree, we will be more likely to care if it is being damaged and be more willing to fight for it and for some place dear to other people.

It is important both to bond to others and to provide good bonding environments—ones that promote caring for others. Schools, workplaces, churches, and families can do that. Environments that encourage bonding have a number of characteristics. They tend to our biological needs, so we feel nurtured. For example, sharing food is an ancient custom that signifies friendship. Think of the custom of bringing food to a family that has suffered a death. Across many cultures, we comfort and care with food. Good bonding environments also allow us to play—to share happy times. They give us emotional safety and reassurance and permit us to share losses, to grieve together. Good bonding environments encourage caring for those with special needs in ways that highlight their commonalities with others. Schools that mainstream physically and mentally challenged children often provide just such bonding opportunities. They do this by bringing these especially challenged children into the community of the classroom. The other students get to know them as individuals, and social psychologists tell us that we come to like people more simply by seeing them more often and interacting with them more. When the students have the opportunity to help each other, to work together on projects, they come to appreciate one another, and the especially challenged students become part of the in-group of the class. They bond. Mainstreaming also allows more able students to learn helping skills they can use in other situations with different people.

STEP 2: PRACTICING EMPATHY

In order to empathize with how someone else is feeling, we need to clarify our own feelings and values. It may seem impossible that we might not know what we are feeling ourselves, but in fact, we can be very good at ignoring or distorting our own emotions. For example, fear is often interpreted as anger. Rwandan Hutus who saw their Tutsi neighbors being brutalized by the military may have experienced their fear as anger toward the victims, rather than fear of the military. To admit fear of the military is to acknowledge that you too might become a victim, so it is psychologically safer to blame the victim for your discomfort. This, then, might have contributed to those Hutus eventually joining in the brutality. So, the first step in practicing empathy is to be honest with ourselves and to practice awareness. We can ask ourselves, "What am I really feeling now? Why did I say or do that?"

In many Western cultures, there are gender differences in the social acceptance of such introspection. Women are both allowed and trained to identify their emotions, while men are expected to solve problems rationally, rather than understand their emotions. Men may be more encouraged to recognize their own emotions in small groups of friends who ask each other what they are feeling in particular situations and who encourage honesty rather than conformity to rigid gender norms (Oliner and Oliner 1995, 39). We can all learn to be more empathetic if we practice taking the perspective of others. It is a capacity we have as early as the age of three and certainly by the time we are about twelve, but it is one that must be cultivated if we are to put it into practice. Corporate team-building workshops often include just these kinds of exercises, and they are a critical part of what is called nonviolent or non-defensive communications (Ellison 2002, Rosenberg 2000). We can ask our friends or ourselves what other people, especially people different from us, may be thinking or feeling. Role-playing, especially with good feedback from those who are watching how realistic and accurate we are, is very helpful in developing empathy for others.

When we actively imagine another person's feelings or put ourselves in their place, our empathy for them increases, and we are much more likely to act in a moral and helpful way toward them. Social psychologist Daniel Batson and his colleagues showed this in a recent pair of experiments. In the first, they let each participant keep one of two tasks for himself and assign a second task to another (fictitious) participant. One task offered the chance to win lottery tickets, while the second did not and was described as boring. Some of the participants were then asked to imagine how the other person feels waiting to know which task they will receive and how they will feel when they learn it. More than half of these participants gave the rewarding task to that person and kept the boring task for themselves. However, three-fourths of the participants not asked to imagine how the other person feels kept the rewarding task for themselves. In a second experiment, participants were told that they could win two raffle tickets for each correct answer on a task, while another participant could win none, or they could share the tickets so that each participant could each win one ticket for each right answer. Half of the participants were asked to imagine themselves in the place of the other person. Of these, more than 80 percent chose to share the rewards equally, but fewer than 40 percent of the other participants did so (Batson et al. 2003).

Taking the other person's perspective can increase empathy and moral action in many situations. A valuable part of training for nonviolent demonstrations is playing the part of the police officers who control the demonstration. If you can empathize with the police officers, understanding what might make them feel out of control and thus vulnerable, you can craft a demonstration that minimizes the danger of confrontation.

Even young children can benefit from training that asks them to sort out their own feelings, recognize and differentiate among others' feelings, and realize the impact of their behavior. The child-rearing technique called *induction* does this specifically by inviting children to empathize with someone they have harmed. It is a powerful tool in empathy development and can be used with children as young as two years old when the parent points out why the behavior is harmful in terms the child can understand. Pointing out immediate outcomes, such as telling a child, "If you keep pulling her shirt, she will fall down and cry," works for very young children. For older children, pointing out more subtle explanations is appropriate: "He didn't mean to bump you; he was just running after the ball." Or "She was proud of her picture, and you painted on it. Imagine how you would feel if someone did that to your painting." Induction helps develop moral norms by giving children guidelines they can use in future situations—guidelines that make sense to the child. It encourages empathy and concern, which promotes pro-social behavior. In one early study, parents who used inductions consistently had preschoolers who showed more concern for other children who were crying, offering toys and hugs and verbal sympathy (Zahn-Waxler, Radke-Yarrow, and King 1979). Simulations that put people into others' realities for hours or days often have dramatic results. Yoram Binur, an Israeli journalist, became a Palestinian Arab for six months in an effort to understand Palestinian-Israeli relationships from the other side. He began to understand Palestinian humiliation and anger in a way he had never appreciated before and was even more committed to trying to find a peaceful solution to the hostilities between the Israelis and Palestinians.[6]

When we turn off pictures of suffering people (e.g., starving children in Africa) or turn our heads away from homeless people we pass on the street, we are showing *empathy avoidance*. We are acting as if we are all too aware of the power of empathy to motivate us to help. By avoiding the empathy and "not noticing," we eliminate the need to act, especially if the action is likely to be high cost in terms of time or effort (Shaw, Batson, and Todd 1994). If the objective of empathy is to be helpful, then it will be important both to see how others' feelings and experiences are similar to our own and to appreciate how they may be different.

There is an amazing story of the power of this expanded sense of "we" in the midst of war.[7] During World War I, German and Allied (British and French) troops were fighting each other from water- and mud-filled trenches in the freezing days leading up to Christmas 1914.[8] The conditions were miserable, and neither side was winning. The soldiers on both sides were being sent on attacks that resulted in massive losses of lives with no gain in position. Anecdotally, in the months leading up to that Christmas there was considerable evidence of all sorts of friendly exchanges between soldiers of the opposing armies across the "no man's land" between the trenches. The soldiers exchanged jokes and songs, bartered goods, and even reached unspoken agreements not to fire on one another, or to pretend they did not see each other's patrols. One British soldier wrote home that the Germans had called across from their trenches, asking when the British were going to go home and let them have peace, saying that they, the Germans, wanted peace as well. On Christmas Eve, small Christmas trees appeared in the German trenches, despite this action being expressly forbidden. And then the voices of the German soldiers rose in song. In many places where Germans faced the British, the Germans sang, "Stille Nacht, Heilige Nacht," and and from the British trenches came the English equivalent, "Silent Night, Holy Night," and then they were all singing together.

When they finished the hymn, one man stood up waving a white flag of truce, and another man from the other side did the same. Soon, the soldiers were putting down their weapons and were meeting in the center of the battlefield, sharing pictures of their families, trading the contents of the Christmas packages they had received. It is estimated that more than ten thousand troops up and down the line in Belgium and France participated in this truce. When dawn came, the ground was frozen with no more mud, and the sun rose brightly, a wonderful change, and the camaraderie expanded. Some soldiers even moved into each other's trenches. Burial parties were arranged, and prayers were said in German and either English or French, depending on the nationality of the Allied troops in any particular area. Some soldiers wrote home that this was the best Christmas they had ever experienced. In some cases, this truce lasted beyond New Year's Day, and the soldiers only reluctantly went back to their trenches to begin the war again. But the soldiers could no longer attempt to kill the men with whom they had shared pictures of wives and girlfriends and children. Their officers had to move them away from the front and replace them with men who had not come to see the enemy as just like them.

Although the war lasted another three years (and another three Christmas holidays), the truce never repeated itself. There were particular conditions that came together that Christmas time: the British sense of "gentlemanly warfare," the German belief that Germany was close to victory, miserable weather for both sides, shared anger at military superiors on both sides who ordered the soldiers into senseless danger and death, and the fact that many of the men who were at the front were reservists, older men with families. The military hierarchy on both sides of the war understood that this recognition of the enemy as "we" and not as "other" was an impediment to war and to killing, and neither hierarchy wanted to have it repeated. Both sides clamped down on fraternization.

What do we learn from this? If we want to create peace instead of war, we need to find a way to institutionalize these moments where we recognize our common humanity. Peace groups made up of the families that have lost children in conflict have formed in areas of war—for example, in Northern Ireland, Israel, and Palestine. Their shared loss gives them an understanding of the costs of war and thus, sympathy for those on the other side. In less dramatic settings, people who work together to solve common problems come to like each other, even if they first approached the problem distrusting each other. Working with people who seem different from us and making the effort to share equal status experiences where members of both groups share in decision making will open us to an expanded sense of "we."

STEP 3: PRACTICING CARE

Why do we need to practice caring? Ervin Staub (2003) concludes that caring for others is the single best predictor of subsequent care. It is even better than seeing others caring for someone (modeling, which is itself a powerful incentive for caring) or learning about caring. Our values do influence our behaviors, but it is equally true that behavior influences our values and attitudes. There are two factors at work when behavior influences values and attitudes. The first factor is our need for what psychologists call *cognitive consistency*. We like to experience that our behaviors and our values are consistent with one another. When we behave in a caring way, we examine our values to see if they support that caring behavior, and if they do not, we often adjust the values to match the behavior. Why did I volunteer to tutor kids in the local middle school two hours a week for the whole semester when I knew it would really cost me sleep time during midterms? It must be because I am a generous person. That means that the next time someone asks me for help, I will be more likely to give it because helping fits my sense of self. Thus, when we give ourselves opportunities to practice caring, we are increasing the likelihood we will come to understand ourselves as caring persons, we will value caring, and we will act. And this can be true even if the original motivation for the caring behavior is self-serving—for example, if you volunteer to tutor as part of a class requirement and get a grade for it.

The second factor has to do with what psychologists call *the-foot-in-the-door*. If we do something small for someone, we are more likely to do something more for them later, and then something even more than that. Think about offering to help friends pack up the dishes in their apartment when they are moving. Once you are there and the dishes are packed, they might ask you to do the glasses too, and once those are done, they might offer to order pizza for lunch and then ask you to stay to help move the furniture out. And you are more likely to do each additional task simply because you have done the one before. So, if you sign a petition about a cause, you are more likely to help obtain more signatures if you are asked, and then you are more likely to write a letter to your local representative and senators about the cause. Whistleblowers are a good example of how this escalation of commitment occurs. At a 2003 conference at Smith College for seven women whistleblowers, including Cathy Harris, someone asked the group if they had realized all that they would be required to do as the process of their resistance unfolded over months and years. The women all replied that they had not, and that each step they took gave them more skills and made them feel more competent and confident so that they could take the next step. It was the gradual escalation of the cost of the commitment that made their high level of commitment possible.

Opportunities to practice care can be built into the activities of many organizations. An organization's holiday giving program for the poor can be designed to benefit both the recipients and to give the donors the opportunity to practice caring for specific individuals, for example, by buying a coat for a thirteen-year-old girl named Rachel who likes red. This specificity of gift-giving promotes feelings of attachment to that specific recipient, even though the donor and the recipient will never meet, feelings of attachment that do not occur when gifts are designated for general groups, for example hats and mittens for preteenagers. If people volunteer to spend time with a specific disabled person, or to tutor a specific child, that feeling of attachment will be even stronger, and the volunteers will come to feel responsible for the person with whom they are working. This caring builds on itself, and the volunteers come to see themselves as the sorts of persons who care for those in need, and they are more likely to respond to a call for volunteers in the future. High schools and colleges recognize the value of these experiences in their community involvement programs that encourage students to commit to helping for the time period of a semester or more.

It is the most natural of human traits to like people who are like us. There is considerable evidence that we are attracted to people who look like us, who share our culture, our religion, our interests, and even those who come from our same neighborhood. We like people we see more often, even if we don't know who they are. So our second large task on our way to becoming more courageous is to increase the number of people and groups with whom we feel attached and for whom we feel responsible. Remember that we are trying to develop the pro-social attitudes and the networks that will provide us with the preconditions to be capable of becoming a courageous resistor. The following are suggestions on how we can increase our circle of care.

STEP 4: DIVERSIFYING

Diversifying, as the Oliners define it, "is a deliberate effort to connect with groups different from our own for the purpose of seeking mutual understanding. Deliberate means intentional rather than accidental, seeking out rather than being found, and connecting implies forming some type of personal relationship" (Oliner and Oliner 1995, 102–3).

We are more inclined to help members of our own family and to like those who are more familiar to us. An interesting addition to this finding is that we tend to respond to people who were present while we were growing up in much the same way as we respond to our relatives (Wells 1987). Oliner and Oliner (1988) report that rescuers said that as they were growing up, their families had close associations with more people who were of different religions and social classes than they were, compared to matched non-rescuers. This was associated with feeling more connected to a wide variety of people. Asked about their activities fifty years after the Holocaust, rescuers were still helping a greater variety of people and causes than were non-rescuers (Midlarsky and Nemeroff 1995).

So, our task is to increase the number of persons and groups with whom we are connected—to discover both shared and unique characteristics. We can choose to have actual experiences with others who are different, especially equal status experiences, working together on common goals. It is our choice whether we join clubs and social organizations where most of the people look like us and come from the same background, or ones where we make new connections. We should participate in activities that connect us in specific ways to people in different countries or from different environments.

For example, many student and community groups sent work parties to help in the cleanup and reconstruction after Hurricanes Katrina and Rita hit the southern coast of the United States in 2005. These people worked side by side with residents who often represented a community different from the helpers' communities. In another instance, Camp IF (short for interfaith) brings together Jewish, Christian, and Muslim teenagers from Massachusetts to get a personal understanding of religious differences and then asks them to meet throughout the year to work on projects. One camper, returning for his second year, said, "I don't look on this camp as this one little week in the summer that I'll look back on . . .

and say 'Gee that was great.' . . . This is more of a life lesson. I'm taking the values here and carrying them for the rest of my life" (Levenson 2006).

There is considerable evidence that we are all born with the capability to develop our caring capacity to include wider and wider circles of care, even eventually to include all those who suffer. There is much suffering in the world, and there are many opportunities to offer help to those people when they are included in our circles of care. Every day twenty thousand people in our world die from poverty. They lack adequate food, safe drinking water, or the simplest kinds of medical care. The following two campaigns are examples of many that are organized to address world poverty. U2 lead singer Bono helped launch ONE: The Campaign to Make Poverty History. The UN launched the Millennium Campaign to reduce poverty, child and maternal mortality, and to make primary education available to all. Both campaigns have ways in which you can help.[9] It is when we act to help those in our expanding circles of care that we begin to change both ourselves and the world.

STEP 5: NETWORKING

Throughout this book, you have read about people using their current networks or finding and cultivating new networks in order to resist the human rights abuses they saw happening. Every example we have used involved networks in important ways. Rarely is it even possible to practice courageous resistance alone, and it is always easier when we can call on the resources, services, and moral support of others. When Oliner and Oliner (1995) talk of networking in their book, *Toward a Caring Society*, they mean a deliberate effort to find such connections for effective action for a more caring world, and they use, as their model, many concepts that have come from the business world. They offer a series of steps for successful networking:

- Identify the stakeholders, and pick the ones with whom you have the most common goals. Stakeholders are the people who have influence in an organization and those who will be affected by your actions. They are the ones who care. Joseph Darby recognized that he would be more successful in stopping the prisoner abuse at Abu Ghraib if he gave those photos to the Criminal Investigation Division (CID) rather than to his superiors. The CID had special responsibilities, was not in the normal chain of command, and thus was not implicated in the problem.

- Recognize that the problem you are dealing with can best be solved by cooperating with other people or groups. Cathy Harris's stakeholder groups included the local press, civil rights groups, her congressional representative, and the Government Accountability Project (GAP) that assists whistleblowers. She even started her own group that allowed her to work with other whistleblowers and supporters in the U.S. Customs Service. When she went public with her evidence, she engaged all of these groups in her network.
- For networking to be successful, the stakeholders have to find a goal to which they can all commit themselves—a superordinate goal. This was discovered in a classic psychological experiment called The Robber's Cave, in which two groups of boys in a summer camp became hostile and prejudicial towards one another when they were encouraged to be competitive. When they had to cooperate to solve a crisis that affected both groups (a superordinate goal) they came to like one another. Their networking was successful (Sherif et al. 1961).
- Successful networking depends also on the ability of groups to be linked together, to communicate clearly and easily. This usually depends on what the Oliners call "boundary spanners," people who can carry communication between groups. The people of Old Providence, the Colombian island that successfully resisted development, had several "boundary spanners" who helped to connect them with each other and with helpful groups on the mainland. For example, Sandra Gomez, who had moved to the island from mainland Columbia, connected Dr. Fabio Londono, the attorney with expertise in indigenous rights, to the island's activists.
- Successful networking involves cooperation and mutual interdependence, a partnership rather than a hierarchical relationship. This means joint planning, reciprocity, good communication with the sharing of information, and acting as if the relationship will be long-term, rather than temporary. These characteristics maximize the sharing of resources. The activists of Old Providence were especially good at engaging and empowering as many of the people of the island as possible, setting up groups to study the constitution and to learn of their rights and making the local government transparent in its decision making.

So, we should not try to do it alone. We need to find our networks, make connections, and if necessary, make groups ourselves. We can bring together people who share our concerns and values and find our support there, paying attention to the strategies that make networking successful.

STEP 6: PRACTICING SKILLS

What keeps people from responding to an act of injustice or abuse is oftentimes less a lack of concern or compassion than a sense that there is nothing they can do. Studies have shown that a willingness to promote and defend human rights requires a belief that it is possible to improve our world and that an attitude of fatalism inhibits that willingness.[10] This difference is evident in the Rwandan Bishop Misago and Paul Rusesabagina. Bishop Misago felt helpless to save the eighty-two Tutsi children in his school, and he did nothing. Rusesabagina thought there was something he could do, even if he was not sure what it would be. He felt competent and responsible. In his case, he used the skills he had developed as a hotel manager: diplomacy, appeasement of the powerful, organization, and problem solving. And so, part of effective caring involves developing competencies and skills. These can include practical skills, such as construction skills we learn from building Habitat for Humanity houses, skills in talking with people in power, negotiating or conflict resolution, or social skills that help people to feel cared for, respected, and empowered to help themselves. We can also develop specific skills to help us to respond to social injustice: collecting data, web design, writing press releases or letters for Amnesty International, fundraising, and organizing events or demonstrations. Gene Sharp has a list of 198 nonviolent actions we can take that can be found on the web.[11] There is even a video game/simulation designed to teach effective use of nonviolent conflict, *A Force More Powerful*.[12] The more skills we have, the more positive responses we will have, the more empowered we will feel, and the more likely we are to feel responsible.[13]

Our social environments can support our caring norms and make them salient. Eva Fogelman, the author of a perceptive book about rescuers of Jews during the Holocaust, *Conscience and Courage* (1994), said in a personal conversation with author Sharon Shepela that she had joined the particular temple she attended in New York because it had a very active social justice program, and she wanted to be around people who cared about their neighbors and who defined those neighbors broadly. Surrounding ourselves with those who value caring norms—friends, communities, worshiping communities, even movies, books, and magazines[14]—makes those values salient to us and provides opportunities for us to practice them. The world is full of cynics. We have to choose those who have hope.

DECIDING TO BE COURAGEOUS:
LEAPING BARRIERS AT THE CROSSROADS

We may have worked on our attachments and developed skills and increased our circle of care, and still we will not be able to predict when we will exhibit courageous resistance and when we will not. The preconditions have to be present for courageous resistance to be possible, and the institutional supports have to be in place for courageous resistance to be successful, but people must still make the decision at each crossroad, and the steps of that decision are filled with hurdles. If we know what those hurdles are, we will be in a much better position to leap over them ourselves or to help other people get to the next step. This section is designed to point out the hurdles at the crossroads and to get us thinking of ways that we might get over or around them—because people do. All the courageous resistance we have read about in this book involves people and groups who eventually made it over or around every hurdle in their path. In contrast, the passive bystanders and perpetrators took different paths at the crossroads where courageous decisions could have been made.

It is in this transformation of courageous predispositions to courageous behavior where we think that the decision-making model proposed by Latane and Darley, explained in chapter 2, can be useful. Latane and Darley propose that there are five stages we all have to go through in order to act in an emergency. We have added to that to account for sustained courageous behavior over time. The stages are *noticing, interpreting* the situation as needing a response, *accepting* personal responsibility, *deciding* what to do, *taking action, and keeping on* and *reevaluating* your sense of self. Let's take the stages one at a time and see whether we can find the hurdles.

STAGE 1: NOTICING

How could we not notice a gross injustice that is happening in the world? We discussed earlier in these materials how the whole world was aware of the devastation caused by the tsunami in Southeast Asia, while few people knew of the genocide taking place in Darfur, Sudan at the same time. In that case, it was a situation of the media focusing on one dramatic event, while essentially ignoring the other. Some people say that they do not watch or listen to the news because it is too depressing, so it is possible to not notice what is happening even when it *is* being covered in the news if one deliberately turns away. This is *empathy avoidance*.

The political reality is that there are those who do not want us to notice, and so they give artful names to programs and policies that gut environmental protections or penalize the poor or favor the rich. They may distract us with other arguments. It may also be that we are totally absorbed in other problems and issues and are not paying attention. It takes an effort on our part to search out the truth. Connections with others who ask good questions and share information and hold up values in which we believe help us to do that. We must be willing to see that which makes us uncomfortable because it is that discomfort that will motivate us to move to the next step.

STAGE 2: INTERPRETING THE SITUATION AS NEEDING A RESPONSE

If we have noticed something, why might we not interpret it as needing a response? If we think the situation is just normal behavior, we will not think it needs a response. So if we think that some people have always been poor, or that it is their own fault, or if we think that racist or sexist or anti-Semitic or homophobic jokes are just funny, we will not think we need to intervene to change the situation. If we have been convinced that there is nothing to be done about a situation, if we have become hardened to someone's pain or even to our own, then we are not likely to think that a response is called for. If we do not have hope, we may give up.

How do we know when a response is needed? We can use the criterion of whether we would want to respond if this situation were happening to someone we loved dearly. Who is in our circle of care? We can use our networks and discuss and analyze and see what others think. We can question and look to see who is benefiting, who is suffering, and ask how the world will be different if this situation continues.

STAGE 3: ACCEPTING PERSONAL RESPONSIBILITY

In the real event that gave rise to Latane and Darley's work on bystander intervention, a woman named Kitty Genovese was attacked and stabbed multiple times over a half hour, while more than thirty of her neighbors heard her screams from the safety of their apartments in New York City. Not one of them even called for help until she was dead. Each of them thought that someone else surely had called. This is called *diffusion of responsibility,* and it happens in many situations. Psychologists will tell us that it is better to fall and sprain your ankle in front of one stranger than in front of ten because that one person will realize that he or she is the only one who can help you and will accept that responsibility.

To summarize, what are the circumstances in which we are more likely to accept responsibility? We can accept personal responsibility when we know we are the one person who can act in the situation, when we know that our response matters, when we are backed by a network that will support us, when we know that the institutional supports are in place and will be enforced, and when we have a sense of oneness with those who are suffering. It may seem that what we can do as an individual could not matter, but it does because each of us is part of a larger effort. Following the Rwandan genocide, Senator Paul Simon said, "If every member of the House and Senate had received one hundred letters from people back home saying we have to do something about Rwanda, when the crisis was first developing, then I think the response would have been different" (Kristof 2005).

Stage 4: Deciding What To Do

This is often the stopping point. We do not know what to do. Finding the addresses for one's local senators and representatives may seem a trivial hurdle, but it can stop someone who has never written or called their congressional representatives before. What if I do not know how to write a decent letter or have never spoken in public?

How could you get the information you need? Does a group you know have a template of a letter you could just sign? Political groups all along the spectrum of concern have gotten very sophisticated in getting people to act by removing the barriers to action. You noticed because they sent you an e-mail, told you it was critical, said that you could have an effect, and then made it easy for you to send a letter or sign a petition or send money. These were the networks that facilitated other people's courageous action. Groups and organizations have the information you need, the skills you do not have, and the experience and enthusiasm when yours lags. They will help you clarify your values and make your best values salient. We do not need to walk this path alone. Find a group, or, like Cathy Harris, invent a group.

Each action we take will make the next one easier. First we sign a petition, then we sign a letter, and then we can write our own letter, and then we can draft a letter that other people can sign. We learn by acting, and we develop skills that will enable us to learn even more skills. The important thing is to start where we are, to push our envelope just enough so that we can grow. The analogy of exercise is a good one here. Exercise physiologists tell us that if we want to build muscles we need to do micro-damage when we exercise. This means that we need to push ourselves just so it hurts a little. Do too much, and we do real damage that needs long repair time, and that discourages us. Do too little, and you never build more muscle than you had to begin with. With our courageous actions, we need to push our envelope of courage just enough to do micro-damage to our complacency.

Then when we come back, we will be stronger, and the next push will take us further.

STAGE 5: TAKING ACTION

Once we decide what to do, we have to follow through. It is a funny thing about human nature that sometimes when we have decided to do something, we stop. Sometimes it is because we realize the cost—in time or energy or danger—and we have to weigh those costs against the potential benefits. Sometimes there are other impediments specific to us, or to the situation. We need to become aware of what those impediments are so that we can strategize how to overcome them. We can lean on our networks and on our friends to push us into the action we have decided on. It helps to make a public commitment to action—telling people, signing up for a particular time, agreeing to pick other people up—because it is harder to break a public commitment than one we have made privately to ourselves. Compassion is not for sissies. It takes time and energy, and it helps to remember that we are not doing it for ourselves, but for other people who cannot do it by themselves or for a cause bigger than we are. Everything important takes effort, and the satisfaction that we get from a hard job well done for a good cause is our reward. Two and a half years after he turned in the pictures of prisoner abuse at Abu Ghraib prison in Iraq, during which time he and his wife had been in a military witness protection program because his life had been threatened by people in his home town, Joseph Darby said, "I don't regret any of it. I made my peace with my decision before I turned the pictures in" (Hylton 2006).

STAGE 6: KEEPING ON KEEPING ON AND REEVALUATING OURSELVES

Persistence is difficult, especially when there is resistance and drudgery, or when people fight back, or your family protests your absence, or you get tired and you do not succeed. Marion Wright Edelman, president of the Children's Defense Fund, broke down and wept at a lecture she was giving in Hartford, Connecticut, because she had just come from a congressional session in which a bill to protect children, on which she had worked for over a year, had been watered down to the point that it was practically useless, so that it would pass a vote in the House of Representatives. She pulled herself together and said that she would have to go on because the children depended on her, and every step, however small, was necessary. She was resilient and determined and she made the decision to stay the course. Most of the examples in this book are of people who, over and over, made the decision to persist in their courageous resistance.

This can be hard, and we have to call on the values that led us to resist in the first place and call on our friends and networks, and we need to be sure that we are taking care of ourselves so that we do not burn out. It is important to understand what we need to do to care for ourselves and to make the time to do that. It could be going for a quiet walk or going dancing, whatever charges our batteries.

This last stage in our model also includes personal reassessment and is part of the model to account for the evolution of commitment to courageous resistance. Courageous actors sometimes decide to stop after they have completed their courageous task and sometimes decide to dive back in with more commitment, or commitment to an expanded or different goal. The Madres (Mothers) of Plaza de Mayo began to march to protest the disappearance of their children. As they continued these demonstrations, they developed a concern for universal human rights and later offered sophisticated political analysis to justify not accepting compensation from the new democratically elected government (Bouvard 1993).

This reevaluation of the self comes when we see ourselves as having changed because of our action. Fogelman calls this new self-image the "rescuer self" (Fogelman 1994). Staub says that when people behave in even a limited courageous way, they come to see themselves as courageous people, as "heroic helpers," and it is from this new base of self-image that they decide on future actions (Staub 1993). So, courageous behavior can change who we are, at least who we think we are, and that can change our life. It is not guaranteed, it may not be life-altering, but if Staub is right, just starting to work for justice, for others who need our help, will make us think of ourselves in a different way, a self-assessment that can help us to make courageous decisions in the future.

PRACTICAL REFLECTIONS AND CHALLENGES FOR THE SIX STEPS TO TRANSFORMING OURSELVES

STEP 1: BONDING

Reflection

Do you have a place or a group or organization toward which you feel a strong attachment—one that has played a really important role in your life? Imagine that you just learned that it was about to be destroyed or closed. How would you feel? Would you spend time and energy to try to save it?

Challenge

An environmental group is trying to get the responsible company to clean up a toxic waste dump that is polluting the groundwater near your neighborhood at home. Your little sister has been diagnosed with a cancer that her doctors think may have been caused by this dump. Other children you know have been exposed. The group has approached you and some of your friends to commit to work with them a specific number of hours a week, starting now. Are you willing to commit yourself? What kind of actions would you be willing to take?

STEP 2: PRACTICING EMPATHY

Reflection

Think of a topic on which you feel strongly and with which you really disagree with some other people. Make a list of your feelings when you think of having a discussion (or an argument) with them about this topic. Try to be as specific and as honest as you can. For example, when someone says that people on welfare are lazy, I feel angry because my Aunt Millie had to go on welfare when my uncle died, and I know that she worked very hard to support her family and got off welfare in less than a year. Do this for several points that are likely to come up and for the feelings associated with them. Then try to put yourself in the position of the person having the discussion or argument with you, and make a comparable list. Do this with a group of friends, and give each other feedback on how well you put yourself in the other person's shoes and how well you articulated your own feelings.

Challenge

We encourage you to seek out the opportunity to work as an ally with a group that is different from your own, one that is struggling against an injustice. Are you heterosexual? You might work with a gay, lesbian, bisexual, transgender advocacy group. Are you white Anglo? Pick a Black or Hispanic group. Are you middle class? Work with poor people on their issues. An ally is not there to take over or to solve someone else's problems, but rather to work with the group, to help them in ways the group decides. This might make you uncomfortable at first, but discomfort is a good motivation for change. Watch how your attitudes toward that group evolve. Notice changes that occur in your understanding of their situation. Does your empathy change?

STEP 3: PRACTICING CARE

Reflection

We often have caring skills we do not recognize that could be used for courageous resistance. Think of an incident in which you made a considerable effort to help someone, and it worked. What skills did you use then? How could you build on those skills to make them even more effective? What other skills would you like to develop?

Challenge

Imagine the following scenario: Residents of Joseph Darby's hometown are meeting in anger over his actions. They believe he was unpatriotic in choosing to look out for the rights of Iraqis over American soldiers. You attend the meeting and decide to speak on his behalf. What would you say? How would you frame the argument if you were to speak before the community group upset about his actions?

STEP 4: DIVERSIFYING

Reflection

Consider ways you could identify yourself—by gender, race, religion, sexual orientation, age, ableism, social class, political affiliation, major activities, significant skills, and interests. How many people different from you on these dimensions do you know well enough to know important things about their lives? How could you increase your circle?

Challenge

Start where you are. Look at the course guide at your school for next semester, and see what classes you could sign up for that would expand your knowledge of people and areas you know little about. You might start with history, political science, art and music of other cultures, gender studies, or religious studies. Look at cultural events that highlight social groups new to you or clubs that work in your community with groups different from yours. Then follow through—sign up for a course; join a club.

Step 5: Networking

Reflection

This section describes six criteria of successful networking. We have shown you how the people of Old Providence met two of those criteria. Go back to chapter 5, and see whether you can identify which of the other criteria they met.

Challenge

Look at the Challenge section in Step 6. How would you find groups or individuals with whom to network as you respond to this injustice? Use the suggestions for successful networking to plan your response. Who are the stakeholders? Who might be the boundary spanners? Take each step and identify how you would network successfully.

Step 6: Practicing Skills

Reflection

What practical skills and competencies do you have now that you have been able to use to help others? What were the particular circumstances where those skills came in handy?

Challenge

For this group project, consider the following scenario: In the last three weeks in your community, posters for a lecture of a prominent Muslim imam have been torn down, and someone spray painted a hate message on the wall of the local mosque. Several young Muslim girls have been taunted and have had their head scarves pulled off as they walked to school. Strategize what your group could do in response to these acts. Be very specific. What are your goals? One might be to bring as many people as possible in the community to care about these incidents and to want to have them stop. With what groups could you network? How could you help each other? Make a timeline, and then list all the tasks that need to be done and what skills are needed. Will you organize a protest? How will you get the information out? Will you write letters to the editor of the local paper? Will you organize churches to take symbolic or practical action?

We can intervene and, in so doing, begin to change the world. This is the adventure to which we are invited. It is an adventure that ordinary people like us have been taking, one that is helping to make the world a better place. As we quoted from the Syracuse Cultural Workers at the beginning of this section, "Always hold firmly to the thought that each one of us can do something to bring some portion of misery to an end."

NOTES

1. Syracuse Cultural Workers is a peace and justice publishing company. You may learn more about them at http://www.syrculturalworkers.com.
2. Adler represents the analytic approach and Maslow, the humanistic approach to understanding human personality. There are other approaches that do not talk about the concern for others as part of our core personality (Adler 1954; Adler 1964; and Maslow 1954).
3. Ervin Staub may serve as an example for his own theory here. Because of his research on genocide and its prevention, he was invited to Rwanda and, since 1998, has been conducting both research and practical projects there to promote healing and reconciliation in the aftermath of the genocide. In the wake of that effort, Staub accepted an invitation to go to New Orleans soon after the hurricane devastated that city. He helped a community organization develop training programs for both community members and leaders to help heal racial tensions and promote reconciliation, which is now widely used.
4. This list and much of the supporting data and arguments come from Oliner and Oliner 1995.
5. It is important to note that attachment does not always lead to increasing inclusiveness of caring. A problem may arise when our attachment to a local group becomes so focused that it either makes us think that these are the only people for whom we have any responsibility, or it encourages viewing outsiders as enemies.
6. Binur 1989.
7. A movie entitled *Joyeux Noel*, released in the United States in 2005, dramatized this event.
8. The entire discussion that follows is based on Eksteins 1989.
9. The ONE campaign can be found at http://www.one.org. The Millennium Campaign is at http://www.millenniumcampaign.org.
10. Chiu and colleagues (1997) found that individuals with a fatalistic view, who agree with statements such as "Our world has its basic and ingrained dispositions, and you really can't do much to change it," (925) tend to hold a "duty-based morality" and to view morality mainly as loyalty to one's duties. Those who disagree with such statements, who see the world as improvable through human effort, are more likely to hold a "rights-based

morality" and to believe that morality consists of promoting the principles of justice and human rights (923). Those with a fixed view are prone to see violations of social norms as worse than violations of individual rights; those with a malleable worldview see the latter violations as worse. McFarland and Mathews (2005) found that non-fatalists, those who disagreed with statements like that above, were more willing to commit American resources and troops to defend human rights around the world (305–19).

11. This booklet may be downloaded without charge from the Web site http://www.aeinstein.org (Sharp 2003).

12. The video game/simulation is available from the Web site http://www.AFMP.com[0].

13. A student in a course on courageous behavior taught by one of this book's authors sent a note soon after the course ended, saying that she had learned both the value of networks and the practical skill of networking in the completion of her course project. She then reported that she had used those skills to organize a fund-raiser for a family in need in her town and was planning a second one because of her success.

14. *Yes!*, *Ode*, and *The Other Side* are all magazines that focus on social justice actions. Look for others.

Reference List

Ackerman, Peter, and Jack Duvall. 2000. *A force more powerful: A century of non-violent conflict.* New York: St. Martin's.

ACLU. 2005. Newly released army documents point to agreement between defense department and CIA on "ghost" detainees, ACLU says. March 10, 2005. http://www.aclu.org/safefree/general/17597prs20050310.html (accessed May 4, 2007).

Adler, Alfred. 1954. *Understanding human nature.* Trans. Walter B. Wolfe. New York: Fawcett Publications. (Orig. pub. 1927; *Menschenkenntnis* [Zürich: Rascher]; first English ed. pub. 1927 [New York: Greenberg]).

———. 1964. *Problems of neurosis.* New York: Harper Torchbooks. Trans. Philip Mairet. (Orig. pub. 1929 [London: K. Paul, Trench, Trubner]).

Altemeyer, Robert W. 1996. *The authoritarian specter.* Cambridge, MA: Harvard University Press.

Amnesty International. 2005. Report 2005. http://web.amnesty.org/report2005/index-eng (accessed May 25, 2005).

Anna (pseudonym). 1992. Interview by Kristina Thalhammer, Tape recording. October 19. Buenos Aires, Argentina.

Andersen, Martin Edwin. 1993. *Dossier secreto: Argentina's desaparecidos and the myth of the "Dirty War."* Boulder, CO: Westview.

———. 2002. Harry Bingham: Profile in courage. *Insight on the News,* July 22, 2002. http://www.insightmag.com/ME2/Default/asp (accessed March 31, 2007).

Annan, Kofi. 2005. In larger freedom: Toward development, security and human rights for all. http://www.un.org/largerfreedom/ (accessed May 4, 2007).

Arendt, Hannah. 1963. *Eichmann in Jerusalem.* Repr., New York: Penguin, 1992.

Arenas, Rafael. 2003. Interview by Kristina Thalhammer. Tape recording. January 29. Sweetwater Bay, Old Providence, Colombia.

Asch, Solomon. 1956. Studies of independence and conformity: A minority of one against a unanimous majority. *Psychological Monographs* 70 (9): 1–70.

Batson, C. Daniel, David A. Lishner, Amy Carpenter, Luis Dulin, Sanna Harjusola-Webb, E. L. Stocks, Shawna Gale, Omar Hassan, and Brenda Sampat. 2003.

As you would have them do unto you: Does imagining yourself in the other's place stimulate moral action? *Personality and Social Psychology Bulletin* 29 (9): 1190–201.

Becker, Maki. 2004. Soldier who revealed abuse at prison stands for what he believes in. *Knight Ridder/Tribune News Service*, May 19.

Benenson, Peter. 1961. The forgotten prisoners. *London Observer*, May 28.

Bessel, Richard. 1997. Snatched from the jaws. *Times Literary Supplement*, May 16.

Bierman, John. 1981. *Righteous gentile: The story of Raoul Wallenberg, missing hero of the Holocaust.* New York: Viking.

Binur, Yoram. 1989. *My enemy, my self.* New York: Doubleday.

Borwn, Norvel Walter. 2003. Interview by Kristina Thalhammer. Tape recording. January 22. Bottom House, Old Providence, Colombia.

Bouvard, Marguerite. 1994. *Revolutionizing Motherhood: The Mothers of the Plaza de Mayo.* Wilmington, DE: SR Books.

Bowlby, John. 1969. *Attachment and Loss: vol. 1 Attachment.* London: Hogarth.

Browning, Christopher R. 1992. *Ordinary men: Reserve police battalion 101 and the final solution in Poland.* New York: HarperCollins.

Brysk, Allison. 1994. *The politics of human rights in Argentina: Protest, change and democratization.* Stanford, CA: Stanford University Press.

Buchanan, Tom. 2000. "'The truth shall make you free'": The making of Amnesty International. *Journal of Contemporary History* 37:575-97.

Büttner, Ursula. 1988. *Die Not der Juden teilen: Christlich-jüdische familien im Dritten Reich.* Hamburg: Hans Christians Verlag.

Carnahan, Thomas, and Sam McFarland. 2007a. Let's go directly to jail! Personality and volunteering for a "psychological study of prison life." *Personality and Social Psychology Bulletin* (February), http://www.chass.utoronto.ca/~josephf/Pspbrevs2.doc (accessed May 4, 2007).

———. 2007b. Revisiting the Stanford Prison Experiment: Could participant self-selection have led to the cruelty? *Personality and Social Psychology Bulletin* 33:603–14.

CBC News. 2003. Indepth: Romeo Dallaire. October 24. http://www.cbc.ca/news/background/dallaire (accessed March 9, 2005).

Chiu, Chi-yue, Dweck, Carol S., Tong, Jennifer Yuk-yue, & Fu, Jeanne Ho-ying. (1997). Implicit theories and conceptions of morality. *Journal of Personality and Social Psychology* 73, 923-940.

Clark, Ann Marie. 2001. *Diplomacy of conscience: Amnesty International and changing human rights norms.* Princeton, NJ: Princeton University Press.

CONADEP. 1986. *Nunca mas never again: A report by Argentina's national commission on disappeared people.* New York: Farrar, Straus and Giroux.

Conference for Security and Co-operation in Europe. 1975. Helsinki Final Act. August 1, 1975. http://www.hri.org/docs/Helsinki75.html (accessed November 20, 2005).

Constitucion política de la Republica de Colombia. 1996. Ministerio de Justicia y del Derecho, Bogota.Cowell, Alan. 2005. U.S. "thumbs its nose" at rights, Amnesty says. *New York Times*, May 26.

Dallaire, Roméo A. 2003. *Shake hands with the Devil: The failure of humanity in Rwanda.* Toronto: Random House Canada.

———. 2005. Letter to the editor. *New York Times,* August 30.

Daniel (pseudonym). 1993. Interview by Kristina Thalhammer, Tape recording. April 12. Buenos Aires, Argentina.

Danner, Mark. 2004. Abu Ghraib: The hidden story. *New York Review of Books* (October 7, 2004): 44–49.

Darby, Joseph. 2006. Interview by Sharon Toffey Shepela. Telephone interview and tape recording. September 20. Hartford, CT.

Darley, John M., and Bibb Latane. 1968. Bystander intervention in emergencies: Diffusion of responsibility. *Journal of Personality and Social Psychology* 10:202–14.

Donnelly, Jack. 2003. *Universal human rights in theory and practice.* 2nd ed. Ithaca, NY: Cornell University Press.

Drum, Kevin. 2004. Political animal. *Washington Monthly,* May 17. http://www.washingtonmonthly.com/archives/individual/2004_05/003946.php (accessed May 4, 2007).

Eksteins, Modris. 1989. *Rites of spring: The great war and the birth of the modern age.* Boston: Houghton Mifflin.

Ellison, Sharon. 2002. *Taking the war out of our words: The art of powerful, non-defensive communication.* Berkeley, CA: Bay Tree.

Erkut, Sumru, Daniel S. Jaquette, Ervin Staub. 1981. Moral judgment-situation interaction as a basis for predicting prosocial behavior. *Journal of Personality* 49 (1): 1–14.

Evans, Richard J. 1996. Wives against the Nazis. *The Sunday Telegraph,* November 17.

Fisher, Jo. 1989. *Mothers of the Disappeared.* Boston: South End Press.

Fogelman, Eva. 1994. *Conscience and Courage: Rescuers of Jews during the Holocaust.* New York: Anchor Books Doubleday.

Frank, Anne. 1952. *The diary of a young girl.* 1st ed. Garden City, NY: Doubleday.

Froelich, Elke, ed. 1993. *Die Tagebuecher von Joseph Goebbels.* Vol. 7. Munich: K.G. Saur Verlag.

Fry, Varian. 1997. *Surrender on Demand.* Boulder, CO: Johnson Books.

Gamson, William A. 1995. Constructing social protest. In *Social movements and culture,* ed. Hank Johnston and Bert Klandermans, 85–106. Minneapolis: University of Minnesota Press.

Geisler, Astrid, and Felix Lee. Nazis müssen auf der Stelle tretten. *Die Tageszeitung,* May 9, 2005, 3. http://www.taz.de/pt/2005/05/09/a0177.1/text (accessed April 4, 2007).

Glazer, Myron Peretz, and Penina Migdal Glazer. 1989. *The whistleblowers: Exposing corruption in government and industry.* New York: Basic Books.

Glazer, Penina Migdal, and Myron Peretz Glazer. 1998. *The environmental crusaders: Confronting disaster and mobilizing community.* University Park: Pennsylvania State University Press.

————. 2004. *The Jews of Paradise: Creating a vibrant community in Northampton.* Northampton, MA: 350th Anniversary Committee of the City of Northampton.

Gomez, Sandra. 2003. Interview by Kristina Thalhammer. Tape recording. January 25. Sweetwater Bay, Old Providence, Colombia.

Glamour. 2000. Watch-worthy women: Female forces to watch. March 2000, 178.

Glendon, Mary Ann. 2001. *A world made new: Eleanor Roosevelt and the Universal Declaration of Human Rights.* New York: Random House.

Gottfredson, Michael R., and Travis Hirschi. 1990. *A general theory of crime.* Stanford, CA: Stanford University Press.

Gourevitch, Philip. 1998. *We wish to inform you that tomorrow we will be killed with our families: Stories from Rwanda.* New York: Farrar, Straus, and Giroux.

Gross, Jan T. 2001. *Neighbors: The destruction of the Jewish community in Jedwabne, Poland.* Princeton, NJ: Princeton University Press.

Gross, Michael L. 1994. Jewish rescue in Holland and France during the Second World War: Moral cognition and collective action. *Social Forces* 73 (2): 463–96.

Gutterer, Leopold. 1986–1987. Interviews by Nathan Stoltzfus. Tape recording. August 17 and 19, 1986, July 16, 1987. Aachen, Germany.

Haffner, Sebastian. 2002. *Defying Hitler: A memoir.* Trans. Oliver Pretzel. New York: Farrar, Straus, and Giroux.

Hallie, Philip. 1979. *Lest innocent blood be shed: The story of the village of Le Chambon and how goodness happened there.* New York: Harper and Row.

————. 1986. Major Julius Schmahling. In *The courage to care: Rescuers of Jews during the Holocaust,* ed. Sondra Rittner and Carol Meyers, 108–115. New York: New York University Press.

Haritos-Fatorouris, Mika. 1988. The official torturer. *Journal of Applied Social Psychology* 18:1107–20.

Harris, Cathy. 2000. *Flying While Black: A Whistleblower's Story.* Los Angeles: Milligan Books.

Hawkins, Richard. 2003. Interview by Kristina Thalhammer. Tape Recording. January 22. Southwest Bay, Old Providence, Colombia.

Henry, Patrick. 2002. Banishing the coercion of despair. *Shofar: An Interdisciplinary Journal of Jewish Studies* 20 (2): 69–85.

Hersh, Seymour. 2004. Torture at Abu Ghraib. *New Yorker* 80 (11): 42–47.

Hilberg, Raul. 1985. *The Destruction of the European Jews.* New York: Holmes and Meier.

Holzer Elsa. 1987. Interview by Nathan Stoltzfus. Tape recording. July 16. Berlin, Germany.

Huffington, Josefina. 2003. Interview by Kristina Thalhammer. January 16. Sweetwater Bay, Old Providence, Colombia.

Huggins, Martha. 2000. Legacies of authoritarianism: Brazilian torturers' and murderers' reformation of memory. *Latin American Perspectives* 27:57–78.

Huggins, Martha, Mika Haritos-Fatouros, and Philip Zimbardo. 2002. *Violence workers: Police torturers and murderers reconstruct Brazilian atrocities.* Berkeley: University of California Press.

Human Rights Watch. 1999. Leave none to tell the story: Genocide in Rwanda. http://www.hrw.org/reports/1999/rwanda/ (accessed November 9, 2005).

———. 2004. The road to Abu Ghraib. http://www.hrw.org/reports/2004/usa0604 (accessed May 26, 2005).

Hurst, Hannum. 1995–1996. The status of the Universal Declaration of Human Rights in national and international law. *Georgia Journal of International and Comparative Law* 25 (1–2): 289.

Hylton, Wil S. 2006. Prisoner of conscience. *Gentlemen's Quarterly* (September). http://men.style.com/gq/features/full?id=content_4785 (accessed October 2, 2006).

Inskeep, Steve. 2004. Profile: Joseph Darby's politeness and how he handles controversy. *Morning Edition, National Public Radio (NPR)*, May 7.

International Commission on Intervention and State Sovereignty. 2001. *The responsibility to protect.* Ottawa: International Development Research Centre.

Isenberg, Sheila. 2001. *A hero of our own: The story of Varian Fry.* New York: Random House.

Jenni, Karen, and George Loewenstein. 1997. Explaining the identifiable victim effect. *Journal of Risk and Uncertainty* 14 (3): 235–57.

Keck, Margaret E., and Kathryn Sikkink. 1998. *Activists beyond borders: Advocacy networks in international politics.* Ithaca, NY: Cornell University Press.

Kelman, Herbert C., and V. Lee Hamilton. 1989. *Crimes of obedience: Toward a social psychology of authority and responsibility.* New Haven, CT: Yale University Press.

King, Martin Luther, Jr. 1999. Letter from a Birmingham jail. In *Ideals and ideology: A reader*, ed. T. Ball and R. Dagger, 360–70. New York: Longman.

Klandermans, Bert. 1997. *The social psychology of protest.* Cambridge, MA: Blackwell.

Kressel, Neil J. 2002. *Mass hate: The global rise of genocide and terror.* New York: Plenum.

Kristof, Nicholas. 2005. The secret genocide archive. *New York Times*, February 23.

———. 2006. Helping Bill O'Reilly. *New York Times*, February 7.

Kuhn, Rita. 1989. Interview by Nathan Stoltzfus. Taperecording. April 26. Berkeley, CA.

Latane, Bibb, and John M. Darley. 1970. *The unresponsive bystander: Why doesn't he help?* New York: Appleton-Century-Crofts.

Lauren, Paul Gordon. 2003. *The Evolution of International Human Rights: Visions Seen.* 2nd ed. Philadelphia: University of Pennsylvania Press.

Lemkin, Raphael. 1944. *Axis rule in occupied Europe: Laws of occupation, analysis of government, proposals for redress.* Washington, DC: Carnegie Endowment for International Peace.

Leugers, Antonia, ed. 2005. *Berlin, Rosenstrasse 2–4: Protest in der NS-Diktatur: Neue Forschungen zum Frauenprotest in der Rosenstrasse 1943.* Annweiler: Ploeger.

Levenson, Michael. 2006. Religious differences unite campers. *Boston Globe*, August 21, p. A1.

Levine, Hillel. 1996. *In search of Sugihara*. New York: Free Press.

Maier-Katkin, Brigit, and Daniel Maier-Katkin. 2004. At the heart of darkness: Crimes against humanity and the banality of evil. *Human Rights Quarterly* 26 (August): 584–604.

Maslow, Abraham H. 1954. *Motivation and personality*. New York: Harper and Row.

McAdam, Doug, and Ronnelle Paulsen. 1993. Specifying the relationship between social ties and activism. *American Journal of Sociology* 99 (November): 640–67.

McDonnell, Patrick J. 2006. The world, Pinochet loses immunity in abuse case. *Los Angeles Times*, January 21, p. A3.

McFarland, Sam, and Melissa Matthews. 2005. Who cares about human rights? *Political Psychology* 26:365–85.

Medoff, Rafael, and Dov Fischer. 2003. Their father was an unsung hero of the Holocaust. *Norwich (Conn.) Bulletin*, June 15.

Meyer, Norma. 2005. Film shows how one man saved Rwandans from certain death. *Copley News Service*, January 2, http://www.signonsandiego.com/news/features/20050102-9999-m1a2rwanda.html (accessed April 4, 2007).

Michalczyk, John J., ed. 2004. *Confronting resistance in Nazi Germany*. New York: Peter Lang.

Midlarsky, Elizabeth, Stephanie F. Jones, and Robin P. Corley. 2005. Personality correlates of heroic rescue during the Holocaust. *Journal of Personality* 73 (August): 907–34.

Midlarsky, E., and R. Nemeroff. 1995. *Heroes of the Holocaust: Predictors of their well-being in later life*. Poster presented at the American Psychological Society meetings, New York. Cited in D. T. Kenrick, S. L. Neuberg, and R. B. Cialdini. 2005. *Social psychology: Unraveling the mystery*. Boston: Pearson Allyn and Bacon.

Milgram, Stanley. 1965. Some conditions of obedience and disobedience to authority. *Human Relations* 18 (1): 57–76.

———. 1974. *Obedience to authority*. New York: Harper and Row.

Monroe, Kristen Renwick, Michael C. Barton, Ute Klingemann. 1990. Altruism and the theory of rational action: Rescuers of Jews in Nazi Europe. *Ethics* 101 (1): 103–22.

Monroe, Kristen Renwick. 1991. John Donne's people: Explaining differences between rational actors and altruists through cognitive frameworks. *Journal of Politics* 53 (2): 394–433.

———. 1994. A fat lady in a corset: Altruism and social theory. *American Journal of Political Science* 38 (4): 861–93.

———. 1996. *The heart of altruism: Perceptions of a common humanity*. Princeton, NJ: Princeton University Press.

Montgomery, Bruce. 2002. The human rights watch archives. *Peace Review* 14:455–63.

Morsink, Johannes. 1999. *The Universal Declaration of Human Rights: Origins, drafting, and intent.* Philadelphia: University of Pennsylvania Press.

Neuffer, Elizabeth. 2001. *The key to my neighbor's house: Seeking justice in Bosnia and Rwanda.* New York: Picador.

Noelle-Neumann, Elizabeth. 1984. *The spiral of silence: Public opinion—Our social skin.* Chicago: University of Chicago Press.

Oliner, Samuel P., and Pearl M. Oliner. 1988. *The altruistic personality: Rescuers of Jews in Nazi Europe.* New York: Free Press.

Oliner, Pearl M., Samuel P. Oliner, Baron Lawrence, Lawrence A. Blum, Dennis Krebs, and M. Zuzanna Smolenska., eds. 1992. *Embracing the other: Philosophical, psychological, and historical perspectives on altruism.* New York: New York University Press.

Oliner, Pearl and Samuel P. Oliner. 1995. *Toward a caring society: ideas into action.* Westport, CT: Praeger.

Oxfam. 2005. Oxfam welcomes historic anti-genocide move at UN summit. 14 Sept., http://www.oxfam.org.uk/press/releases/unsummit140905.htm?search term=UN%20summit (accessed May 4, 2007).

Peace Media Service. 1992–1993. Germans protest neo-nazism. Repr., in *Albert Einstein Institution Newsletter* 4 (3): 4, aeinstein.org/organizations/org/13_winter92_93-1.pdf (accessed May 4, 2007).

Power, Samantha. 2002. *A Problem from Hell: America and the Age of Genocide.* New York: Basic Books.

Priest, Dana. 2005. CIA's assurances on transferred suspects doubted: Prisoners say countries break no-torture pledges. *Washington Post,* March 17, p. A01.

Putnam, Robert D. 2000. *Making democracy work: Civic traditions in modern Italy.* Princeton, NJ: Princeton University Press.

Rachman, Stanley. 1990. *Fear and courage.* New York: W. H. Freeman.

Rafshoon, Ellen. 2002. Harry Bingham: Beyond the call of duty. *Foreign Service Journal* 79 (6): 16–25.

Reid, T. R. 2005. Trial starts in Abu Ghraib death. *Washington Post, May* 25, p. A2.

Risse, Thomas, Stephen Ropp, and Kathryn Sikkink, eds. 1999. *The power of human rights: International norms and domestic change.* Cambridge: Cambridge University Press.

Rittner, Sondra, and Carol Meyers, eds. 1986. *The courage to care: Rescuers of Jews during the Holocaust.* New York: New York University Press.

Robertson, Arthur Henry, and John Graham Merrills. 1996. *Human rights in the world.* Manchester, England: Manchester University Press.

Robertson, Geoffrey. 2000. *Crimes against humanity.* New York: New Press.

Roby, Pamela Ann. 1998. Creating a just world: Leadership for the twenty-first century. *Social Problems* 45 (February): 2–3.

Rosenberg, Marshall. 2000. *Nonviolent communication.* Encinitas, CA: Puddle Dancer.

Rosin, Hannah. 2004. When Joseph comes marching home. *Washington Post,* May 17, p. C10.

Ruddick, Sara. 1989. Mothers and men's wars. In *Rocking the ship of state*, ed. A. Harris and Y. King, 75–92. Boulder, CO: Westview.

Rusesabagina, Paul, and Tom Zoellner. 2006. *An ordinary man: An autobiography*. New York: Penguin.

Ryan, Donna F. 1996. *The Holocaust and the Jews of Marseilles*. Urbana: University of Illinois Press.

Sanchez, Domingo. 2003. Interview by Kristina Thalhammer. Tape recording. January 29. San Isabel, Old Providence, Colombia.

Sauvage, Pierre. 1988. *Weapons of the spirit*. VHS. New York: First Run/Icarus Films.

Schelling, Thomas. 1968. The life you save may be your own. In *Problems in public expenditure analysis*, ed. S. B. Chase, 127–62. Washington DC: The Brookings Institute.

Secrecy News. 2004. Honoring Joseph Darby. In *FAS Project on Government Secrecy* 2004 (89), http://www.fas.org/sgp/news/secrecy/2004/10/101204.html (accessed May 26, 2005).

Sharp, Gene. 2003. *There are realistic alternatives*. Boston: The Albert Einstein Institution.

Shaw, Laura L., C. Daniel Batson, and R. Matthew Todd. 1994. Empathy avoidance: Forestalling feeling for another in order to escape the motivational consequences. *Journal of Personality and Social Psychology* 67:879–87.

Shepela, Sharon Toffey, Jennifer Cook, Elizabeth Horlitz, Robin Leal, Sandra Luciano, Elizabeth Lutfy, Carolyn Miller, Grace Mitchell, and Emily Worden. 1999. Courageous resistance: A special case of altruism. *Theory and Psychology* 9 (6): 787–806.

Sherif, M., O. Harvey, B. White, W. Hood, and C. Sherif. 1961. *Intergroup conflict and cooperation: The robber's cave experiment*. Norman: University of Oklahoma Institute of Group Relations.

Sikkink, Kathryn. 1993. Human rights, principled issue networks, and sovereignty in Latin America. *International Organization* 47 (3): 411–41.

Sikkink, Kathryn, and Ellen L. Lutz. 2000. International human rights law and practice in Latin America. *International Organization* 54 (3): 633–59.

Slevin, Peter. 2002. At state, giving dissent its due. *Washington Post*, June 28.

Small, Deborah, and George Lowenthal. 2003. Helping a victim or helping the victim. *Journal of Risk and Uncertainty* 26:1, 5–16.

Smith, Jeffrey R., and Josh White. 2005. Soldier who reported abuse was sent to psychiatrist. *Washington Post, March* 5, p. A15.

Snitow, Ann. 1989. A gender diary. In *Rocking the ship of state*, ed. A. Harris and Y. King, 35–73. Boulder, CO: Westview.

Staub, Ervin. 1974. Helping a distressed person: Social, personality, and stimulus determinants. In *Advances in experimental social psychology*, vol. 7, ed. L. Berkowitz, 293–341. New York: Academic Press.

———. 1989. *Roots of evil: The origins of genocide and other group violence*. Cambridge: Cambridge University Press.

———. 1991. Psychological and cultural origins of extreme destructiveness and extreme altruism. In *Handbook of moral behavior and development*, vol. 3, ed. W. M. Kurtines and J. L. Gewirtz, 425–46. Hillsdale, NJ: Lawrence Erlbaum Associates.

———. 1993. The psychology of bystanders, perpetrators, and heroic helpers. *International Journal of Intercultural Relations* 17:315–41.

———. 2003. *The psychology of good evil: Why children, adults, and groups help and harm others.* Cambridge: Cambridge University Press.

Stenner, Karen Lee. 2005. *The authoritarian dynamic.* Cambridge University Press.

Stoltzfus, Nathan. 1992. Dissent in Nazi Germany. *The Atlantic* 270 (3): 86–94.

———. 1996. *Resistance of the heart: Intermarriage and the Rosenstrasse protest in Nazi Germany.* New York: W. W. Norton.

Taguba report. June 6, 2003, http://www.publicintegrity.org/docs/AbuGhraib/Taguba_Report.pdf. (accessed May 26, 2005).

Task Force on the United Nations, Newt Gingrich and George J. Mitchell, Co-chairs. United States Institute of Peace. June 2005. American interests and UN reform. Washington: Endowment for the United States Institute of Peace. http://www.usip.org/un/report (accessed May 4, 2007).

Taylor, Shelley E., Laura Cousino Klein, Brian P. Lewis, Tara L. Gruenewald, Regan A. R. Gurung, and John A. Updegraff. 2000. Biobehavioral responses to stress in females: Tend-and-befriend, not fight-or-flight. *Psychology Review* 107 (July): 411–29.

Tec, Nechama. 1983. Righteous Christians in Poland. *International Social Science Review* 58 (Winter): 12–19.

Thalhammer, Kristina. 2001. I'll take the high road: Two pathways to altruistic political mobilization against regime repression in Argentina. *Political Psychology* 22 (3): 493–519.

United Nations. 1942. Declaration by the United Nations, January 1, 1942. http://www.yale.edu/lawweb/avalon/decade/decade03.htm (accessed March 3, 2007).

———. 1945. Charter of the United Nations. http://www.un.org/aboutun/charter/index.html (accessed March 31, 2007).

———. 1948a. Convention on the prevention and punishment of the crime of genocide. http://www.hrweb.org/legal/genocide.html (accessed March 31, 2007).

———. 1948b. Universal declaration of human rights. http://www.un.org/Overview/rights.html (accessed March 31, 2007).

———. 1998. Rome statute for the international criminal court. http://www.un.org/law/icc/ (accessed March 31, 2007).

United Nations General Assembly. 2005. 2005 World Summit outcome. http://daccessdds.un.org/doc/UNDOC/GEN/N05/487/60/PDF/N0548760.pdf?OpenElement.

Veiga, R. 1985. *Las organizaciones de derechos humanos.* Buenos Aires: Centro Editor de América Latina, Biblioteca Política Argentina.

Vogelin, Eric. 1999. *Hitler and the Germans.* Ed. Detlev Clemens and Brendan

Purcell. Columbia: University of Missouri Press.

Waller, James. 2002. *Becoming evil: How ordinary people commit genocide and mass killing.* New York: Oxford University Press.

Webber, Francis. 1999. The Pinochet case: The struggle for realization of human rights. *Journal of Law and Society* 26:523–37.

Weissbrodt, David, and Maria Luisa Bartolomei. 1991. The effectiveness of international human rights pressures: The case of Argentina 1976–1983. *Minnesota Law Review* 75:1009.

Wells, P. A. 1987. Kin recognition in humans. In *Kin recognition in animals,* ed. D. J. C. Fletcher and C. D. Michener, 395–416. New York: Wiley.

White, Josh. 2005. Reported abuse cases fell after Abu Ghraib. *Washington Post,* March 17, p. A17.

Williamson, Elizabeth. 2004. One soldier's unlikely act: Family fears for man who reported Iraqi prisoner abuse. *Washington Post,* May 6, p. A16.

Women of courage: Whistleblowers in the public interest. 2003. Kathleen Ridder Conference, Smith College's Project on Women and Social Change. Northampton, MA, February 7–8.

Wyman, David. 1984. *The abandonment of the Jews: America and the Holocaust, 1941–1945.* New York: Pantheon.

Zahn-Waxler, C., M. Radke-Yarrow, and R. M. King. 1979. Child-rearing and children's prosocial initiations toward victims of distress. *Child Development* 50:319–30.

Zimbardo, Philip G., Craig Haney, W. Curtis Banks, and David Jaffe. 1974. The psychology of imprisonment: Privation, power and pathology. In *Doing unto others,* ed. Z. Rubin, 61–74. Englewood Cliffs, NJ: Prentice Hall.

Zoroya, Gregg. 2004. Whistleblower asked mom's advice. *USA Today,* national edition, May 12, p. A4.

INDEX